PRAISE FOR

Cruise Confidential

by

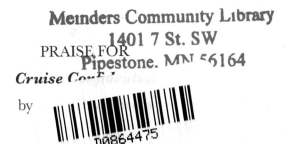

Benjamin Frank [illegible] **the Year**

***GOLD Medal, ForeWord's* Book of the Year**

***New England Book Festival* Book of the Year - Finalist**

"Part *Love Boat*, part *Mutiny on the Bounty*, *Cruise Confidential* does for the cruise industry what *Animal House* did for higher education."

- J. Maarten Troost, author of *The Sex Lives of Cannibals*

"I found it absolutely hysterical!"

- Peter Greenberg, *Today Show*

"*Cruise Confidential* is a deliciously addictive read... a blistering kiss-and-tell about the dysfunctional life working on-board Carnival Cruise lines. We get a good look into the orgy-like crew parties, a frightening management style that's a mix of Old Testament and Mafia."

- Doug Lansky, *Travel Channel*

"I couldn't put it down."

- Chicago Sun-Times

"This is a very funny, behind-the-scenes exploration of a cruise ship."

- Booklist

"*Cruise Confidential* is a juicy tell-all. The crew deals with the 'sweat shop' conditions by indulging in massive amounts of alcohol and sex."

- Cleveland Plain Dealer

"Spray crashing, thunder blasting, bodies rolling around a heaving floor. Ship on the rocks? No, just a typical midnight party 'under-the-waterline'... the funniest travel book I've read in years."

- Peter Mandel, author of *Boats on the River*, and *My Ocean Liner*

"A really entertaining true tale [about the] bizarre world of cruise ships..."

- San Francisco Chronicle

"Bruns doesn't hold back when it comes to discussing his experience of working on cruise ships..."

- *Thomas Cook Magazine* (United Kingdom)

"...the real party is going on in the crew's quarters..."

- USA Today

"Bruns is an excellent writer able to show you raw emotions and the nasty underbelly of what goes on..."

- Thomas Duff, *Amazon.com* Top 50 Reviewer

"Witty and self-deprecating [Bruns] has a flair for dialogue, and his book is chock full of whacky characters..."

- Blogcritics Magazine

Cover design by Brian David Bruns

Interior layout by Steven Urban

Library of Congress Cataloguing-in-Publication Data

Bruns, Brian David
1st ed.
ISBN: 978-0-9745217-2-5
Library of Congress Control Number: 2011929797

1. Cruise Ships—Humor. 2. Travel/Essay
3. Cruise Ships—Employees

Ship For Brains

Brian David Bruns

World Waters

Las Vegas - Ottawa

ACKNOWLEDGMENTS

The author would like to thank Traveler's Tales; the scrutiny of Larry Habegger, the acumen of Sean O'Reilly, and the vision of James O'Reilly. Also many thanks to the efforts of Jeffrey Morris, Jr., and the generosity of time by Dan Halsted and Chuck Martin.

CONTENTS

Part III: The Fun Ships

Part IV: The End of the Beginning

Appendices

This book is lovingly dedicated
to Aurelia

Eu voi fii intotdeauna maimuța ta

Part 1: The Widow Maker

"If you are going through Hell, keep going."
—Winston Churchill

1. SURVIVAL TRAINING

Cruise ships rarely look guilty. They should. If bulkheads could talk, revealed would be month after month of menial labor, little pay, and less sleep. The dining rooms bear witness to gastronomic atrocities of the highest order, and crew cabins? Booze and sex are taken to criminally insane levels. But luxury liners are never penitent because they are built nose in the air, then vindicated with expensive champagne smashed on their puffed up chest. Like the rest of us, they are oblivious to what happens in their own bowels.

I was already nervous when I approached *Majesty of the Seas* to sign on as crew. The sea was a harsh mistress and had already broken me once, but like a good masochist I returned obediently for more. Not a particularly flattering metaphor, but accurate. Horrendous shrieks rose from the ship, and memories of the damned toiling ceaselessly in her depths flooded over me. But that was just the swell rubbing the ship up against the pier.

Because the pier was level with the opening in *Majesty's* hull, crossing the crew's gangplank was like walking across a horizontal step ladder. Tiptoeing rung to rung loaded with luggage is a little nerve-wracking, especially when directly above Volkswagen-sized bumpers being ground into hamburger. The protective net below was for catching falling wallets, not arrogant Iowans. But cross I did, one with the Idaho potatoes and Samsonite, though as a crew member I was first patted down by security.

Attractive wooden paneling and brass accoutrements made it clear that this first spot was intended for guests, whereas the dirty plastic flaps blocking a doorway indicated our lot. A young, brown-haired man in a lime green Tommy Bahama polo waited for me, munching on a handful of Tums as if they were peanuts. He rushed forward to greet me, shooting words like the rat-a-tat-tat of a machine gun. This is not to imply aggression, but that he perhaps thought his words would vanish if not expelled fast enough.

"You're Brian, eh? I'm Shawn the art auctioneer. Just the suitcase and a backpack? Bob's your uncle. My gay boys will join us soon. Don't worry about the purser."

His speech ended so abruptly I wasn't sure if he was through. But Shawn was already moving, so I followed. He ducked through the flaps accessing the crew corridor and led me into the bowels of the ship. We passed stacks of pallets heavy with plastic-wrapped contents. Open doorways made gaps between the towers of supply, like a long Cheshire cat smile with missing teeth.

Shawn was a cheery soul, babbling nonstop about all sorts of subjects.

"Where you from?"

"I'm from Iowa."

"Go Buckeyes!"

"Close," I complimented. "That's Ohio. Iowa is the Hawkeyes."

He leaned his head charmingly sideways, like a confused puppy. "Did I mention I was from Canada? Survival's in the cinema. Busy day today. My gay boys are busy, too, but we won't work you too hard yet. You know about the I-95, eh?"

Over the noise and the chaos, his choppy speech was incredibly hard to follow. The crew corridor, known as the I-95, was terra incognita for guests because it housed the mess, the purser, the crew bar, and access to crew cabins below the waterline. Surprisingly, the name was not a reference to an Interstate, but referred to the immigration papers the U.S. requires of foreigner workers, Form I-95.

"Gene said you know ships already, eh?"

"I've been on three Carnival ships," I answered slowly. I tried to slow him down without being rude or, for that matter, appearing like the dullard my ex-wife insisted I was.

"Oh, all ships are the same," he said, giving me a lopsided smirk. "Only the officers are different. Carnival's are Italian, so they are easy to handle. They demand respect and tail, you know. Nothing else matters, especially the rules. Just kiss their ass and you are in. But on RCI they're all Dutch. That means rules first: people last. They love protocol and formality and all that. This is a problem with a lot of Americans because you're all so casual and hip hoppy."

"I believe the technical term is hip hop-*like*," I replied helpfully.

Suddenly a small, handsome man bullied past in obvious agitation. Beneath a striped bandana, his forehead flushed red with anger and he hammered his fists against the bulkhead as if it was a speed bag. Shawn dropped his typically explosive speech pattern and called to the fuming man with incredible, almost mocking sweetness.

"Why, hello, Amor! Out in port today?"

The man glanced up, surprised. He outwardly calmed himself, but the quivering of his dimpled chin revealed pressure yet brewing. His face contorted, trying to find the right spot between anger and horror. Shawn suddenly remembered introductions.

"This is Amor, the bartender I hired for the auctions. He's from Greece. Amor, this is Brian, the new art auctioneer."

No doubt Amor had not really heard anything, lost as he was in rage. He nearly struck his head into the wall, apparently feeling his fists were not appropriately expressive. Shawn prompted with sugary innocence, "Is there a problem?"

"The problem," Amor answered venomously, "is that all Americans are gays."

I blinked in surprise. Shawn gave me a sly smile and bowed with grand flourish, indicating the rebuttal was mine.

"That may, in fact, be an exaggeration," I replied with amused patience. "I am American and am not gay. However, I hope this explains why my ex-wife so thoroughly avoided me in the bedroom."

Amor glared at me a moment, obviously not convinced. Finally he sighed to release some tension and began his tale.

"I was there, to east. All buildings had flags in front with bright rainbow colors on them. These ones," he added, indicating the crisp new bandana he wore. It was striped with the entire color spectrum.

"I thought how cool everyone in America is, they are always so happy. Nobody shows bright colors in my country. We are not all sad, but we are not all happy like you Americans. Colors like this are so happy and full of life."

I bit my tongue, perhaps for the first time in my life.

"I want these rainbow flags to send home to my family, show how different America is. I enter a bar selling these flags and buy this bandana also. In there a man approach me and buy me a beer. I think, what a nice place this Key West, where a stranger buy you beer."

I burst out laughing. I couldn't help it. Shawn grinned widely, and Amor's face clouded as he tried to understand why.

"Amor," I explained. "You were in the gay district. Key West is famous for that. Those rainbow flags mean you are a supporter of gay and lesbian rights."

His face darkened and he exploded, "But I am obviously not a gay!"

"Obviously," I agreed, trying not to roll my eyes. "Amor, you don't have to be gay to be a supporter of gay rights. Surely this dastardly deed of buying you a beer isn't why you are so angry?"

"No," he said sullenly. "The man asks me questions the way all Americans do. Where I from, what I do, what my name. I tell him I am Greek, I am sailor, and I am Amor. Then for no reason he try to kiss me!"

Amor stormed off with an indignant slap at the bulkhead, a kick of some luggage, and a mutter at how humiliating it was that 'every American in the bar was a gay.'

"Well, then!" Shawn said brightly. "Welcome aboard!"

Survival training was an amusing label for the watching of a few videos on watertight doors and garbage separation. That excitement was usually followed by quizzes on how many kilojoules of energy each survivor on a life raft was allocated per day. Such was the way Carnival Cruise Lines handled it. But, to my surprise, Royal Caribbean provided a much more interactive session. While not a dress rehearsal for the next season of *Survivor* or anything, it was still exciting enough to leave me limping away from the ordeal, humiliated and bleeding.

First, of course, was film. But this was a far cry from the dry narration of a policy procedural. This shocker was reminiscent of what I saw on graduation day at my high school driving class. 'Blood Flows Red on the Highway' became 'Blood Flows Red on the High Seas.' I endured simulations of sinking ships and drowning people more intense than even James Cameron's *Titanic*. There were also sections where fires burned the unwary, crowds trampled the weak, and pirates attacked everybody. My personal favorite was the watertight door slicing a cow's leg in two.

After the gore fest, we were led up to the open deck on the bow of *Majesty*, which was brutally exposed to the tropical heat of May in Key West. My eyes watered at the brightness reflecting off the lumpy white paint thick on everything, and the sunlight hammering the metal deck burned through my shoes.

RCI's *Majesty of the Seas* was an old-school beast and, like those great liners of the past, the *Queen Mary* or even *Lusitania*, this open deck above the boson's area was filled with unsightly things like cranes and hatches. Yes, Kate and Leo had to navigate all sorts of hazards to get to their first amazing kiss in *Titanic*, romantic things like extra anchors, propellers, and engine parts.

A single, bright orange life raft rested upon the humming deck. Three steps led up to a platform before the opening in the angular, tent-like peak. There lounged a Dutch officer in a clean and pressed white uniform. By lounging I mean he was merely idle, for he was not slouching by any stretch of the imagination. He stood ramrod straight, out-starching his own uniform. He was of medium height and of slight build, with sandy blond hair feathered back over a youthful middle-aged face. He was very handsome and his ice-blue eyes were magnetic.

"My name is Roosevelt Reddick," he said as the motley gathering of new crew gathered below him. His English was as crisp as his uniform and correct as his posture. I always found Dutch accents pleasing because they were obviously not American English, yet I could never actually identify what made their speech different.

"I am Chief Officer," he continued. "Welcome aboard *Majesty of the Seas*. This ship was commissioned in 1992, is 74,000 tons and is of Bahamian registry. She carries 2,750 passengers and 830 crew members."

"Working at sea and serving our guests is a wonderful privilege, and it is earned by keeping their safety first and foremost on our minds. Here, you are not a cabin steward or a waiter or a singer or a cook: you are crew who safeguard the lives of our guests. That means lowering lifeboats and directing panicked people, it means man overboard training. It may even mean fighting pirates."

Aha! Mild-mannered art dealer by day, pirate-smashing crime fighter by night. I always wanted to be a superhero. I'm cool with the tights.

"Each of you will be certified as 'personnel nominated to assist passengers in emergency situations' according to the training objectives of the International Maritime Organization, Resolution A770. This includes basic first aid, survival craft basics, fire fighting skills, and human relationships training."

"Now!" he ordered brusquely. "Everyone into the raft!"

I moved forward like everyone else. Well, not exactly like everyone else: I was the only white guy in the crowd. I was used to that on ships, and certainly used to being the only American present. Barring one Jamaican lady, the crowd was entirely Asian. It was easy to see, as I stood a head or two taller than everyone. More and more bright floral prints and Caribbean T-shirts disappeared into the raft, like the old clowns-fitting-in-the-funny car gag. As soon as Reddick's X-Ray eyes caught mine, however, he motioned for me to step outside the queue.

This allowed me the rare opportunity to review a ship's inflatable life raft. It was a shockingly large thing, considering how it compressed so snugly into keg-sized canisters on deck. The base was two thick black rubber tubes bent into octagonal shape, and the top was a highly visible orange. The entrance was high up to prevent waves from entering, and ropes snaked around everything to assist people doing so.

The line began to slow, and Reddick urged the crew in with sharp words until everyone except me was inside. "Do not be shy! Make room! This life raft is designed for twenty-four!"

Grunts and complaints, and waves of heat and moisture, all rose from inside. Reddick glanced down emotionlessly at the squirming mass of flesh below him. His eyes were cold and brilliant in the sun, like an iceberg —captivating, dangerous.

"Tomorrow this raft could save your life!" Reddick shouted. "Imagine this raft rocking at sea for unending hours under the hot sun."

"It *is* under the hot sun!"

Reddick let the hoots and jeers subside with exacting patience. He was by far the most comfortable person on the open deck, after all, and at his leisure he chose the best moment to emphasize another point. "This raft will hold twenty-four crew and guests. There are currently only twenty-three of you in there. How does it feel?"

Angry mutterings and cynical jokes answered him.

"That is correct, it is difficult to fit all of you in."

Reddick motioned for me to step up. I leaned forward and reviewed the conditions inside with anxiety. Bodies filled the space like sardines in a can. Though people crammed at the sides were neatly arranged, the middle was nothing more than a mosh pit.

"I said this is for crew and *guests*," Reddick emphasized. "Now, can anyone tell me what the difference is between each of you and the average American?"

Alarm bells went off in my mind when Reddick placed his foot on my behind.

"About one hundred pounds!"

Reddick launched me through the air, and through the whistling wind I heard someone cry, "Ahh! Big Mac attack!"

Groans rose as I crushed entwined legs and smashed into bodies. The hapless crew writhed and squirmed to get out of my way. Laughter from those safe at the edges turned to hollers as the shockwaves of my inglorious entry radiated outward, with elbows elbowing and knees kneeing. When all the hubbub died down, I wriggled into an awkward position atop four Indonesian and Filipino men and propped my back against the Jamaican woman.

"Now listen up. As you can see, survival is about everyone. There is no room for anyone to focus solely on himself. You are all crew and obey, but can you imagine this raft filled with complaining guests? They are scared and do not know what to do, they may be separated from loved ones, and they certainly are not comfortable. Imagine this filled with Americans and not Indonesians!"

"Or da rats with ESP!" cried the Jamaican behind me.

Ice blue eyes blinked slowly as the odd statement was processed.

"Excuse me?"

The bold Jamaican shook her head with emphasis, loose beads buzzing around her knit cap like a swarm of bumblebees. A few braids smacked me in the face.

"Rats always leave da sinking ship first," she proclaimed. "I know for fact two ships in da south Carib sank and da rats left first. For fact! Now how dey know what's up? Dey gots the ESP, mon, and they get in da raft!"

The Chief Officer pondered a moment, then finally replied with a painful lack of animation. "I *have* heard old maritime reports of rats abandoning ship by the dozens prior to the crew even being aware of a problem. Perhaps on less modern ships, such as are likely from

Venezuela or Columbia in the south Caribbean, this still happens.

"Rats would most likely live in the bilge area at the bottom of the ship, which is also likely to be the first place to take on water. Hence rats would move to higher decks. Once on top they would be scared by all the human activity and panic, eventually jumping overboard. A short time later the crew will also learn that the ship is sinking and the uneducated or superstitious may believe the rats can see into the future. Yes, ESP, I believe it is called. I can assure you that there will not be any rats with ESP joining you in the raft."

Satisfied, she nodded with a click of beads, several of which continued to rap against my head. Reddick continued in lecture mode.

"If the ship sinks, guests will look to *you* for safety. They will assume you are an able seaman, even if you are only a waiter. They will not even see past your nationality. 70% of survivors from maritime accidents are reported as bewildered and using impaired reasoning. 15% will actually panic and exhibit irrational behavior. Panic leads to pushing, shoving and trampling, which leads to broken bones. Can you imagine being stuck in this raft, rocking on the high seas, with a broken arm or leg? *You* must be ready to lead."

"Is dis da poop deck?" the Jamaican interrupted. "You know, where people would *go* off da boat?"

The Chief's handsome face became stone, but his eyes flashed dangerously.

"No," he replied tersely. "The poop is the deck *above* the rearmost cabin. The name comes from the Latin word for 'stern', not from any bodily functions."

With a glare at the woman, which included me by proximity, Reddick continued, "There is no reason to panic, anyway. Passengers practice boat drill every cruise, and the International Maritime Organization's guidelines require that all passengers can be lowered into the ocean within thirty minutes. Barring a deliberate bombing, the sinking of a ship of this size will take many hours."

"A bombing?" someone asked, concerned.

"Yes," the Chief explained. "After the terrorist attacks of September 11th in the United States—"

"What about pirates?" the Jamaican blurted, interrupted again.

Reddick's lips compressed as he tightly asked, "Pirates?"

"Dey in the Caribbean, mon!"

"Only at Disney World," the Chief replied sharply. "Or around Somalia and the South China Seas. No pirate, no matter how desperate, would attack a ship of *this* size, with such a preponderance of trained crew. Pirates seek large, slow vessels with minimal crew and maximum payload, such as oil tankers or cargo haulers. In those cases they have a mere two dozen men to overcome. On *Majesty of the Seas*, pirates would need to secure nearly one thousand crew. Still, the wealth on this ship is immense and kidnapping two thousand Americans is surely worth a high degree of risk."

"*Ya der* be risk, *mon!*" the Jamaican boomed. "And the Bermuda Triangle? Tell me—"

"Everybody out of the raft!" Reddick ordered curtly. "We are going to the pool!"

With amused snickers, we all struggled awkwardly out of the raft. The floor beneath bowed under our knees, but enthusiasm to escape the stifling heat was more than enough to propel us out. A long line of sweaty men trudged after Reddick through the corridors, up ugly metal crew stairs, and finally to the pool deck, which was cordoned off from guest use. He ordered everyone to grab a lifejacket and encircle the pool, upon which another life raft lazed.

"Now," Reddick said. "There are two things we have left to cover. The first is simple, but important: jumping from the deck of a sinking ship."

The Chief Officer motioned me forward, and I asked cautiously, "You're not going to kick me into the pool, are you?"

His answering grin never reached his eyes.

"This time we will *start* with the big guy," he called to everyone. "Jumping into the sea may seem simple, but if you do it wrong you can seriously hurt yourself. No, you won't break a leg jumping ten meters into the ocean, but you may damage something more important, so make sure you cross your legs!"

Reddick motioned for me to illustrate, but when he reached towards me I panicked. Legs crossed, I hopped awkwardly on the pool's edge and accidentally fell over with an ignominious splash. When I spluttered to the surface, I was greeted with an embarrassing wave of laughter.

"The last thing to cover today again involves the life rafts," Reddick called out. "If *Majesty of the Seas* sinks, the hydrostatic release will loose all the life rafts in the white canisters on deck. Their painter lines are attached to the ship and designed to snap under strain, which self-inflates the rafts so they float to the surface. But sometimes they do so upside-down.

"It is very easy to flip a raft right-side up when empty. With people inside, it is impossible to flip, regardless of how high the waves are. Grabbing the rope encircling the base of the raft, you flip it using leverage, not strength."

Following Reddick's orders, I swam over to the raft and lumbered up onto the wet rubber bottom with surprising difficulty and finally lay there, like an elephant seal on a bobbing rock. Salt water dribbled into my eyes and I squinted in the sunlight reflecting off the waves generated by my unwieldy motions. The raft rocked like mad and I was nearly pitched off the side.

"The raft is unstable in this position, so lay your body flat. Grab the rope. OK, now just stand up."

"Huh?"

"Just stand up," Reddick repeated. "You will see."

Still holding onto the rope, I adjusted my weight as if simply getting up from the floor after watching TV, like when I was a kid. The raft flipped so fast that I was flung backwards into the shallow end. Somehow my hand caught in the rope and instead of being tossed back to safely land in the water, I plunged beneath and cracked my knee against the bottom. Wincing terribly from the pain, I struggled to the surface with a gasp.

Embarrassed and bruised, I extricated my hand tenderly from the line. My fingers throbbed from the throttling and rope marks blazed in red and white across my wrist. Pain lanced up my leg as I limped to the edge of the pool. I was sure I had sprained it.

"Like that!" Reddick exclaimed, "Only do it better. Smart people let go of the rope so they don't hurt themselves!"

⚓

An hour or so later, *Majesty of the Seas* pulled away from the pier and churned towards the open sea. Somewhere across its thin, roiling surface was my Bianca. She had been my original reason for going to sea with Carnival. She inspired my aspirations as an art auctioneer. She was my motive for everything.

Bianca was a cruise ship waitress from Romania who worked at sea eight months a year. I was a smitten American who followed her like a puppy the *entire* year. We came from dramatically different worlds, but had resolved to come together. That wasn't as easy as either of us wanted. Against all precedents, I had fought a whole year in Carnival Cruise Line's restaurants to be with her. I slogged seven days a week at menial labor for less than minimum wage, and endured international politicking that involved denial of medical care and even food. But after no less than *fifty* straight fifteen-hour days, and still no closer to my Bianca, I finally admitted defeat.

Yet when one door closes another always opens. I was now training to become an art auctioneer for Sundance at Sea. I had endured much for this job already, including the single most stressful week of my life during auctioneer screening. All my strengths and weaknesses had been brilliantly exposed at Sundance's main gallery in Pittsburgh, but I had shown enough potential to be sent here to learn from the Rookie of the Year. The stakes were high, but self-awareness was a powerful force for soothing nerves.

The sobriquet of auctioneer was yet a long way off. I would be an unpaid trainee for a full month while on *Majesty*. During that period Shawn had first call whether or not to promote me into the next step, that of associate.

As an associate, I would be a glorified auctioneer's assistant. The lion's share of learning would happen there, and would last for untold months or possibly even years. But what a living it would be! Associates' wages were entirely sales-based and most did quite well. It was still second class citizenry, to be sure, but regular crew life was about ninth class.

To become a full auctioneer on my own ship required the blessings of my managing auctioneer first, followed by the fleet manager, then the endorsement of the supreme fleet manager, and then ultimately the owner of Sundance. I needed to reach these goals while alone, but once the position was secured, I would finally be able to bring my Bianca with me. I had already suffered thirteen months at sea to be with her, what was another year? I would wait a lifetime!

2. SHIP LIFE

My walk-in closet at home was literally larger than my crew cabin. True, it never stank or had condom wrappers crammed into the nooks, but such things were to be expected on ships. I inherited my cabin on *Majesty* from Shawn, who arrived late and more than a little disheveled. He rifled through his pockets and dumped all manner of revealing evidence of ship-style revelry on the floor: bits of napkin with numbers hastily scrawled upon them, breath mints, a condom, and several cherry-flavored Tums. Finally he found his key and opened the door with a look not unlike a dog caught chewing slippers.

"The maid won't come on home port," he apologized. "They move all the guest luggage, you know."

"As long as there aren't any naked men inside, it will be just fine."

"My reference to '*my* gay boys' is just an expression, eh."

"I had a recurring problem with naked men popping up in my room while with Carnival," I hastily explained. "I'd rather not talk about it."

"Please don't," he agreed. "But as an auctioneer you have your own cabin."

My home for the next month packed two bunks, two lockers, and a small desk in about ten by six feet. A slender aisle separated the bottom bunk from the desk, providing all sorts of painful opportunities to hit my sprained knee. The top bunk was occupied by about four dozen art prints in matting stacked liked books. My bunk was lost beneath heaps of clothing roughly categorized by cleanliness, purpose, and designer label. Cheap, dog-eared posters of generic beach scenes were taped aggressively to the walls and nearly hid the entrance to the tiny bathroom, which crammed a shower, sink, and toilet all in the space of a phone booth. Yes, the toilet was actually *in* the shower.

It was a typical cabin in most regards, but it did have one exciting feature: a port hole! The round window let in a stream of sunlight and a horrendously dusty artificial plant absorbed it all indifferently.

"A window!" I squawked. "Crew cabins have windows? I don't believe it!"

"Staff cabins, eh. Not crew," Shawn corrected. "Crew are packed into little closets and stuff. You know, the ships are contractually obligated to provide a guest cabin for auctioneers. They found a loophole to deny me one, but now that we have an associate coming I get it. So thanks for that, eh."

"We have an associate?"

"We have you," he answered, shrugging. "I dunno. I'm sure you'll be fine as an unpaid trainee for a month and stay on as associate. I don't really know what they have in mind for you, because this is new for all of us. But I could use the help, man. I'm burned out. Really, I'm done. I could hardly get it on last night, and I still have three more Steiners to bang."

I chuckled. Steiners were the crew who worked in the ship's spa. Invariably young women, they had a reputation as being very accommodating. Not in the Biblical sense.

"Just one more month and I get four months off. Damn, I need it."

"I hear you have done very well. Sounds like your hard work is paying off."

"You got that right, brother. I'm clearing shitloads of money. I'm moving my ass as far away from Calgary as I can get. Buy me a house in the Bahamas."

I nodded, not really listening. I was thrilled to finally have my own cabin. Living on a ship was a trying experience in a lot of ways, but having a private space to call your own could possibly be the difference between success and insanity.

In the past I had been forced to shack up with a Thai couple with a penchant for Chinese martial arts movies, an incomprehensible Costa Rican with the size and tendencies of a gorilla, and an insomniac Reborn-Christian from India who quoted scripture until dawn. Those had been the only cabin mates who refrained from having sex parties while I was trying to sleep, anyway. The art in the other bunk wasn't going to bring a different foreign woman in here every night. *That* was not nearly as intriguing as I would have thought when I was a teen. Yes, this was the life. This was, without a doubt, the mother of all cabins.

"So, here's the deal about food in here," Shawn explained. "We are contractually allowed room service in our guest cabins but, again, they hosed me on that. I tip so much, though, that they sneak it in for me. No one is allowed food in their cabins these days. Big drama.

Roaches. And for God's sake, don't put any food down the toilet!"

"Why would I do that?"

"The Asians do it all the time. They take food from the mess and bring it to their cabins. Then to hide the leftovers they put all sorts of bones and fish heads in the toilet. It clogs, of course, and screws up the whole system. You know how ship toilets are super sensitive. That's why the crew mess literally smells like shit all the time. It's not the food."

"You have got to be joking."

"No, really. You'll see. You know ships, you know how different some of these cultures are. Just be real careful, OK? Hot Man will make cabin inspections. What kind of clothing do you have with you?"

"Not much," I admitted, nearly caught off guard by his odd segue. "I didn't want to bring the wrong things. I have my suit, but that's about it."

"Bob's your uncle," he said, for some reason I could not fathom. "I am very casual. During the days I wear pants and polos. They have a Banana Republic in Key West, so you can get some stuff there. I think Gene mentioned that trainees don't get any money for their first month, so if you need some cash, just ask."

"No, I'm all right. Thanks."

"Bob's your uncle," he said.

"I beg your pardon?"

"Bob's your uncle," he repeated, as if that explained everything.

"I presume that is some sort of top secret Canadian military code?" I asked, adding cryptically, "The moose is at the door."

"Anyway," Shawn continued. "You can watch my gay boys. You don't have to do boat drill. One of the perks. Anyway, first night's auction is tough because everyone is new and confused and lost and all that. But we have my gay boys."

He looked at me expectantly. I just stared blankly at him, trying to sort through everything he had just said. He spoke a mile a minute and hopped back and forth from subject to subject without any rhyme or reason. I sensed that though this be madness, there was method in it. Of all the nationalities I had worked with at sea, numbering about sixty, I was having the biggest communication problems with a Canadian!

"So, uh, Bob's your uncle?" I offered slowly.

"Bob's your uncle!" he agreed firmly. "Anyway, speaking of gay boys, how was your meeting with Roosevelt? He did your survival training, eh?"

"Uh, yeah. Survival training. Uncle Bob. Gay boys. Shawn...*what the Hell* are you talking about?"

He cocked his head again for his Basset-Hound look. "You'll meet them. The guys I hired to set up and assist the auctions, Denny and Jesse. They're a dancing couple. By that I mean they are dancers *and* a couple. They are awesome man, absolutely sweet. I pay them a shitload of money but they are worth every penny. I think they used to own a flower shop or something, because they make everything so pretty."

"Yes, I believe the rules require all gay men to work as florists at some point," I said sarcastically. "Barring those who don't heed the call of being hair dressers, needless to say. So what does that have to do with Reddick? Is he gay or something?"

"No, of course not. He's Dutch. Kinda like your uncle."

"You're losing me, man."

"The Dutch are like the world's leading nation for accepting gays," he explained. He looked me up and down for a moment and added, "I figured you would know that."

I snorted in response.

"They have a monument to gayness in Amsterdam and stuff," he continued. "You Americans don't get out much, do you?"

"Apparently less than Greeks," I replied. "Anyway, yes, I just met Reddick Roosevelt. He seems nice enough for a Chief Officer, but a bit stiff."

"*Seems* nice enough, sure. It's Roosevelt Reddick, by the way."

"Isn't that what I said?"

"No, Roosevelt is a first name in the Netherlands."

I was used to the switching of family names and given names in Europe. Bianca and I had all sorts of difficulty because she never knew what her first and last names were. In Romania the family comes first, so they say Pop Bianca, and not Bianca Pop as we Americans would. While summering in Romania I had a similarly difficult time referring to myself as Bruns Brian. They were completely flabbergasted at my middle name.

"He gets mad at Americans who think it's his family name. I know you had a president with that name, but trust me, the Dutch were around first and that matters a lot to them. When America was brand new it was the Dutch who gave them their first loan. I hear that all the time, so I guess they feel you still owe them. Anyway, Roosevelt seems nice until protocol is broken. You'll see it. Break the rules and you'll face hell."

"You had problems?"

"Me? No way, eh. Everyone loves Canadians."

"Well, I'm a good boy, I follow rules. I was a boy scout and everything. Troop 63, don't you know. Bob is most definitely my uncle."

"And Fannie's your aunt!"

Unfortunately, Shawn's warning about the importance of protocol was more accurate than I would ever imagine. Within a month I would be embroiled in such a far-reaching problem that the captain himself would have to step in... *and* top-tier Royal Caribbean... *and* the owner of Sundance Auctions at Sea.

My entire first day on *Majesty of the Seas* was a blur, but it was better than being a waiter. I once had to return to *Carnival Conquest* from Bianca's house in Transylvania. That involved a gypsy-filled train to Bucharest, a turbulence-shaken flight to Frankfurt, an ear-bleeding Transatlantic flight beside screaming children to Chicago, then an ear-*busting* party flight with Mardi Gras-minded revelers to New Orleans, and then finally a bus to Gulfport, Mississippi. One hour after that I began a twelve hour shift with nary a five-minute break. When I finally returned to my cabin for a blissful six hours of sleep—after a solid *fifty* hours on the go, my insomniac Reborn Christian cabin mate quoted gospel until dawn. The punchline? I am an atheist. Ship life.

Still, I was surprised Shawn chose to auction the very first night, because there was no time for advertising and guests were usually tired, hungry, and confused. They couldn't find their cabins, let alone a specific lounge for an auction. Then again, some people can smell free booze with more accuracy than a bomb-sniffing dog.

But this was the Widow Maker, and Shawn had to move fast lest he fail like every preceding auctioneer. *Majesty of the Seas* was in port a whopping seven days a week. Sundance demanded we make tens of thousands of dollars in sales to guests tanning on Bahamian beaches or shopping in Key West. With such little guest time, no wonder Shawn developed such rapid-fire speech!

His genius lay in identifying the one and only time guests were sure to be aboard: dinner. While hungry guests impatiently waited for their tables, Shawn gave them a semi-welcome distraction. Outside the restaurant's two decks was an area called the Centrum, and this was completely overtaken by the art auction.

The Centrum was an astounding open atrium of seven stories ringed by balconies, shops, and lounges. Hovering in the air was a piano platform accessed by exposed staircases spiraling up to multiple levels. This impressive, corkscrewing open-air labyrinth funneled all attention to the platform, which floated before the two-level entrance of the dining room. But no longer did classical music caress the ether, for it was buried beneath a load of art.

It was chaos.

On two levels, first-seating guests poured out of the dining room even as the second-seating guests pushed in. Even higher decks flowed with people pulsing through densely arranged artwork, only to cascade like a waterfall down the staircases to pool at the platform or lower levels. Above their heads huge canvases spread like a canopy, held aloft by the trunks of countless easels, while at their feet scores of small canvases snaked away like gnarled roots.

The jungle metaphor was particularly apt because life teemed on decks, above, level with, and below. Passersby leaned over rails to view the action, gibbering excitedly like monkeys in treetops. I saw on a documentary once that monkeys sometimes urinated on people below them, but I felt safe because this wasn't a crew party.

And there, on the platform groaning beneath the weight of countless canvases, was the rock around which all the disarray flowed. Shawn was master of the bedlam he created, and upon his cool demeanor confusion smashed into spray. All eyes were drawn to this singularity of control, who commanded guests on no less than four levels simultaneously. He invited to participate, instructed on procedure, dripped data about art, and reassured that more free champagne was coming.

The champagne was my only responsibility. While 'Shawn's gay boys' Denny and Jesse assisted the auction, I coordinated with the bartender. This was Amor, the disgruntled homophobe I met immediately upon boarding. This small but forceful man from Greece had a head shaved clean to the scalp, and finely arched eyebrows looking out of place over such a hawk-like nose. Yet with a delicately dimpled chin his face, he turned out quite handsome. I could not tell if his bronzed skin was natural or from a tropical tan.

Amor iced the champagne in a makeshift station and unloaded racks of champagne flutes. Absently polishing the glasses, he stood next to me and watched the maelstrom swirl through the Centrum.

"Look at those two?" he said, gesturing to the two dancers. His tone was somewhere between an order and a question. He did not smile, but his brow arched ever higher to apparently indicate pleasure. "I like them. They are very nice and always smile."

I marveled that Amor had not observed their obviously being gay, but opted not to mention it. We all live in denial, after all. Instead I quipped, "That's because they aren't European. Europeans rarely look happy."

Amor barked a laugh, but did not smile. "Maybe with American dentist, we smile more. Ever think of that? I am ready with champagne."

"OK," I said. "How does this work?"

"I serve to crowd from tray. End of auction you sign for bottles used."

"Shawn told me the standing order was for fifteen bottles, with a case in reserve. You will only pour what is needed, right?"

"Yes," he said simply.

I left him to his work, and wandered the scene in order to learn. The auction block was a single easel on the platform, brilliantly lit by a portable light box. Shawn's arms flapped riotously between his many duties; pointing to the art, punching numbers into his laptop, and speaking into a microphone to acknowledge bids. His finger jabbed at bidders below on deck three, stabbed at those on the stairs, and then thrust up to those on decks four and even five.

My head swam from all that was happening and I wondered how I would learn to control it all. Back when I first saw the craziness of ship restaurants, I had been confident I could handle anything. Sure, things were different at sea, but I had mastered every level of dining rooms over the previous decade. Yet in the end I had been completely devoured by cruise ship restaurants and failed every single goal I set. If I could be humbled so brutally by something I had already mastered, what had art auctions in store for me? I resolved to stick with Shawn until I knew every detail perfectly.

Eventually the action moved from auction to billing, and I sought out Amor. He was cleaning up the portable bar he had created from a cart and a table cloth. The large ice bin bristled with a dozen open bottles of champagne. Twisted foil and bent cages lay scattered everywhere and the smell of champagne was cloying and sweet. A waist-high stack of glass racks dripped with the golden fluid.

"Is that what we went through?" I asked. "A dozen bottles? Why put the empty bottles back in the ice?"

"No," he explained, gesturing to two cases on the floor. "Empty bottles in boxes there."

I frowned. "So these iced and opened bottles are the reserve case? Why did you open all twelve?"

"In case you need," he explained, handing me an invoice for twenty-seven bottles, from which he received a handy commission. "Orders were to pour only as you need. You never said not open *until* you need. I am nice and I prepare for you."

Amor's lips split into a huge smile.

"Now that they open and auction over," he added tartly, "Why you not let me have bottle or two?"

The next morning, Shawn appeared disoriented and fumbled with the keys to access to the purser's area. He even dropped them, twice, while behind him I strained to pass a heavy frame from hand to hand. The wires were digging deeply into my flesh, and my hand still throbbed from the mishap in the pool. Now I could add bleeding to my list of minor annoyances.

"This is where all the important stuff happens," Shawn explained tiredly. "The bridge is just for navigation. Hot Man is here. This is the heart of the hotel and all business decisions are made here."

A dozen cubicles shouldered against each other for space just like in any other office, though they all enjoyed an entire wall of windows. It was incredibly rare for crew to enjoy natural sunlight.

"Just so you know," he said, gesturing to a bank of community printers. "You can use these copiers if you need, but you're supposed to bring your own paper. Since I slept with a purser, you probably won't need to worry about it. Unless she wants you to follow protocol, if you know what I mean."

"Meaning bring my own paper?"

"Meaning sleep with the purser."

"Ah," I said in understanding. "Ship life."

"Bob's your uncle," he agreed with a grin. "The far cubicle has a computer we can use for email, but we share it with the photogs, uh, photographers. Remember: all emails are screened and archived by RCI, so never criticize them and never talk about money. Believe me, they *do* check. Auctioneers have been booted off RCI ships because of personal comments before."

He rapped a hand on the desk of the only empty cubicle. "This is where your savior works, the ship's accountant. I assure you, this is the nicest accountant you will ever, ever meet, so treat him well. He works graveyard, so twice a week you'll have to meet him at 1:30 to finalize paperwork."

"1:30?" I asked. "In the morning?"

Shawn merely grinned and led me into a painfully clutter-free office with a huge window overlooking the port.

Shawn motioned for me to take down a large Caribbean-themed painting from the wall.

"Hot Man just signed off," Shawn explained. "The hotel manager. He's the most important man on the ship besides the captain, and is arguably *more* important. The previous Hot Man, Rodrey, was Jamaican and very, very cool. He's the reason I am allowed to conduct my auctions in the Centrum, because he saw how much money I make when given some freedom. I am the first auctioneer on *Majesty* to actually reach our sales goals, and that's entirely because of the Centrum. We lose that, and the Widow Maker takes another life. The problem is that the new guy is Dutch, and not even remotely interested in revenue. That's funny, because hotel managers are judged by the revenue their departments produce, just like the rest of us. We'll have to work on the new guy and see what turns him on, because he's already made noise about denying us the Centrum."

Together we hung the heavy, gold-framed art that was straining my arm. The actual art itself was only a tiny etching in heavy black ink set into a vast field of cream matting. But even without knowing *what* the art was, the ornate gold-leafed frame made it clear it was important.

"There!" he exclaimed. "If he doesn't like a centuries-old, original Rembrandt etching, then we're in trouble."

I whistled, not realizing the age of the work I had been mentally swearing at. Suddenly it seemed even heavier. "A contemporary Rembrandt, then?"

"No," he said. "It was made just after Rembrandt died. This is from his own copper plate, by those entrusted to them. *Not* from the plates taken by the banks during his bankruptcies, who then cranked out thousands of cheap copies. Of course, even the cheap copies are worth something now that they are nearly three hundred years old. Anyway, since the new Hot Man isn't here I'll swing by later and pretend I forgot to take the inventory number or something. That way I can educate him discreetly about how special we think he is. Politics, eh? Learn them well because it's a huge part of life as an auctioneer."

As we left, Shawn pulled a huge plastic bottle from his pocket and downed a handful of Tums.

"Too much to drink last night?" I asked.

He looked back, startled. "Hmm? Oh, no, I can handle huge amounts of booze nowadays. I'm an auctioneer, eh. I just didn't sleep much. No ties to wear last night, you know. You have to take advantage of casual while you can. You have a girlfriend back home?"

"Not back home, but I have a girlfriend, yes."

"She hot?"

"She's so cool that she's hot, you know? Euro-trashy dress, wild hair, black eyes, red lips and a cigarette. What more could I ask for?"

"Ah, met her on ships, eh? Sweet! She'll understand you doing what you have to do."

"Which is…?"

"You gotta bang those chicks, man. You know how on ships everyone screws everyone. Plus we have a dozen dancers who'll screw anything that moves: men, women, and anything in between. That's pretty cool. And Steiners? Bob's your uncle! You scored yet?"

"I got here yesterday, Shawn."

"So? Try the spa girls, they're always ready. Your girlfriend will understand if she's on ships."

"No doubt," I said drily, but knew Shawn was probably right. Bianca had insisted on a 'don't ask, don't tell' policy when I promised to be faithful before joining Carnival. I had thought that dubious, but soon discovered it was wise. It was far easier to find an attractive, ready partner on a ship than a good meal. She just wanted to ensure I came back to her.

Shawn babbled onward as if reliving a memory.

"Oh yeah, baby. Steiners are always fun. Working on a ship and not sleeping with a Steiner is like being in the rain and not getting wet."

"Is that some sort of clever 'raincoat' reference?"

"Ha! Well, I definitely recommend a raincoat with a Steiner. Double bag it if you can. Wait a minute. Are you saying that you really didn't hook up last night?"

"I heard German porn through the walls. Does that count?"

"Tonight's formal night, so if you want some action you'll have to wear a tie. I don't do ties, so no go for me, and I really need to sleep tonight. Well, we'll see. I got Steiners calling, two left on my list. Oh, and vacation is calling me! I am so goddamn burnt out. Been at sea for eleven months straight."

"Eleven months! They said auctioneers had only six month contracts because it was too stressful for more than that."

"Damn right it is, but I made so much money on *Oosterdam* that they tested me on the Widow Maker. They figured it'd break me like everyone else, but it didn't so they won't let me leave. That's Sundance. If you succeed somewhere, you better run with it as far and fast as you can or Bob ain't your uncle."

"Several times now you've said the 'Widow Maker'."

"Yeah. This ship broke a dozen auctioneers until I came along. It was tough man, tough to make it work. I mean, come on: they want us to bring in $30,000 in three days *without* a sea day! That's bullshit. I would never have made it without my gay boys. I pay them $200 a week. I could get about six Filipinos for that, but they're that good at arranging the art. You know, they are all flowery and gay and stuff."

"Of course," I replied with an amused smile. "Gay men are required to have good taste. It's in the rules."

"I don't mean to sound too cocky," Shawn admitted, "But, really, me and my gay boys are the first ones ever to survive on this ship. I'll teach you everything I can, but I'm really burned out and leaving in only four weeks."

"I'll follow you everywhere," I said.

"Not everywhere," he replied, giving me a lopsided grin. "I'm meeting two Steiners tonight."

3. HIGH SEAS ULCER

Later that day I returned to my cabin to find a man wearing officers' whites bent over my desk examining the contents of the top drawer.

"Can I help you?" I asked irritably. While there was no pretext of privacy on a cruise ship, having my own cabin had given me delusions of it. Who knew the number of keys floating out there, from my room steward to Shawn's Steiners.

The man shoved the drawer shut and snapped to his full height. At first I thought Chief Officer Roosevelt was pawing through my belongings, but this man was much taller. In fact, he was about three inches taller than me, about six foot four. His extremely slender physique added to the characteristic, somewhat like a reed rising from a ditch, were not his stance so unyielding.

"Cabin inspection," he said curtly with a Dutch accent. "I have reports that you routinely order room service. This is highly improper and will not continue."

"Oh, not me," I defended. "I just signed on a few days ago. The previous auctioneer may have, I don't know."

"Indeed," he said severely. "You will obey the rules, even if your predecessor did not. We have a cockroach problem in the stern deck, and I will not have it spread into this section of the ship."

"Of course," I agreed softly, wondering at the man's intense behavior. Only then did I conclude who he was. Cabin inspections were conducted by each department head and, since Shawn and I *were* the department heads, there was only one man above us.

"You are the hotel manager," I exclaimed in understanding. "It's nice to meet you, sir."

"Yes," he answered brusquely, ignoring my extended hand. He did not even offer his name, but merely waved me aside in order to check the toilet. He muttered to himself as if I were not present. "The boson is not happy. Not happy at all."

"Hey!" I cried. "I can assure you, sir, that I touched nothing in the boson's area."

Ignoring me, Hot Man dropped the toilet lid with a slam. He tried to hide his disdain behind a professional countenance, but the grimace worked through.

"No fish bones," I said cheerily.

"I am seeking a shoe."

I blinked. "Um… shoes?"

"*A* shoe!" Hot Man corrected sharply. He stormed out of my cabin, calling the explanation over his shoulder. "The entire sewage system is backed up ship-wide because a crewman flushed a shoe down the toilet this morning."

Suddenly alone, I sat on my bunk and shook my head in wonder.

Majesty's crew bar was the first such I had encountered that was not a dark little hole oppressively noisy and smoky, hidden deep within the bowels of the ship. The mysterious 'shoe in the toilet' happened in this area, however, so the subsequent stench of feces sticking to everything made ironic any metaphors about bowels. Luckily the dinner hour was over, as the crew mess was back here.

The crew bar was outside, a gorgeous area swathed in teak comprising the entire stern deck of *Majesty*. Lining the rail was a series of tables enjoying an unparalleled view of the tumultuous, dark sea. The faint afterglow of day tinged the horizon, glistening blood red off the roiling surface of the ocean. The bar itself, a mere window really, was nestled all the way beneath the overhanging deck.

The only lit tables were the few large rounds beneath the overhanging deck, and there I found Shawn, staring at a squat bottle of beer. In the center of the brilliantly lit table bristled nearly a dozen bottles perspiring in the humid evening.

"Dude," Shawn greeted me weakly, holding up a beer. "Red Stripe."

I happily joined him, being rather partial to the Jamaican beer, no doubt because it was so strong. Certainly that was how Shawn rated his alcoholic beverages.

"A dozen bottles?" I asked. "Expecting a herd of Steiners or something?"

"Don't talk to me about any goddamn Steiners."

His huge puppy-dog eyes implored support from his bottle, not me. I let it be, knowing he would eventually explain. But for now, Shawn talked shop.

"The gay boys are joining us after the show. Backstage is right above us, eh, so they'll be here any minute. Tomorrow I'm gonna have you finish the auction. From now on, once I reach Goal One all auctions are yours. Bob's your uncle?"

"Definitely," I replied.

Auctioneers had two sales goals per cruise. The amount of these goals varied radically from ship to ship, based on a billion tangible factors and more than a little Sundance whim. To say the goals were aggressive was an understatement. Once Goal One was reached, an auctioneer could somewhat relax, but reaching Goal Two was the only way to remain employed. Our auction today had been dismal, but afterwards we sold an expensive lithograph from Marc Chagall, mercifully putting us over both goals. We had been very lucky.

Yet Shawn's face was creased with worry. His youthful features sagged and his puppy-dog look was all droopy, like a Basset Hound. He fished in his pocket for comically long minutes until pulling out his ubiquitous jar of Tums. He popped two in his mouth and chased them with a slug of Red Stripe.

"You hit those a lot," I prodded.

"Yeah, I have an ulcer. Got it here on the Widow Maker. When I get on vacation back in Canada I'll have it looked at."

"The food?"

He chuckled, but shook his head sadly. "The stress."

"You really do look like Hell. Your vacation's in three weeks, right?"

He jiggled the plastic bottle in his hand. "Yep."

We sat in silence for a while, sipping our beers. Shawn seemed enthralled by his Tums, while I stared out at the awesomeness of the wine-dark sea. I sighed with the beauty of it, and breathed, "Holy Chicken, is that one beauty of a sunset."

Slowly Shawn glanced up at me. "What did you just say?"

"Hmm? Oh, I'm sorry. I learned that in Romania."

"I know they believe in vampires and shit, but you're sayin' they worship chickens, too?"

"No, no, it comes from 'what the chicken,'" I answered, smiling. "In Romanian, the term for 'what the fuck' is one letter away from 'what the chicken,' so you say that to not be offensive. You know, like saying 'shoot' instead of 'shit'. So it's a habit now, even in English."

"You are a strange man, Brian."

"At least I didn't say Holy Cat."

Shawn paused, then let his shoulders drop in defeat. "All right, do tell."

"On Carnival, you aren't allowed to use any language that invokes religion, whether praying or swearing. I thought 'Holy Cow' would be safe, but an Indian thought I was mocking him. I finally discovered that Holy Cat only offended my Born Again roomie, and that was too fun to pass up. Surely it pleased my cat to no end. In fact, that's why I made the switch to 'what the chicken'. My cat was already too cocky."

"Let's not talk for a while, eh?"

"Now you sound like my ex-wife."

Time passed, and eventually Shawn broke the silence.

"Did you meet the owner of Sundance during auctioneer training?"

"No," I said regretfully. "There were rumored Frederick sightings, but the way everyone was so scared of him perhaps it was for the best. They act like he's the messiah."

Shawn tilted his head to the side. "So they didn't show you Frederick's formula? I'm sure you heard he is a genius scientist. Seriously, he consulted for MIT, for Christ's sake."

"Cat's sake," I corrected.

"He came up with a formula for making a profit from art, which as you probably know is among the highest markups in the world. He's so confident of his mathematical formula for success that he shows it to everyone. If you can figure out the two dozen variables and shit, you are welcome to use it, he says. So, yeah, he's got it all worked out."

"Why did you ask if I'd seen him?"

"I wondered if he gave any clues about what's going on. Sundance is shuffling a lot of people because of you associates. It means more competition for the auctioneers. They used to throw auctioneers to the wolves and, if you survived, you made a fortune and banged a lot of chicks. Now every month there is a new crop of kids coming out, complete with training and verified as beautiful or they couldn't even get *into* auctioneer screening."

"Don't feel bad: they still throw us to the wolves."

"For sure. But now survival means splitting commissions with associates. For every one auctioneer there's now two trained and eager associates who want the job. Talk about stress, I can't even get it on anymore. How am I supposed to do my job while politicking with cruise lines, politicking with international management, politicking with Sundance *and* politicking with my assistant?"

"Nah," I said. "Don't worry: I'm way too inexperienced to be an auctioneer. My week in Pittsburgh involved little learning and more breaking, you know? I'm here to learn from you, yes, but in it for the long haul. I screw this up and I'll never get my Bianca with me."

"Look man, you're cool and all, but my ulcers are getting a lot worse with you aboard. This ship was one of the last to get an associate. I know two veteran auctioneers who failed G1 just twice in a row and lost their ships to their associates. Years of experience was immediately replaced by kids straight out of Pittsburgh."

"Twice? Holy Chicken!" I replied incredulously.

"And you're freaking me out with all that Holy Chicken shit!" he exclaimed.

"Holy Chicken Shit," I laughed. "Gotta be someone out there offended by that one."

"Laugh it up, chicken man. Carnival Corporation is thinking about leaving Sundance and doing art auctions in house. We would go from one hundred ships to about thirty. What will they do with all those auctioneers that aren't in the top tier? Fire them, that's what. Screw it. I'm so burnt out I don't care anymore. Screw the stress. Screw the auctions. From now on you can do most of them."

"I would love the opportunity," I replied. "But seriously, Shawn, chill. Your auctioneering manliness has me humbled."

"Manliness?" he barked abruptly. "Ha! I'm so goddamn burnt out, I'm impotent!"

"Whoa, Shawn," I said leaning back and trying to lower his escalating volume. "I love to talk dirty and all that, but-"

"Really!" he interrupted with tremendous agitation. "That's why I need you to finish the auctions. I've only got one goddamn Steiner left to bang. Just one, and I can't get it up anymore. I don't want to be impotent. Help me out, man!"

As Shawn shouted the last words, I looked up to see Denny and Jesse standing over us, sweat-glistened from their performance on stage. Blonde Jesse's handsome features stared at Shawn in open surprise, whereas Denny had a smug look of satisfaction.

"See?" Denny said to his partner. "I told you he would come around. It must have been Brian's pretty eyes."

At 3 a.m. my phone rang, and Shawn groggily ordered me to meet him at the purser's office in two hours. At the last minute, credit was denied to the guest who had purchased the Marc Chagall lithograph. Because he was cleared for early debarkation, we knew he would likely be off the ship before 6 a.m. If we did not personally meet him and secure payment, we would lose *both* our sales goals for the cruise.

I hung up and pondered the reality of being an art auctioneer. Mere hours earlier Shawn had climbed into bed, perhaps with that elusive Steiner, confident of a payday and a job. In a blink both were in jeopardy. While crew slaved seven days a week for months on end, I realized that auctioneers *stressed* seven days a week for months on end.

Shawn was Rookie of the Year by age thirty. He was young, handsome, and monied, but he was also impotent, alcoholic, and ulcered. What was it about cruise ships that even the best job was a nightmare? For the first time I fully realized that I would *never* be in control of my destiny while at sea. Any such feelings of being on top in the past had been woefully incorrect, and now my idealized future promised more of the same. This was not a new insight, of course, but it still stung. Even with Bianca at my side, this type of life was going to be nerve-wracking.

Fortunately, we found the guest in time and secured payment. All was well.

Or was it? That day in home port our fleet manager, Mary Elizabeth, stopped by for a surprise visit. Despite my having three plus weeks left of unpaid training, she promoted me to associate. Lest I suffer the delusion this was because of Shawn already praising my abilities, Mary Elizabeth told me point blank it was only because Shawn was being sent to another ship. It was merely underperforming in sales, but to Sundance this was an 'emergency' and required the Rookie of the Year, vacation be damned.

Poor Shawn. After a brutal eleven months of unrelenting pressure, he just wanted to pull back those last few weeks and ease me in. I had been looking forward to learning from the best. But instead his overwhelmingly earned vacation was denied indefinitely. He was leaving in three days.

There's a lot of damn chickens in Key West. Not happy farm animals, mind you, but roving packs of thug chickens, ready for some shit. I seem to have a penchant for finding menacing wild animals in the strangest places. I was literally cornered on a rainy mountaintop by a rabid dog in Romania. I was nearly trampled by a wild stallion in the high deserts of Nevada who thought I wanted his fillies. And one dark and stormy night I was nearly killed when an entire horde of suicidal bunny rabbits leapt onto a lonely Nevada highway one hundred miles from nowhere. None of those are jokes or exaggerations, and I survived each incident a bit wiser.

But really, on my first visit to Key West, to get attacked by a goddamn chicken?

It was a beautiful, warm day when I finally had a chance to escape *Majesty*, even if only temporarily, in a port of call. Propelled by the increasing wind, thick clouds were approaching and threatened an afternoon shower. After a solid two hours of wandering, my leg was beginning to hurt. I still had not fully recovered from my knee cracking against the bottom of the pool during survival training. It galled me that I could not run regularly, as it was my preferred manner of keeping mentally sharp and physically trim. The rapid-fire changes of ship life kept me alert, and as for staying trim, I safely relied upon *Majesty's* horrid food.

I sat wearily on a public bench beside a heavyset, heavy-bearded man with more than a passing resemblance to Jerry Garcia of the Grateful Dead. His tie-dyed shirt was still brilliant in the growing gloom of a tropical rain.

Sudden pain jolted me and I jumped from my seat, blurting, "Ow! What the chicken!"

A flurry of feathered wings disoriented me and a chicken raced away, flapping and squawking. I watched it rush across the street, past several parked cars, and safely into a parking lot. After a quick examination of the throb emanating from my foot, I concluded that the chicken had mistaken my toe for a worm. I sat down sheepishly, shooting an embarrassed peek at my neighbor. I wish I had yelled out something a bit manlier.

"Would you look at that?" I asked him. "That's a wild chicken. Here, in town."

The grizzled man just looked at me through his tinted sunglasses.

"Why did the chicken cross the road?" I prodded, trying to salvage some dignity. He made no motion.

"To get to the donut shop!"

No reaction.

"Look!" I urged, now thoroughly embarrassed. "That's a donut shop across the street."

The man slowly rotated his shaggy head to review where the chicken had fled to.

"The chicken ran over there? You know, crossing the road? That's funny," I defended lamely. He remained silent, however, and I was forced to move on because the humiliation throbbed worse than my toe.

Key West is a very beautiful place. I loved the lush foliage of the trees and the brilliant, succulent flowers everywhere. Being a restaurateur, there were few things I appreciated more than a patio café surrounded by blossoms dripping from verdant trees above. Key West was loaded with them. I settled upon one such establishment for lunch, to be accompanied by an art catalogue. I sat at a small round table with a mosaic top beside a whitewashed fountain. The table sat crookedly upon the hand-laid bricks, so whenever the wind gusted the ice in my drink clicked and spun.

This was exactly the kind of patio that Bianca and I enjoyed so much. We would waste hours sitting in a place like this, her with coffee and cigarettes and me with cognac and a cigar. In Romania we took advantage of the exchange rate and indulged in imported luxuries like fine Belgian and German chocolates for our afternoon talks. I missed those days, and not just because of my usual pining for Bianca. I was also pining for funds. There was no pay for the auctioneer screening or my time on *Majesty*, and I had just bought an entire new wardrobe to fit the job. Fortunately as an American I was blessed with credit cards.

Ah, for those long afternoon discussions and laughter! Currently our interaction was limited to snippets of love letters sent via email. I had been ecstatic to discover that her ship visited Key West, but alas, our port stops were off by one goddamn day. Talk about frustrating! All I could do was read and reread her every charmingly misspelled word. English was Bianca's third language and entirely self-taught via movies and music. I loved her misspelled words, but could do without the hip hop lyrics.

"Look who's here!" a voice called out from nearby. I looked up from my catalogue to see the dancers Denny and Jesse. Jesse, the head dancer, was short and of medium build, but oh what a build. This man had perfected the balance of being buff yet slender and smooth. His hair was a bit too blonde to be authentic but it matched his bright blue eyes well. He was, in a word, beautiful. Dark-haired Denny was the same height as his blonde companion, but nowhere near the same build. Rather, the outspoken backup dancer had a skinny kid-next-door look.

"Hello boys!" I greeted. "Care to join me?"

"Next time," Denny said regretfully. "We just finished lunch and have a rehearsal."

"Oh? Recommend anything? Certainly I need whatever Jesse here is having."

"Jesse is having me," Denny quipped. "Be careful what you ask for, you just might get it."

"Denny!" Jesse gasped. "Manners!"

"Oh, he's gay," Denny scoffed. "How can he not be with eyes that pretty? It's just a compliment."

"Most men don't think of it that way," Jesse replied with an apologetic glance to me. "You've met Amor."

"Fret not, my dear dancer," I laughed. "A compliment is a compliment."

"Well I don't recommend the chef's salad," Denny continued with an overtly sour expression. "It's loaded with pounds of ham and cheese, with only a little wilted lettuce. Ugh! There's nothing I hate worse than limp carrots!"

After hearing Jesse's disapproving sniff, he wisely opted to change the subject by asking, "So, Brian, where are you from?"

"Iowa."

Both men stared at me. I waited for the inevitable jokes about corn or, from the badly informed, potatoes. Nor would any references to corn-holing be beneficial at this juncture.

"We owned a flower shop in Cedar Rapids!"

"Wha- really? That's where I'm from! What flower shop?"

"The Flowerama on Beaver Street."

I was so surprised I nearly missed the irony of two gay men working on Beaver Street. Amazingly, that was only a mile from where I lived during my college years! What a small world. Perhaps Shawn's stereotype was right, that gay men really *did* always have a background in flowers.

"You doing homework?" Jesse asked, eyeing my art catalogue.

"Yes. We don't know what to expect now that Shawn's leaving, so I thought it would be a good idea to learn all the art in case I have to do an auction."

"You'll learn it in no time," Denny said, as they pulled away. "We're thinking of becoming auctioneers ourselves, in fact. We can study together sometime."

"I'd like that," I said, bidding them farewell.

They departed, leaving me with one hundred artists and one thousand works of art. This was not as intimidating as it could have been, thanks to a merciless and rather unkempt professor from the University of Northern Iowa. My final lesson before graduating as an art historian required an insane amount of memorization in only one week. He showed us slides of fifty paintings, and we had to identify the artwork's name, year, and movement, as well as the artist, his country, his teacher, and, when appropriate, the name of his dog. Yes, really. The professor loved dogs and would frequently highlight masterworks featuring canines, from English hunting hounds to Parisian poodles. Upon reflection, *Dogs Playing Poker* was conspicuously absent.

Thus, my great opportunity to work with Rookie of the Year devolved into a college-like cramming before a final.

Not surprisingly, my thoughts turned to my Bianca. She would memorize this stuff in record time. Bianca was a product of communist Romania, a flower that somehow managed to blossom in the shadow of the Iron Curtain. Her crappy society had required a significantly higher level of education than our United

States of America, a point which humiliated me to no end. How funny that Romanians were forced to assemble the tools for bettering their lives but forbidden to use them, whereas in rich America the opposite was true.

The irony of it all was that my chances of becoming an art auctioneer were slim without Bianca to help. She was the natural salesperson, not me, and smart as a whip. But while I was free to give this a shot, she had to support her extended family back in Romania. If she joined me before things were secured and failed, I would be damning multiple generations of Pops! No, I had to do this alone. Indeed, I felt more alone than ever.

At sea, friendships were short and intense, then gone. Every cruise meant dozens of different faces from all over the earth. But *Majesty* was new to me because I interacted with only a handful of people. Now the one I was closest to, with whom I had the greatest expectations of learning my craft, he, too was being torn away.

My success in getting the job and, thusly, my girl, was really to be shaped by the auctioneers I worked with. I had come with high hopes for working with the Rookie of the Year, but, alas, he was already a wreck when I met him. But what did the new auctioneer promise? Could I learn from him, or would he also be a man shredded by his ambitions and the pitiless sea? The Caribbean waters may not be so cruel, but the men who plied them have always been so, and would always be so.

The next afternoon, while moored at the Port of Miami, Shawn stared in disbelief at the security guards closing down the gangway. Four Filipino men in sweaters with epaulettes pulled up power cords and folded down trays. When the X-ray machine was safely secured, they hauled back the gangplank and dropped it to the carpet with a heavy clang. The look on Shawn's face was nearly indescribable. Thunderstruck was the only word that came to mind.

"Son of a goddamn bitch," he breathed. "He isn't here. The new goddamn auctioneer isn't here."

"What does this mean?"

"Bastard!" he cried suddenly, ignoring me. A security guard glanced up, but Shawn was apparently addressing the heavens. "I'm so goddamn burned out, and now this! I am so screwed!"

"Shall I invoke the Chicken?" I asked calmly.

"Fuck the Chicken!" Shawn snapped.

We had waited all afternoon for the arrival of the new auctioneer and with each passing hour grew more and more agitated. Shawn had rubbed his silent cell phone obsessively between numerous calls to our fleet manager, Mary Elizabeth. She was the go-to gal in case of situations like this. But she had no idea of the whereabouts of this new auctioneer, this Charles. All she knew was that he was flying in from Turkey.

A handover to an oncoming auctioneer was a very stressful process that always required more time than was available. Even had Charles been waiting on the gangway as soon as it was cleared in the predawn by the port agent, time would have been tested. Arriving in the afternoon was unheard of. Not arriving at all was devastating on so many levels.

Auctioneers were by nature adaptable and could take most aspects of a handover in stride. After all, they were expected to maintain a constant revenue stream despite being dropped onto a foreign vessel with a foreign layout and foreign customs; all while being assisted by foreign employees and filling out foreign paperwork. And this was usually done under extreme jet lag, to boot. None of this fazed an auctioneer. But missing the ship, that was a new thing entirely!

"I'm screwed!" he howled again. "I can't sign off with three million dollars of art still here. Until Charles signs for it, anything missing is out of my pocket. So now my flights are screwed. My hotel is screwed. My sign on tomorrow is screwed. That means my first cruise on the new ship is screwed. And my vacation was *already* screwed. Damn it! Damn it! Damn it!"

Shawn took a deep breath to calm himself. He appeared about to speak, but instead hurriedly fumbled the bottle of Tums from his pocket. While chomping on cherry-flavored salvation, he explained our plan of action.

"OK, OK. I'm calm. First, I need to call Mary Elizabeth and tell her the bastard didn't show up. My cabin was reserved for him, so I'll have to talk to the purser to ensure I can remain another night. It's a good thing I didn't set foot off the ship, because then they could not legally allow me back on board without a signed form from the Chief Officer. That would have sucked beyond all comprehension.

"Anyway, tomorrow we are in Nassau. I'll sign off there because surely the new guy, what's his nuts… Charles… will sign on then. I'll have to call and cancel my flights and hotel reservations and see when I will be allowed to sign on my new ship. Instead of flying to Maine, I'll sign on at the next port of call. I think that's St. John's. Great. Goddamn great."

"What can I do?"

"You need to get an auction going. Ordinarily we would already be setting up the auction in the Centrum by now, but the inventory nixed that. We need to play this like a normal cruise now and get haulin'. Call the boys and then start pulling art for the auction. You know the drill."

"Why bother? Leave it for the new guy. You're already overworked. Just be done with it."

"You don't get it," Shawn replied, shaking his head sadly. "What if he doesn't show up at all? This is only a three day cruise. If there's no revenue this first night, and whats-his-nuts doesn't show up at all, then it goes on me as a failure. In fact, you do the auction. I lied to Mary Elizabeth that you did one already, anyway."

"Thanks for that," I said honestly. "But I still don't get it. Surely you or Charles won't be judged by revenue on only half a cruise?"

"Damn right we will!" Shawn snorted. "You don't know Sundance. I once got a reprimand for bad sales on a ship that I never even set foot on. Gene laid into me for ten solid minutes before realizing his mistake. He never apologized. Our fat checks are apology enough. So start pulling the art now, so when the boys get here they can start hauling it to the Centrum."

"Just chill, Shawn," I said. "It's my auction now, so you just do what you need to do."

"What I *need* to do is a Steiner!" he cried as he rushed down the corridor. "Ha! Good luck with that, eh?"

So we went about our tasks with energy, if annoyance. The worst case scenario had just occurred and now it was time to deal with it. Setting up an auction required more time than we had, but with such talented and energetic assistants as Denny and Jesse we would survive. Usually the auctioneer preselected artwork with care, based upon cruise-long strategy, but today would be grab and go.

All too soon the many levels of the Centrum buzzed with guests browsing and carousing the art. Because there are so many little details to keep track of before an auction, I was too busy to be nervous about it. Not having my name on the bottom line surely helped that. But I was unnerved by Shawn taking up position by the champagne and downing glass after glass with abandon.

"The auction begins soon, folks!" I finally said into the microphone. It was strange hearing my own voice echoing over several floors. A dream come true, my ex-wife would surely have said. I wasn't sure where to look as I spoke, because lines of people pushed into the dining room on one deck and poured out on another. As usual, I babbled ever onward.

"This preview is the time to see the artwork up close and personal. Anything you want to see on the auction block, just put a tag on it. There's no obligation: it's just a little sticky note on the frames, folks. When you register for the auction, you'll get a bidding number, some tags and some free champagne. Take advantage of this time to see the art and ask questions! Don't you worry, I'll explain how it all works at the beginning of the auction."

Denny and Jesse flitted around in a graceful swirl, grabbing tagged artwork and arranging it next to the auction block on the raised platform. Shawn, champagne in hand, spoke with a guest over the sales laptop. Amor plied the crowd with champagne. Time flew and I was in the zone. Of course, whenever I start talking I *think* I am in the zone.

Delusions of things going well usually don't last long in auctions. The specter of bad luck still haunted us, a huge brute lurking in the wake. Just minutes before gavel time, Shawn rushed up to me with the sales laptop. His forehead was creased with worry and his puppy-dog brows expressed concern.

"Brian!" he whispered fiercely. "We need the art data!"

"What?" I asked, surprised. "You've been using the laptop for all preview. If there is no art data, what are you looking at?"

Shawn kept rolling his eyes as each wave of stress washed over him. Though bad timing, it was an easy fix. His capacity for handling the unexpected was nearly exhausted.

"It's my fault," he repeated with quick jerks of his head. His breath reeked of champagne. "To do the inventory for the handover, I kept last week's art data. If we use last week's art data it will overwrite my sales! I'm not losing my commissions from last cruise for this bastard."

"His name is Charles," I supplied in a soothing voice. "We have ten minutes, so just go swap the data now."

"I'm busy talking to a guest," he dismissed hurriedly. "Can you do it? Yes, you do it! I'm too busy to do it."

"OK, OK," I said exasperatedly. "Give me the diskette and I'll be back in two minutes."

"Bob's your uncle!" he cried. He hurriedly exported the old art data onto a 3.5 inch diskette and handed it to me. "Fly, my pretty bird, to the ship's computer. Fly!"

To illustrate, Shawn flapped his arms and hurled himself off the platform. He tumbled headlong into a group of guests who squawked and scattered with alarm. Too drunk to notice them, Shawn began raving, "I'm the chicken of the sea! The Holy Chicken of the sea! Bob's your uncle and Fannie's your goddamn aunt!"

Amor casually moved away from the prancing auctioneer, apparently convinced that he, too, was gay.

Swapping the art data was easy, if nerve-wracking. Exporting the old data encoded the file, so until new data was loaded, the laptop was blank. Thus the data was emailed days early. If it was running late, an auctioneer would stress. If it had not arrived by embarkation day, an auctioneer would panic. But I knew Sundance had safely emailed us the new data already, and it was waiting on the ship's computer. I skipped behind the purser's desk without a concern in the world, but suddenly stopped dead in my tracks.

Two computer technicians were squatting over the disjointed pieces of a computer, heads shaking solemnly, like surgeons who had just lost a patient in the OR. It was the ship's computer, our computer, the *only* computer with the art data.

I ran back to the Centrum and found Denny and Jesse trying diplomatically to stop Shawn from sucking down yet another glass of champagne. I quickly yanked it from his grip and exclaimed, "Shawn! The ship's computer is dead!"

Jesse gasped, but Shawn just blearily looked my way, too drunk to focus.

"There's no art data! The ship's computer is toast. We need to auction in five minutes!"

Shawn gaped at me for a long moment as the magnitude of things pushed through the champagne. Some eighty guests were signed up and waiting, and the balconies teemed with waiting guests as well.

"Wha- what?" he asked, rolling his eyes again. The waves of stress no longer washed over him, but crashed wildly upon the reefs and shoals. Clearly he was about to lose it.

"Can we cancel an auction this late?" I asked.

"Can we stop gathering tagged artwork?" Denny asked.

"Can you make an announcement?" Jesse asked.

"Can I have a bottle of champagne?" Amor slipped in.

Shawn's eye flopped every which way, like a fish out of water. Finally he raised his arms wide and cried out with great drama to the heavens. Or, rather, the guests on the balcony above.

"Why?" he boomed. "Why didn't that bastard auctioneer show up, what's his nuts."

"My name," a rich voice answered from behind us, "is Charles."

4. THE CHICKEN OF FATE

We whirled to see a tall, slender man parting the crowd with his approach. He strode forward with such gaunt grace and expensive accoutrements that I wondered if he were a vampire.

Charles was extremely thin, a feature amplified by a ponytail of solid grey hair so long that it touched the small of his back. Yet his features were young and his skin white as if never yet touched by sun. A neatly trimmed goatee smirked beneath his pointed nose. I had seen a pencil-thin mustache before, but this was the first pencil-thin goatee I had ever seen. He wore an expensive, smartly cut three-piece suit, though wrinkles revealed it to have just been pulled from luggage.

"You're Charles?" Shawn asked, gaping. "Bob's your uncle pluckin' chicken! When did *you* get on-board?"

"Twenty minutes ago," he answered with his sepulchral voice. "My wife is with the purser right now. He said an auction was already going, so I didn't bother calling but instead got dressed."

"W-where the Hell have you been?" Shawn demanded.

"Port security," Charles deadpanned in a slightly British accent. "I'll explain later. We used the guest gangway at the last second. So, shall I do the auction now that I am here?"

"I wish! No art data."

Charles raised an eyebrow in surprise and viewed the crowd with wonder. "You went this far without art data?"

Shawn's face clouded and I feared a meltdown was imminent. I jumped in first and said, "We'll explain later. I have a paper catalogue in my cabin. Can we use that?"

"No way," Charles replied, shaking his head with a swish of grey ponytail. "It's hard enough doing an auction with new art using the computer. With a paper catalogue after twenty-six hours of travel would be impossible."

"I'll do it," Shawn said abruptly. "I know all this artwork like the back of my hand. I'll do it from memory."

Charles whistled in admiration. "Surely not! Can't we cancel or do something smaller than a full auction instead? How long is the cruise?"

"Too short," Shawn answered. "You can invoice tomorrow. I'll explain the Widow Maker later."

"Sounds like much explaining will be happening later," Charles observed drily.

Shawn's infamous, lopsided grin suddenly sprouted and the twinkle blossomed in his eye. The transformation that occurred before us revealed exactly why this man had been the Rookie of the Year. He grabbed the microphone and strode up to the auction block. All evidence of champagne was gone.

"Ladies and gentlemen!" he called smoothly. "We are ready to begin. My name is Shawn and I want to welcome you all to the *Majesty of the Seas*. This cruise you are all in luck, because you get three auctioneers for the price of one! Tonight I'll be hosting the auction, but tomorrow you will have Charles, the man with the ponytail over there. There is also our associate Brian, the big guy with the stupefied look on his face."

Shawn was dazzling during his final performance on *Majesty*. I watched from behind a tangle of plants and was ready with the catalogue should he need it. Yet at each work of art brought to the auction block, Shawn rattled off without hesitation the name, the artist, and the year. Only twice did he pause and wait for me to verify the opening bid, and both times he was spot on. Awed, I double-checked his every statement by flipping through the cumbersome printout catalogue of some forty pages. He never once erred. His confidence and speed increased as he progressed, no doubt amplified by showmanship and champagne.

When the gavel struck for the final time, Shawn stumbled from the auction block like a soldier who had fought through an entire battle wounded. Charles and I both supported him with heartfelt compliments, but we all knew there was yet much work to be done.

The checkout process, normally chaotic, was now a nightmare. Many who purchased artwork were grateful to defer finalizing details until later in the cruise, but we had to fabricate a paper system to placate others, including the ship's accountant. Ordinarily Denny and Jesse packed up the auction while Shawn and I closed sales, but tonight everyone was needed for maximum communication and minimum confusion. Hours slogged by, and eventually the dancers had to leave for their stage performance.

Thus it was extremely late when Shawn, Charles, and I finally slid the last work of art back into the locker. Shawn ceremoniously handed the keys to Charles, whose long, thin fingers gripped the keys. Charles intoned, "I don't know about you, but I could use a sly drink."

"Amen, brother!" Shawn bellowed.

"And you can have these Tums back."

Sheepishly Shawn snatched back the scattered antacids that he had pulled from his pocket along with the keys. Charles smirked, but clearly understood.

We commandeered a large round table that looked comfortable upon the teak deck of the crew bar, but the effect was ruined by harsh lighting and its radiant glare upon the lumpy white paint of the nearby bulkhead. The reflective tape on the numerous lifejacket bins was blinding, and the lamps buzzing above also destroyed our view of the night sea. Charles indicated a preference for the smaller tables near the aft rail, under the stars and away from the bustle of the crew, but this was Shawn's night.

"As I was saying," Charles said, continuing the narration of his delays. He had been interrupted by a shop girl who felt the need for one last kiss on Shawn's forehead. "Your Homeland Security leaves much to be desired. I was cleared by one group only to be detained by the next, neither of which communicated with the other. Had I chosen to run, I doubt any of those obese men could have caught me. Considering England is your one and only ally in Iraq right now, I would think you would treat me a bit better!"

"Hey now," Shawn rebutted. "I'm Canadian."

"I jest," Charles continued. "My wife, whom you will meet tomorrow, is Turkish. No doubt we were detained because of her. I certainly don't blame you: Turks can be deceitful, tricky bastards."

"Your wife is on-board with you?" I pressed excitedly. I could finally get to see the reality of my dreams for auctioneering with Bianca.

"Yes. She is sleeping. If she gets less than fourteen hours of beauty sleep a day, she is, well, a Turk. It's all right, though, because as the Bard says, '*Baby got back*'."

"Huh," I said in wonder. "All these years I had no idea that 'the Bard' was a reference to Sir Mix-A-Lot."

"Shows what you know," Charles mocked with his deep voice.

"It still sounds suitably English," I replied with equal sarcasm. "Anyway, it's a good thing she is in the cabin right now if you're ripping on Turks."

"No doubt she would agree with me," Charles replied non-nonplussed. "She receives poor enough treatment in England, but I get the shaft in Turkey. No one there trusts anyone, whether English or Turkish or Arabic. I honestly don't know what they want."

Charles leaned back and smiled sardonically. "But at least they aren't French."

"I must say, Charles," I said, changing the subject, "Even though I have lived in Transylvania, you are the first undead I have actually conversed with. Certainly you are the first with a penchant for hip hop lyrics."

"I'm on Turkish time," he replied. "I may look like a zombie and certainly feel the part, but couldn't sleep if I tried."

"I was referring more to your image. I think Anne Rice would adopt you."

His thin goatee curved into a smirk. "Auctioneers need to have presence. It helps to command a room full of vacationing, champagne-guzzling passengers. I'm not a forceful type, so I use my image to capture attention. Besides, I like getting second glances."

Not long after, Denny and Jesse joined us after their performance for a final round or three of Red Stripes. It was customary for departing crew to get almost no sleep, so Shawn pushed ever onward. A queue of Steiners paraded by over the hours to say their goodbyes, and Shawn dutifully wrote down email addresses on a napkin. By 3AM's arrival, the subdued festivities came to a close.

"Here you go," Shawn said as he handed me the napkin scrawled over with emails and phone numbers. Also included was a hundred dollar bill.

"You presume much," I said.

"On the back is my address in Calgary," he explained. "I need you to send my Marc Chagall and the two big art books there for me. I didn't have time."

"Don't worry about it. Just go forth and prosper."

He rose tiredly and gave me his last puppy-dog turn of the head. "And if you want to keep those emails, be my guest."

I staggered back tiredly to my little cabin, while Charles climbed a deck higher to where his guest cabin awaited. Because there were no vacancies among the crew cabins, Shawn strode off to the infirmary to catch a nap on an examination table before his 6 a.m. departure.

⚓

As a rule, auctioneers are fiercely independent and unique in character. It was too early to tell if Charles and Tatli were the former, but they had the latter in spades. The morning after the crazy auction-from-memory, I joined the new auctioneering couple for breakfast. We sat at a quiet table away from the other guests on deck eleven at the Windjammer Café.

If Charles resembled the walking dead, Tatli was the embodiment of healthy life. She was pleasantly rounded with flowing sandy hair. Her skin was a radiant, natural bronze that practically glowed from within. Not a blemish was visible upon that skin, not one mole, pimple, or freckle. Such purity is so rare that I was continuously struck by it. Her round face had rounder cheeks and boasted pretty, dark eyes. She was the Raphael angel to his El Greco ghost.

Somehow I sensed that Tatli was a reserved person, yet this morning all evidence was to the contrary. She had not eaten at all during their lengthy travels and had slept through both dinner and the night. The abused remains of numerous melons lay discarded about her, and she eagerly sliced and devoured still more. Charles looked on with obvious distaste, but only after several fish were destroyed and she focused on a pile of greasy bacon did he finally speak.

"Tatli, please," Charles said as he nibbled on his toast and marmalade. "Slow down."

"Apparently you've never been to an American barbecue," I quipped.

"No, but I've seen the effects," he sarcastically. "Anyway, it seems we've got our work cut out for us on this Widow Maker, as they call it. Even so, I will not work day and night seven days a week like Shawn did. I saw that we are in Nassau from sunup 'til after sunset every other cruise. I intend to take that day off, or at least work only evening. We have enough time for that."

He eyed his wife snarfing down greasy bacon and amended, "Unless my wife dies of indigestion. In that case, I guess it will become the Widower."

"I am a fool for bacon myself," I said. "But, Tatli, as a Turk are you not Muslim?"

Tatli paused only long enough to give me a quick smile, bacon-filled cheeks like a squirrel storing for winter. She shook her head, and Charles answered more fully on her behalf.

"She is a modern Muslim. She drinks, too, but not as much as I'd like. Tatli may be very quiet but she is a solid thinker. She does all the math for us and makes all the negotiations. In fact, she does everything that matters. I'm lazy and just stand out and talk a lot. And look good, of course. But she gets things done. I would be lost without her. Which is why I am going to take away the remaining bacon."

Giving action to his words, he reached over and removed the last four pieces of bacon from her plate. He dropped them with a greasy thump onto his own and pushed it away. Tatli, mouth too full to stick her tongue out, taunted him with a mocking wrinkle of her face.

After graciously assisting their little quarrel by devouring the debated bacon myself, I began to compare their apparent relationship with mine and Bianca's. I did not focus on the constant, good-natured ribbing, but on other parallels. Already Charles had admitted his own inferiority in business details. I fear I was very much the same, and certainly gave great credence to Bianca's brains and ability to conduct business. Both our ladies also boasted a shared strength over us poor Western men: they came from bartering cultures and could negotiate circles around us. Charles and I, English and American respectively, were at a severe disadvantage while at sea. Luckily for us, our positions gave us a great equalizer common to members of our societies: money.

Thus, by the end of the bacon, I had already made up my mind about Charles and Tatli. Hasty decisions were the norm at sea, after all. They wore their relationship on their sleeves for all to see. So I saw, and I liked what I saw. They were a product of their respective cultures yet found a way to mix the two. He necessarily acted in charge but was in fact not. I sensed this suited them both. I also sensed this was the nature of most relationships anywhere, just not as overt.

Unfortunately, I was not alone in my quick measure of the new auctioneers. Hot Man voiced his assessment from the first, and his body language needed no megaphone.

"Obviously you don't know anything about ships," he said crisply from behind his desk when we met him after breakfast. He ignored Charles' outstretched hand, but at least gave him the courtesy of standing up to berate him. "That ponytail is completely inappropriate and will be cut off immediately."

Charles retracted his hand. Indignant, he responded in an equally terse manner.

"Hello," he said tartly. "My name is Charles and it's a pleasure to meet you. And I *have* been on nearly one dozen ships, including two from Royal Caribbean. Not once has there ever been a problem with my hairstyle."

"We have rules for crew," the hotel manager said with a dismissive wave of his hand. "Rules that apply to all crew. Do you think you are above the rules on your very first day? Nearly missing embarkation, I might add."

"I was *early*, in point of fact. Port security supersedes ship security," Charles retorted, crossing his arms behind his back and standing stiffly defiant. "Regardless, such rules as you quote apply to crew, not concessionaires."

"The rules apply to whomever they apply to," Hot Man answered in a huff. "In this case, they apply to you. If you are not an entertainer, you are bound by the same hygiene rules as the crew."

"I am in a guest cabin for a reason," Charles answered smoothly. "Auctioneers have a wide variety of latitudes over other concessionaires. It is in our contract with the cruise lines."

"My ship means my rules," Hot Man said forcefully. "You have until the end of next cruise to comply or you will be ejected. After that point, you are free to take up this issue with the corporate office."

With those final words, the hotel manager sat back down and pointedly ignored us in favor of his paperwork. Several files covered the name placard on the front of his desk, and it occurred to me that I did not even know this man's name. He had refused introductions from Shawn and me as well. He was only referred to by others as Hot Man. We departed primarily in silence, barring Charles' gnashing of teeth and low growl.

Because the previous day had been so crazy, Charles had not seen the locations about the ship where art was displayed. I suggested a quick ship tour so he could walk and cool down. During the entire walk from Hot Man's office on deck four up to the Champagne Bar on deck seven Charles fumed. Fortunately, the lounge was closed at this hour so no one observed his rage when he finally cut loose.

"I've had this ponytail for ten years! I have been on dozens of ships, and never has any German asshole had a problem. I hate this ship already."

"He's Dutch," I corrected.

"He's an asshole."

"That is our only original Tomasz Rut painting," I said, trying to change the subject. I indicated a large, lusty painting of a nude male struggling to tame a rearing stallion. Both figures rose from the dust and blackness, magnificently powerful with skin glistening and muscles pulsing with heat.

Charles stared at the painting for long, slow moments, gaunt figure swept continuously by his ponytail thrashing like the mane of the agitated horse. Finally he said, "Can you believe the nerve of that man? I am so insulted I can't even begin to speak of it. What kind of a greeting is that, anyway?"

"I don't deny the asshole behavior, Charles. But you'll want to keep your voice down about such things in here," I warned. "This is where the officers congregate."

Charles sunk into one of the deep chairs of the quiet lounge, all sharp knees and elbows at acute angles. He pursed his lips in thought for a moment and settled down. Finally he asked, "Artwork displayed only here, in this one lounge?"

"Correct."

"Not even a full line of easels in the Centrum area where we conduct all the auctions?"

"Four easels only, two on each side. Actually, half the auctions are in the Paint Your Wagon Lounge, when we aren't kicked out for karaoke."

"Lovely. No real display of art that we can show the guests. Here we have three paintings, in the lounge that no doubt gets the least guest traffic. No desk upon which to even display a catalogue. No time off from port of call."

"Hence the Widow Maker," I said.

"Hence the Widow Maker," he repeated quietly.

"This lounge gets few enough guests," I offered. "But they are invariably loaded. That's why our best works are here. Sell one of these bad boys and we clear G2. I used to work this lounge in the evenings."

"Doing what? Surely not conducting an auction?"

"Networking. I am a natural schmoozer."

"Yeah, you look like an ass-kisser. How's that working for you?"

"Not as well as I'd like," I admitted. "I just came from auctioneer screening a week ago and have only been an unpaid trainee. But I generate a little interest and get qualified bodies to the auctions. It's breaking my bank, but it's beneficial."

"So you have to pay for that, too? Let me guess: full guest price on drinks. The handover report indicated the costs on this ship are extremely high. I pay nearly double for champagne here. Shawn said he paid $80 a month for online access to guest credit, though every other department gets it free. *And* I have to pay the printer to make our flyers for the guest cabins *and* I have to pay for the room stewards to put them there."

"But we get free paper because Shawn porked a purser," I offered. Charles ignored me.

"In fact, I have to pay for my own laundry here, too. What kind of officer has to do that? 80¢ for a T-shirt, my underwear is 40¢ and, get this, they charge 15¢ a sock!

I'm sure I'll have to pay extra for ironing. Unless, of course, you have an ironing board."

"It's funny you mention that," I said with a little pride, "Because I actually have an ironing board autographed by M.C. Hammer."

Charles had been burying his head in his hands, but slowly looked up at me.

"Not with me, of course," I quickly added.

"Why, I do believe that you are serious," he said. "All right, I'll bite."

"I used to work at the best hotel in my hometown in Iowa," I explained. "M.C. Hammer came to town for a concert and booked the entire top floor of suites for him and his entourage. Remember those huge, baggy pants he wore? Can't exactly send those to the cleaners, you know? So they needed a full length ironing board and the hotel only had the short, portable ones. I was dating the Guest Services Manager in charge of getting one on the fly, and I happened to live nearby. So I ran home and got my ironing board, but insisted that he autograph it. Otherwise, who would believe me?"

Charles regarded me skeptically a moment, then chuckled. "Who would believe you indeed? But that story is way too stupid to be made up."

Hoping to have cheered him up a bit, I smiled and added, "As your Lord Byron noted, 'The truth is strange: stranger than fiction.'"

Distraction over, Charles leaned back and stared at the ceiling. "Jesus, is there anything I don't have to pay for on this ship? No doubt I'll have to pay top dollar at the spa to get my haircut for Herr Assmunchen."

I remained silent, completely unqualified to comment. One expense that Shawn had not included in his handover report was the cost of having me on board. As a trainee I was unpaid, but with Charles' arrival I was now an associate and would get a sizable chunk of his sales commissions. I opted not to mention that at the moment.

"And the two art movers?" Charles continued with mounting disgust. "My God, did I really read that they are paid $200 a week? I can get six Filipinos for that money!"

This topic, however, I knew enough about to comment. "Denny and Jesse are worth every penny, believe me. You never saw them in action because yesterday was so whacked out. But they do far more than move all the art: they handle everything from top to bottom. They are fully qualified to close sales on their own and man the check out desks."

"I understand," Charles dismissed with a grunt. "I'll have to let Tatli look at the numbers, but unless we consistently reach Goal 2 I don't see how we'll make any money on this ship. As the Bard says, *'I've got my mind on my money and my money on my mind.'*"

"*Sir* Snoop Dogg," I agreed, recognizing the lyrics he sang.

"Shawn made G2 regularly?"

"More or less," I answered.

Charles loosed a long, slow sigh before rising. No doubt he wanted to crawl back into his coffin. We wandered down to the purser's area and saw that the computer doctors had revived their patient. We greedily loaded the fresh art data into our computer, but then Charles' pale face somehow got paler. Disdainfully, he tossed me the laptop.

"Brian, can you see anything changed here?"

I noticed a change. A big, nasty mother chicken of a change.

"The goals have gone up!"

He clapped me on the shoulder and gave me a predatory grin. "Learned a lot in the last week? You, my friend, had better be worth it."

Quick to change the subject yet again, I glanced once more at the resurrected ship's computer. "I see there is an email from the powers that be."

"Powers that be?" he asked, amused. "Is that Ebonics?"

"Says here that Denny and Jesse will be attending the next auctioneer screening. They leave in one week!"

Charles released yet another long sigh and said drily, "At least I no longer need worry about how expensive they are."

That afternoon I had to set up the art auction more or less alone. Denny and Jesse were scrambling to make preparations to sign off *Majesty of the Seas* and fly to the Sundance Art Gallery in Pittsburgh.

Setting up for an auction had many challenges, far beyond merely hauling artwork. First we had to clear the auction, no matter how routine, with Hot Man *and* the chief officer, for some reason that defies explanation. Then we notified the housekeeping manager, who allocated crew, stackable chairs and folding tables. Then the bar manager had to requisition cases of champagne and a bartender.

These avenues did not involve bribery, barring our redoubtable Amor. Because he received a commission on every bottle of champagne he opened, a preventive bribe of five dollars spared us the expense of entire cases of wasted champagne. We also bribed the printing manager to print our flyers, no doubt because sleeping with him was out of the question. We bribed the housekeepers to distribute the flyers to the cabins, because there were too many to sleep with. With twelve hundred guest cabins even on the modestly sized Widow Maker, there was no other practical way to do it.

By far the most important spoke of the bribery wheel was the cruise director. He placed our ads in the daily papers and spoke about us during various events, including the all-important PA announcements. We were always on the lookout for new and appreciated ways to express our gratitude. But the biggest challenge on *Majesty* was the unavoidable lack of bodies on board. Who would give up all day in the Bahamas for an auction in the karaoke lounge?

The art locker was ten feet deep and extremely narrow, with only a single lightbulb above the door to cast the corners in shadow. Both sides were lined floor to ceiling with tiers of carpeted shelves, all spilling artwork. The larger compartments on the bottom were packed with huge frames arranged like books. The top tier stacked frames two high in this manner, and any open gaps were stuffed with smaller artwork. The locker was so narrow that pulling out the large artwork was impossible until all the other works were first removed, in order to angle them out.

True to his word, Charles was lazy. He stayed in the locker selecting artwork, leaving me to cart it all to the lounge all the way in the stern. Each load turned the art cart into a porcupine-looking creature of bristling frames and edges, and every doorway tried to snag one. On a ship equal in length to *Titanic*, that was a lot of doors! Even worse were these damnable ridges of soldered metal unevenly placed in our hallway. These stupid lips served no apparent purpose, such as connecting metal plates. What, the builders thought if deck *three* was underwater, an inch-high ridge would stop the ship from flooding? Those little bastards tripped me up several times, dumping artwork everywhere. Oh, lipless hall, where art thou?

The elevators were a nightmare. The dancers had overcome this problem by working in concert: Denny literally put his back to the wall and pushed with *both* legs, while Jesse simultaneously hauled up the front wheels over the threshold. But I worked alone and had to muscle the whole thing myself. My back did not thank me. Neither did Charles, I noticed.

As loads of artwork began to fill the lounge, Tatli arranged it on the reclining seats to taste even as she oversaw the housekeepers arranging the chairs and tables. The dance floor soon flowered into rows of seats facing a future auction block. Tatli was also in charge of all the little things an auction needed, like sticky notes, bidder cards, Sundance Credit applications, art catalogues the guests can take and art catalogues they cannot. She ensured an internet card was handy to process credit card applications during the auction. Tatli was unbelievably smooth.

Meanwhile, I was getting my ass kicked by the damnable easels. They were too awkward to transport via art cart, so I had to shoulder them. These annoying creatures had more kicking legs than a millipede and hooked on every doorway. I could handle a stack of five of the unruly beasts, but with our bungee cords continually being stolen by crew members, more than that was hopeless.

After several hours of hauling and arranging, we had the Paint Your Wagon lounge ready for an art auction.

It could hold over two hundred people. We hoped for fifty. We got ten.

That night we three weary auctioneers sat around a table on the open deck, far removed from the lights. It suited our moods to be in the dark, beneath a rumbling, unquiet sky. Beside us a rail kept back the thrashing ocean, and before us champagne kept back the thrashing stress. We were well on our way to getting drunk and eager to solve the world's problems, but before we could do that we had to first solve our own.

Ten people do not an auction make, so the afternoon had been a gallery-style operation. Despite specific instructions and bribery to the contrary, Amor had opened enough champagne for two bottles per guest. That was the only problem of the day we found underwhelming; hence a tabletop laden with champagne bottles. G2 was hopelessly out of reach, but Charles was grudgingly satisfied with our possible gaining of G1 by tomorrow, the last day of the cruise. Still, his mood was as turbulent as the sky.

"One thing is for sure," Charles said as he refilled my glass yet again. "We need some art movers. I can't have you schlepping artwork all day and night. We need you free to sell artwork. These higher goals are gonna kill us."

"I quite agree."

"That's my job, but I need your input. Usually ships have a Filipino cover band that is happy for the extra income during their daytime off-hours. But *Majesty* doesn't have one that I am aware of. Stage entertainers are the second usual source, because they are the only members of the crew who have the free time outside of their regular duties. Like Denny and Jesse, for example. Think that will work?"

"Doubtful," I warned. "Denny didn't have much nice to say about the reliability of the other dancers. He says they are all drunkards, and I believe it. Living in their hallway is one continuous party. I don't mind the half-naked hotties prancing from cabin to cabin in their panties. I *do* mind that they keep missing my cabin."

"Perhaps an upgrade to a guest cabin?" he offered teasingly. "I could handle a parade of women." He was trying to bring himself out of his melancholy, and Tatli gave him an elbow in the side for support.

Thunder rumbled over our heads, and we all glanced out into the black night tailing the ship. Muffled flashes of lightning revealed lumpy clouds in purple. The gusting wind dropped the scent of salt in favor of fresh water. It was entrancing. A moment of silence ensued, and we all pondered the electric, tropical night.

"I love rain," Charles murmured. "There isn't any rain anywhere in Turkey. But the storms of the Caribbean are the best. They are unique and powerful, completely unlike the rain in London. There it just drops all day and night, boring and oppressive. Here it is alive."

"Boring and oppressive?" I teased. "Is that not the very definition of 'be British'?"

Tatli barked a laugh before she could contain it. Charles snorted and gave her a mock scowl.

"That reminds me of a question I've always wanted to bounce off an Englishman," I said slowly and carefully. "You are welcome to not answer, of course."

"Well, what is it?" he asked impatiently before downing another glass of champagne.

"You've got some great beer there, with awesome English pubs to enjoy it in. British theatre, even aside from Shakespeare, is surely the best in the world. I think every British actor has won an Oscar or deserves one, like Anthony Hopkins, Ian McKellan, Kate Winslet, or Judy Dench. Skip Hugh Grant. Your movie directors kick ass, with Ridley Scott and Alfred Hitchcock. Your literary figures are magnificent, with Austen and Dickens, Agatha Christy and H.G. Wells, and so many more. And music? Few musicians have impacted the planet more than the Beatles, and you've got George Michael and Elton John to boot. Skip Boy George. You with me so far?"

"Yes, yes, of course. England has the best entertainment on Earth."

"So is this obsession with entertainment because A; the weather is so shitty, B; because your food is so shitty, or C; because you're too uptight and proper to have some good ol' nasty sex?"

Charles stared at me for a long moment. Lightning flashed above to reveal a face frowning in rumination. I wondered if I had offended him, but after a long deliberation he answered with a deep voice.

"All of the above," he deadpanned. "Why else would I marry a Turk?"

Another flash of lightning lit the night, burning a brilliant impression of the couple I sat with. Only then did I realize the real reason why Charles was so gloomy.

"You cut your hair!"

In the dark, I had hardly noticed that his long ponytail was missing. His grey bangs were still pulled back over the ears, but a few tangles now fell over his forehead. He looked quite handsome, actually. Certainly less vampiric.

"Thank Tatli for that," he answered morosely. "She was so damn excited for me to lose the ponytail that she made me an appointment for immediately after the auction. She's been hounding me for three years to get it cut. As always, she gets things done."

Another flash of lightning burst over the scene, and for one instant every detail was dazzling. I smiled, loving a good storm, but Tatli was anything but pleased.

"Just a storm, darlin'" I consoled, assuming she was frightened by the weather. I had met many Mediterranean women who were for some reason scared of the violence above. I never figured that one out. But then, the thunderstorms over the Great Plains where I grew up were extremely powerful and probably inured me.

"No, no," she replied. "Did you see all those bugs on the deck?"

Sure enough, in the poor light we hadn't noticed the deck was fairly swarming with fingernail-sized bugs. They were of a light color that matched the teak.

"Oh, those are the cockroaches everyone bitches about. Welcome aboard."

Tatli shivered, and Charles shook his head.

"I hate this ship already," Charles said mournfully. "Did I mention I hate this ship? Yes, I certainly do hate this ship."

The storm groaned about *Majesty* all night, not unlike the auctioneers, but did not finally break into a hard rain until the morning. Today's port of call was Royal Caribbean's private island of Coco Cay. It was just one of hundreds of gorgeous little Bahamian pearls scattered across the sand bars and turquoise waters, but that doesn't matter much when the rain falls so hard that you can't even see it. Thus no one tendered to port. With this surprising flow of bodies on-board, the auction was a fair success. Charles managed to close enough sales to clear G1, but even this beneficial influx failed to hit G2.

As promised, Charles canvassed the ship for potential art movers, and stumbled upon the Calypso players. Of course, Tatli made the financial arrangements with the Jamaican duo, and, also of course, Charles took full credit for everything.

These two men were both young and handsome, with sleek black skin, generous smiles, and brilliantly tie-dyed shirts. The steel drummer was named O'Neil, whose long, beaded hair would rattle with ecstasy at the Caribbean folk music. His partner, Kelvin, wore his hair in tight curls around his head. Kelvin's instrument, the electric keyboard, was preprogrammed so he just stood behind it all day, obviously bored. They were good musicians, but as art movers they sucked. They were about as dynamic as a pair of zombies.

Their first cruise as movers was a mess. It went something like this: I explain what to do. They say 'no problem, mon.' They act and demonstrate a complete lack of understanding. I explain what to do. They say, 'no problem, mon'. Disaster resumes, repeat, ad nauseum. It was exasperating. Obviously playing *'Everything Will Be All Right'* by Bob Marley 1,000 times a day had melted their brains.

What Shawn's 'gay boys' did in an hour, the Calypso boys needed three. After multiple auctions this did not change, until Tatli reminded them that they were paid per auction, not per hour. That helped, but even then their exquisitely toned muscles were seemingly incapable of lifting the lightest loads. Having worked with many Jamaicans before, I always wondered if it was island attitude that prevented those beautiful muscles from accomplishment or if they were more like Italian clothing, designed for looks only.

Once, when Kelvin was hauling a distressingly underloaded cartload of artwork, he was suddenly brought up short by one of the soldered ridges on the deck. How he lacked the momentum to coast such a light load over the lip was a testament to ineptitude, as was his not yet having learned to push the art carts backwards to prevent everything from spilling out the front. Out of sheer, perverse curiosity, I watched from afar as Kelvin leaned upon the cart to casually survey the damage. He was not perturbed in slightest. After a while, O'Neil arrived and began picking up the pieces, bobbing to the music in his head. He sorted through a gnarl of wires tangled around broken frames, eventually retrieving two punctured oil paintings.

In awe, O'Neil held up the canvases speared by broken frames. Kelvin gave a hearty laugh.

"*Coo 'pon dat!*" Kelvin cried, meaning 'look at that'.

"*Bamboclat!*" O'Neil berated. "*Dey not donuts, mon! Yu try carry paintins on a stick?*"

"*Dey just a likkle off, mon. Ev'ry-ting I-rey.*"

"*Ev'ry-ting* not *I-rey, yu dam lagga head!*" he cried, meaning, 'everything is not all right.'

Charles rushed forward, and all bickering stopped as they looked up at the gaunt, towering figure. He pursed his lips and frowned at no less than four damaged Rembrandt etchings. A grey-shot eyebrow rose inquiringly at the two pierced oil paintings.

"It appears, gentlemen," he began slowly in his deep voice. "That the Rembrandts are unharmed, barring the frames. But the oil paintings…."

Kelvin tensed, sensing he was about to be struck.

O'Neil tensed, sensing he was about to be fired.

I tensed, sensing I was about to be an art schlepper forever.

"Those are original paintings from Jean-Claude Picot…" he began with heavy drama. Suddenly his thin lips split into a wolfish grin. "Good! Further penance for the French's failure during World War II."

Things slowly got better. Eager to prove I was worthy of skipping my month as unpaid trainee, and fully aware of the strain Charles was under, I stepped up. During auctions I became a large supporting figure and even gave Tatli a run for her money. My biggest contribution, however, lay in schmoozing guests in the Champagne Bar. I am a social butterfly and naturally flitted about the room making contact with everyone. My confidence progressed along with the cruises, and soon I was selling my share of artwork outside the auctions.

Fortunately, Charles did not share in Shawn's misgivings about being replaced. As I sought more duties, Charles gladly obliged. By his own admission he was lazy, and if others performed a job better than he, so be it. Our first few cruises were bruising failures, but eventually we began to tread water just enough to occasionally pop up and snag G2.

Maybe, just maybe, the curse of the Widow Maker could be lifted.

5. MISERY OF THE SEAS

Charles, Tatli and I officially adopted that dark, quiet table beside the rail on the crew deck for our nightly meetings. After the sun set we always met for a sly drink, as Charles would say, and watched the other cruise ships slip off into the blackness. These waters around the Bahamas always offered tantalizing glimpses of brightly lit ships passing in the night. Under this dramatic setting we would discuss the day's events and plan for the morrow.

At first, the buying of a round of Red Stripes launched Charles on a tirade about the costs of running his department. Tatli solved this problem by routinely bringing entire bottles of auction champagne, which ironically cost less than the beer. Thusly Charles congratulated himself for lubricating our thoughts for less. Tatli somehow refrained from rolling her eyes.

"I received an email from Sundance," I began over the champagne. "Regarding the paintings destroyed by Zero Degrees Kelvin? They were rather annoyed."

Charles asked, "You *did* tell them it was due to the rocking of the ship, as I said, yes?"

Tatli had presented that idea, of course.

"Yes," I said. "I was chided for improper stowing, but insurance will pay for it all."

"Good," Charles said with satisfaction. "Say, what do you mean by calling him Zero Degrees Kelvin?"

"Perhaps he means Kelvin is close minded," Tatli suggested.

"How do you figure that?" Charles asked.

"A closed circle has zero degrees of angle," she said simply.

"Good thought, Tatli," I said, impressed. "But I was referring to temperature. Absolute zero is the absence of all molecular movement."

Tatli nodded in understanding, but Charles' brows knit together in confusion.

"You know," I explained. "As things get colder their molecules move slower. That's why when vapor cools the molecules slow and it turns to water, and when that cools it turns to ice. Absolute zero is the cessation of all molecular movement, and theoretically impossible. I thought you, not Tatli, would have the First World education. Didn't you go to school?"

"What the Hell, man?" he protested. "Zero degrees is just freezing."

"That's Celsius," Tatli said quietly.

"Right. The Kelvin scale is the most accurate scale for measuring such things. I thought their names were so odd for the Caribbean. O'Neil and Kelvin? Anyway, Kelvin moves so damn slow I assume his goal is to reach absolute motionless."

"Brian," Charles said drily, "With talk like that it's a wonder the bitches don't line up at your door."

Near midnight the open deck was frequently commandeered by all the Jamaicans on-board, regardless of position. The usual suspects of crew bars; the entertainers, Steiners, and waiters, were replaced by room stewards, bar backs, and cooks. These crewmen did not come to drink, but something else entirely. They would muscle two or more tables together, thus proving that strong Jamaican arms really *could* function when they chose, to create a small arena. All evidence of what happened within that arena was blocked by a tight crowd of standing spectators, cheering and jeering.

Occasionally over their great emotion and greater volume, a boastful cry would rise, *"I BE FLASHIN' BLOOD!,"* followed by a thundering slap, like a body slam. Then a bellow from the Jamaicans would deafen us from afar.

Eventually Charles and I were intrigued enough to try for some details. We pushed into the crowd with not a little trepidation, fearing nothing less than a cockfight.

Just as we approached, O'Neil rose to his feet and held a closed fist over his head with great ceremony. The crowd began to jostle in agitation, and he called, *"Where da bangarang, buoys?"*

The crowd hollered louder and louder, but O'Neil kept his fist up high, calling for more and more 'bangarang' with a shake of his braids. When the pitch was just right, he suddenly swept his hand downward so powerfully that his legs actually lifted from the ground. He slapped the table with great clout, pitching it madly and tossing its contents pell-mell. Above the monstrous roar of approval he stood triumphant and panting, daring anyone to challenge his supremacy.

"What the Hell is going on here?" Charles asked, bewildered.

"They're playing dominoes," I said, observing at last the tiles scattered across the deck among the roaches. The Jamaicans scooped up the dotted tiles and readied the table for another match.

"Come!" O'Neil invited. "And watch me flash some blood on these *rasclats*."

"Nuh," someone protested. *"Dis be for Jam-down buoys, mon!"*

"Nuh, yu be too red eye, mon." O'Neil answered. *"Don't want no harbor shark watchin', nuh?"*

"What did he just say?" Charles wondered aloud.

O'Neil grinned at us. "He want to keep da game for us Jamaicans. We be *Jam-down buoys*. I said he be jealous of you comin' to take da glory. Come, *duppy*, you my white boy. I teach you."

"What does *duppy* mean?"

"Ghost," he answered with a flash of pearly teeth.

Thus was our introduction to the domino scene. Four men settled around the table and drew from the pile of dominoes. The first man began by laying a tile in the center of the table, and each man would place his answering domino with a violent slap. A crisscrossed network of dominoes grew with alarming rapidity, as each man seemed to know exactly what the next move would be before it happened. As the table filled to capacity, play slowed and sweat would bead on the brows of the players.

When O'Neil said, "I be flashin' blood," he had placed a tile that he anticipated could not be answered by the next man, in this case Kelvin. O'Neil would gesture with his tile as if he were dashing drops from it onto the spot that Kelvin could not fill. Then Kelvin would sheepishly admit, "I be wet."

These men had mastered dominoes in a way I had not thought possible, and their over-the-top theatrics were a great joy to behold. How Kelvin could accurately count dominos, to the point where he knew what was left within one or two tiles, yet be unable to program his own synthesizer was beyond me.

"Kelvin," I admitted in awe, "If you counted cards instead of dominoes you would surely be living on the top floor of Caesar's Palace in Las Vegas. It's ludicrous!"

"When I move, you move!" Charles suddenly blurted.

Cheers resounded from the crowd at his words. Now it was my turn to knit brows in confusion. The Jamaicans watched me with amusement.

"Yeeeessss," Charles boomed with the mock gravity of a professor. "You said ludicrous. Thus I quote the song from Ludacris. Surely a man as knowledgeable as you would know Ludacris? No? Jesus, Brian, stick to your damn science books. No wonder you can't get laid."

The Jamaicans bellowed with approval, forcing me to confess, "I be wet."

Two weeks passed before we shaped the Jamaicans into a nominally functioning aspect of our operation. We could smell things improving, even if we had not yet tasted it: four G2 near-miss cruises in a row were technically failures all. The Widow Maker began sucking the soul from another auctioneer, but hope fluttered in the dark like a lone candle.

Yet Charles, too, was beginning to crack under the strain and began drinking heavily and complaining heartily. He ate almost nothing, making his already gaunt frame even more emaciated. Fortunately I had no indication of his sexual potency. Though he had boldly claimed an occasional half-day off upon arrival, only now did he actually take it.

Majesty of the Seas docked nearly twenty hours in Nassau, giving ample time for play. Some damn fine beaches were in the Bahamas, and we were damn happy to lay on one. Near the cruise ship port, on the aptly named Paradise Island, stretched a white sand beach of tropical fantasies everywhere. The taxi ride, however, was a nightmare. Charles tried to purge his frustrations entirely before reaching the beach. If this allowed us a few unmolested hours at play, great, but I feared that he would not stop bitching once he got started. So Charles griped and moaned all while in the taxi and also throughout the walk to the beach.

Rarely did a day pass without Charles expounding upon his disappointment with this assignment. He was always the vocal one, of course. He liked to pat himself on the back for having married a strong woman who spoke her mind, but actually cut her off every time she attempted to do so. Tatli reflected her culture by accepting this quietly, letting him blather on without seeming to take offense. Eventually she would make some amusing demonstration to indicate she was finished being his sounding board.

I was thoroughly interested in watching an auctioneering couple function, but worried about being intrusive. When stress swelled and tempers flashed, I was invariably nearby. Indeed, our three fates were so closely linked as to be family. Only when they seriously discussed quitting Sundance did I feel my presence was inappropriate. Yet each time I rose to leave, they insisted I remain.

A ribbon of spotless, fine sand undulated onward in both directions. Our rear flank was protected by thick palm forests, while before us stretched the aqua-green of a perfect sea. The water was simply amazing, with gyrating phantoms of sunlight spearing down all the way to the clean bottom.

With Charles still griping, we unloaded our beach bags of the essentials. For Tatli: designer sunglasses and imported tanning lotion. For me: a cigar and Civil War History magazine. For Charles: a little plastic baggy holding… something.

"What the Hell is that?" I asked, trying to identify the damp clump inside the kitchen bag. "I swear I just saw it move."

"Don't ask," Tatli answered with a roll of her eyes. Charles abruptly stripped naked right there on the crowded beach.

"Is that your swim suit?" I asked, astounded. "In a plastic baggy. *Wet?*"

"Yes," he answered with his sepulchral baritone. He gave a wiggle and a hop, then lamely explained, "Not easy to put on wet clothes."

"Isn't that, like, *really* uncomfortable? And a little creepy? And can't you hide behind a towel or a tree or something, for cryin' out loud?"

"You get used to it," he defended simply.

"I don't know, man," I said doubtfully. "Sounds like a bad horror movie. *The Creature from the Wet Baggy.* Tatli, if you are as freaked out as I am by that thing he's wearing, I happily volunteer to put the sunscreen on your back. Or anywhere else, for that matter."

"Oh?" Charles retorted. "You aren't afraid of *The Bride of the Creature from the Wet Baggy?*"

For the first time I saw that the skinny Englishman was painted with dozens of tattoos. On each breast was inked a matching image of some strange crossover between a seahorse and a scorpion. His navel was ringed with a tribal sun, and his upper arms were covered with numerous individual works, as well.

"Wow," I breathed. "How many tattoos do you have?"

Charles chuckled. "I had forgotten about them, they are so old. I don't know how many I have. Tatli, do you remember?"

She shook her head in the negative.

"And Tatli?" I inquired innocently, "Anything you would like to show me? Please?"

"I don't think her bikini hides much," Charles rebutted drily as he slid onto his beach towel beside her.

A welcome moment of silence settled over us as we regarded the surf. Waves thumped into the shore closer and closer to our feet with each successive effort. Foaming crests surged over the white sand. The humidity hugged us close, but our sweat seemed right at home under the hot tropical sun.

Tatli, caught up in the vibrant beauty, whispered, "What a magical and wonderful place."

"I'll take you to a magical and wonderful place, baby," I quipped.

Tatli giggled, bringing a snort from Charles. "Must you hit on my wife, Brian?"

"Oh, I don't *have* to," I replied heartily. "I just prefer to."

"As I was saying," Charles continued griping with a huff, "That goddamn Hot Man...."

Charles began his bitching again, and Tatli gave me a profound look. I did not understand the meaning, but I would soon enough!

A strong Bahamian man approached along the surf. The hair on his upper body was tightly curled, like a spattering of freckles across his burly chest. Atop his head he toted a large, beat up box. He was all smiles as he scrunched over the sand towards us. In his hand was a dinner knife with the handle swathed in tape.

"Piña colada in a coconut?" he asked with a grin. His teeth were brilliant white and nearly perfect, had he not been missing one. "Ten dollars! Don't like piña colada? Got rum punch, too!"

Abandoning Charles and his griping, Tatli approached the Bahamian. He swung the box from his head down onto the sand and squatted over it, as did Tatli. They conversed, but were too far away to be heard. As his expression changed, I sensed this was not a usual haggling. First he registered excitement at a sale, then surprise, then became desperate as a fish caught on the end of Tatli's line.

He cracked a coconut for the drink by tapping it with the handle of his dinner knife, then expertly popped the top off. He slid the dull blade along the lid to pull the coconut meat away cleanly. He held this morsel up to Tatli and, to our shock, fed it directly to her in a decidedly arousing manner. Charles raised an eyebrow.

The Bahamian held the coconut high as Tatli leaned back and opened her mouth wide. Luxuriously he poured the milk into her open, craving mouth. Clear liquid dribbled down her face and smooth neck to mingle with her sweat. The hot Bahamian beach just got much, much hotter.

Charles watched silently, his Adam's apple bobbing up and down.

"After seeing that," I asserted, "I am gonna flirt with her *all day.*"

A moment later Tatli slipped delicately over the sands with a piña colada in her hand and a devilish grin on her face. The Bahamian bounded along behind her with drinks for Charles and I. Needless to say, there was no erotic milk pouring ceremony for us.

Afterwards, the Bahamian returned to his box of supplies and looked down on it with a rueful shake of his head. Suddenly he leaned back and roared with laughter. A cluster of seagulls flapped off with a screech, and the crashing surf sang a duet with his guffaw. Satisfied, he hefted the box back onto his head and trudged on down the beach, hawking his stuff anew.

Quite self-satisfied, Tatli settled onto her towel between us.

"So," Charles began, his baritone rising with amusement. "How much?"

"Three for one," she answered with a deceptively innocent-sounding giggle. Tatli's performance had the desired effect, and Charles quickly dropped all griping about money. I vowed that, from this point on, I would never again mistake Tatli for a Rafael angel.

The sun sank deep into our skin, and sweat crawled over our curves lovingly. Time surged like the waves: fear crashed over us, that we should be working, then calm came as a soothing drain back into the great expanse of the sea. Tatli was content to bake all day long, but after the growing waves forced us to retreat further up the beach, Charles and I opted for some water time.

We sloshed through the fabulous blue/green to where the swells rose above our heads. A mere twenty feet from the rioting edge of surf and sand, the waves broke over themselves at some eight feet high.

Though neither of us had body surfed before, the play came naturally. We worked away from the beach, swimming and splashing, until the swells and surge rushed towards the beach. We tried to position ourselves before the crest, which rocketed us towards the beach. It was an amazingly smooth ride, from swell to sand, and we both found ourselves preferring the messy, foam-choked ride on top of the crest. The water burbled and spit all about us as we were forcibly dumped onto the beach like so much flotsam.

Perhaps Freud would have something to say about my preference for the chaotic, tumultuous ride atop the wave rather than before it, and my joy at each violent smash into the sand. Again and again I rode and tumbled and smashed face-first into the beach. My skin blazed with the sandblasting, and salt stung every agitated inch. I loved it.

Eventually the waves grew unusually violent for the Bahamas, but we were already inured to the rough tumbling. Powerful waves forced an odd mixture of invisibly fine sand and water directly into my nose, and I could feel sand literally pouring through my nasal passages. I would stand up shakily and blow my nose, bringing a small handful of sand to my palm.

All told, Charles, Tatli and I spent five hours on the beach. If life is made of moments, this was one to cherish. Amazingly, the good time coasted even through the taxi ride back to the ship, even if Charles got naked again. The sand in his throat made his deep baritone exceptionally gravelly. He would have made the perfect narrator for a horror story. He dabbed his towel gingerly over a nasty scrape across his forearm and said, "Brian, did I mention that I talked to Gene yesterday?"

"*The* Gene?" I replied, surprised. "Isn't that kind of a big deal?"

"Yes," he agreed. In the back of the taxi he began awkwardly removing his bathing suit, despite the presence of me and the untold filth on the seats. Sharp elbows jabbed at both Tatli and I as he worked the cumbersome article off and stuffed it into his little plastic baggy.

"There!" he growled with pride as he zipped up the top. "Ready for next week."

For a moment he sat naked in the dirty taxi, apparently having forgotten where he was or what he was doing. His untanned derrière glowed white and was caked with sand. Tatli fished through her beach bag in search of his shorts.

"Ah, yes: the phone call. Gene wanted to get a firsthand report of the difficulties on *Majesty*. I took the opportunity to give him a verbal review of you. He didn't seem surprised at all when I told him how good you are. In fact, he said he had a good feeling about you all along."

"Awesome! That's the impression I got, but I've been fooled by less."

"He said that your being promoted to associate was technically premature, even though Mary Elizabeth OK'd it. So he got it officially cleared by Frederick, still before the normal four unpaid weeks, I might add. Congrats. Doesn't change anything, of course, but believe me, it's a good thing any time Frederick hears your name."

"Wow," I mused. "I can still recall, ever since I was a little boy, what my father told me. He said, 'Brian, someday you will be sitting in a filthy taxi in the Bahamas with a naked, wet Vincent Price. And he will offer you a promotion.' But I never really believed it would happen."

Charles raised an inquiring brow at my sarcasm, but before he could answer Tatli threw his shorts into his face.

That night I schmoozed at the Champagne Bar, my favorite aspect of work. After all, I could show off my well-tailored suit, drink martinis, and smoke cigars. What more could a man ask for, barring perhaps Angelina Jolie? Even better, my task was to talk about art appreciation with like-minded people. As an art auctioneer, that was surprisingly rare.

The bartender made a mean martini called the Yvette: equal parts Ketel One vodka and Gran Marnier with an orange slice. It was a heavy, aromatic drink; smooth but potent. And expensive. Alas, the price gouging of *Majesty* continued. I received no crew discount and had to pay twelve bucks for a Bahama Mama like everyone else. My sweet Yvette was even more, so I sipped slowly and lovingly.

The Champagne Bar was quiet, but was usually so. The vibe of the room catered to only truly formal occasions, which generally turned off all but the richest guests. Many were further dissuaded by the presence of numerous officers in starched white jackets and shiny accoutrements standing stiffly and speaking quietly with each other. I recognized Roosevelt Reddick among them.

Before lighting my Partagas Black Label cigar, I wandered over to join one of the few guests present. A man with a double chin was admiring our Picasso lithograph placed as bait. A spot light focused on the item to great effect, but he did not seem particularly impressed with the tornado-like scratching that cunningly depicted a minotaur standing over a naked woman.

"That is an original Picasso," I said to the man wearing an unbuttoned brown blazer that fell to the sides of his ample belly. He frowned at the etching a moment longer, then shrugged.

"I don't get it," he said. "I like to look at art, but I don't always get it."

"Picasso is not easy stuff," I agreed. "I spent years in college learning what was up. I'm Brian, the art auctioneer."

He introduced himself as John and said, "I always stop by the displays. Sometimes I take pictures of what I like. I have some nice backgrounds for my computer that way."

"That's an interesting idea," I said. "I never would have thought of that. Of course, the real thing is orders of magnitude better than anything else."

While John reviewed the Picasso further, I noticed the group of officers had split. Only Chief Officer Reddick remained. From across the room he stared at me with ice-blue eyes.

"So," John said lightly, with a shiver of chin. "On *Majesty of the Seas*, do you have any real art?"

"I daresay most people would define an original Picasso as real art."

"No, no," John said. His jowls wiggled gravely as he shook his head. "I mean by someone who can at least paint. This guy is no Michelangelo."

"Oh, I quite agree. He's much better."

"How can you possibly say that?" John scoffed. "I've seen some of Picasso's stuff. My eight year old granddaughter could do it!"

"You are of course referring to his later works," I said. "Though you may not know it. Picasso would thank you for that because simplicity was his goal at the end. Picasso began as a traditional painter, you know. He could out-paint Michelangelo younger than I could legally drink a beer.

"Now, Michelangelo was amazing, to be sure. He mastered both sculpture and painting, from his perfect statue of David to the wondrous Sistine ceiling. He was also an architect, by the way."

"Yes," John said, nodding vigorously. "That's what I'm talking about. A real master."

"He was indeed, but he never achieved anything even close to what Picasso did. There is one simple, tangible reason why Picasso is the greatest artist who ever lived. He did something far beyond the wildest dreams of Michelangelo and Da Vinci."

"And that is?"

Before I could answer, I was interrupted by Reddick's frantically waving me over. I tried to gesture him off, but he was obviously impatient and adamant to speak with me immediately.

"Hold that thought, John," I said. "The chief officer is calling for me. Would you please excuse me a moment?"

I left John hanging, and walked over to Reddick. As I approached, my internal alarm bells began to toll. Reddick launched into me even as I approached.

"What are you doing here?" he demanded.

"I am working."

"You are drinking."

"I am networking," I explained. "This is a huge part of the art world. Buying art is as much about the dealer as the art, because provenance and reputation are paramount in large purchase decisions. This is where I establish a rapport with qualified buyers."

"Don't be ridiculous," he scoffed. "If that man wanted to buy your art, he would come to your auctions. He doesn't want you pestering him here."

"We were having a conversation about Pablo Picasso," I defended.

"This lounge is for high level officers," Reddick continued. "Two stripes only. Not supernumeraries, other than the ship's doctor. The only thing more inappropriate than your presence is your drinking alcohol while conversing with a passenger. I suggest you focus your time to conducting art auctions."

"We work seven days a week!"

"Not today," Reddick replied smoothly. "You left the ship in the afternoon. You forget that all auctions are ultimately given permission by the hotel manager and myself. I did not sign off on any auction this day."

I blinked at him in surprise. He was checking on us? Cold blue bored into me.

"Well," I said, stumbling for a defense. "The auction schedule is not my decision. As long as we make the ship's sales goals, how we go about it is our own affair. We've done that successfully. And I assure you, sir, that a casual drink with an interested passenger can be far more effective than an auction."

"Irrelevant," Reddick snipped. "This lounge is not for those of your stature. You will leave immediately."

"I see," I said, backing down. "Well, let me finish my conversation with John and—"

"*I* will finish your conversation for you," Reddick interrupted. "You will leave immediately and not return to this lounge. Ever."

That night, in an effort to ease my annoyance with the ship's officers, I watched a movie. The crew channel featured *Lost in Translation,* and I was profoundly affected by it. The rendering was all too accurate in loneliness, alienation, and culture shock. The gut-wrenching need for human connection echoed my life on ships painfully.

Bill Murray portrayed a man whose work brought him to Japan, and whose wife hardly noticed his leaving. There he met the significantly younger Scarlett Johansson, who was staying at the same hotel with her own equally disinterested spouse. These two travelers were each in a unique situation, and their loved ones' lack of empathy amplified their loneliness even more than the foreign culture they were stuck in. They became deeply connected and rekindled a joy of life through play that was not unlike an affair, though sex was never involved. Fate had created a moment in time for them as profound as any other in their lives, but the spontaneous forces that created that moment inevitably killed it when they had to separate. They would never be able to explain what was lost to anyone else, for few could ever understand.

When they parted at the end of the movie, they left as lonely and misunderstood as ever. Both knew they would never see each other again, yet were somehow leaving more whole than they were before. Yet their powerful, bittersweet, final moment was quickly eroded by Bill Murray's tedious drive to the airport, where passing neon and buildings and foreign crowds screamed to break his reverie. But he probably didn't let it. Much like a Hollywood movie, fate had created pockets of paradise for Bianca and I, and we loved with the intensity of a lifetime in each. We never knew when, or really even if, we would see each other again.

I wanted so much what Charles and Tatli had : each other. Sure they had issues, but together they could work them out. When Bianca and I shared a cabin on *Carnival Conquest*, we went to bed angry because our conflicting shifts denied any time to hash things out. And speaking of beds, at least they could share one! That little bit of normalcy was a dream on ships. Instead of snuggling with my Bianca after a hard day, I slept with my Samsonite.

And here I was, early June on *Misery of the Seas*. Bianca's contract ended in September. That was so far off, and then how to coordinate across the continents? Oh, how quickly I would abandon the beaches of the Bahamas for the castles of Transylvania! As Frederick Douglass said, 'Alas! Between me and you the turbid waters roll.'

I fell asleep, deeply disturbed by those long, painful minutes of Bill Murray's taxi ride. How long could the power of a goodbye kiss carry you above the onslaught of reality? How many months of exotic newness could I navigate and still hold on to my last kiss with Bianca?

6. BIRTHDAY HUMPING

Several times I returned from a late, sly drink to see my neighbor's door open and the entire coed cast of the stage show inside, all happily watching hardcore porn. The art lover in me was titillated by the pile of aroused, entwined, and lithe dancers. Yet sex was rarely a result of these events. Why? Because all the men involved were gay. Other times the staff corridor late at night *did* echo with a chorus line of sexual activity, but here I usually declined any voyeuristic urges. Why? Because all the men involved were gay.

The pornography espoused in *Majesty's* staff hall was probably more than most folks could bear, or so I guessed, because after a year on ships I could no longer tell. There's only so many times a sexual orgy happens in the bunk above without you learning to tune it out. Thus, strange as it may seem, tolerance for pornography *does* come from being a waiter at sea.

Actually, it's not because there is so much sex on ships, although I maintain that college dorms ain't got nuthin' on crew cabins. It's not even about pornography at all. Tolerance grows from the self confidence that comes from accepting what you can't control. Or, more accurately, not being scared by it.

On ships, it begins with the complete lack of personal choice and space, such as the inability to eat when or what you choose, or complete lack of temperature control. As a waiter on Carnival I could not shower when I wanted, or even go to the toilet. I was denied proper sleep for months and the four hours nightly I got were compressed between my luggage and the cramped bunk. Until then, I had not realized the huge emphasis that we Americans placed on comfort. Thus the strengthening of my tolerance muscle began with lack of physical comfort, which was really a fear of not being in control. Now that I was outside of the States, I *had* to relinquish control of my environment.

For working on cruise ships is indeed living in a foreign country. Suddenly I, like everyone else, was a resident of the Carnival nation. My safety was in the hands of Italians, my orders from Indians, my food from Jamaicans, my clothing from Indonesians. Simply put, strange people with strange ways were in control of me every minute of every day, including my bodily needs. And it was OK. This led to patience when situations did not conform to my ideas, which led to acceptance of other ways of achieving the same ends. This is a difficult perspective to cultivate in a nation as huge and successful as America.

Growing tall in the fertile educational system of Iowa, I was imbued with the just idea that all races, colors, and creeds are equal. Of course, when everyone all around was exactly the same as you it was easy to so preach. For example: the black population of Iowa in those days hovered around 2%. The tiny section of Cedar Rapids that was not white was unconsciously avoided. Perhaps this was because the vast majority of crimes were committed there, but more likely it was to avoid something different and potentially uncomfortable. I did not even realize that what I was taught and what I was practicing were two different things. It resulted in a young man fiercely posturing acceptance and yet strangely uncomfortable in the rare occasions when surrounded by black men.

But now, as a resident of the sea, I've walked my former talk. Ships break barriers far faster than on land, beginning with enforced physical proximity but quickly broadening with dependence upon, and growing respect of, people of all stripes. And my childish nerves about being surrounded by blacks? I was nightly getting mopped up at dominoes and loving it. Being adopted by Jamaican blood flashers is an excellent way to expand your horizons.

Thus I found that my comfort zone was actually *inside*, not outside. I learned self confidence in a way that roamers have, an adaptability that many armchair critics lack and lash out against in righteous naiveté. I could now observe things I did not care for without being bothered by it, things like gay porn, ignorance, or perhaps even Rush Limbaugh.

During home port Charles and I would leave *Majesty* to drop off the paperwork for the cruise while Tatli got her beauty sleep. We enjoyed our stroll to the nearby Fedex drop-box because getting off *Majesty* was not so easy with this itinerary. Upon returning, however, we were brought up short by a yelp from the computer as we scanned in our IDs. The short, brawny Filipino security officer finished patting us down, and explained.

"Says here the hotel manager wants to see the auctioneer."

"Now what?" Charles whined, thin shoulders drooping. "I already saw him this morning. It's only ten o'clock in the morning! Can't I have just one untrammeled day?"

"Untrammeled," I congratulated. "Good word."

"No, not you," the Asian said to Charles. "The other one."

He meant me. "Now what would he want to see me for?"

"Just go," Charles ordered disconsolately as we strode down the I-95. "Try to find out his name, will you? On second thought, I don't care. He'll always be Hitler to me. Why, you ask? Because he's a dick. Hitler was a dick, too. See the connection?"

"Wow. Did you just say that Hitler was a dick?" I repeated, awed. "That is, without any doubt whatsoever, the greatest understatement in the history of the English language."

Soon I was at the hotel manager's door and nervous. Needless to say, I did not expect this was a call to congratulate me on anything.

"Good morning, sir."

"Ah, the auctioneer," Hot Man said blandly as he fished through the copious paperwork on his desktop. Again his name placard was hidden beneath papers. He rifled through the profuse piles for a while, ignoring me. Eventually he found what he was looking for and read it silently for another long moment. I waited patiently and silent, curiosity eating me up.

"You missed boat drill," he finally said, setting down the paper.

"I did not," I defended. "I was at crew drill."

"Not according to the safety officer."

"I was there. My muster leader signed off on it."

"If you are referring to *crew* boat drill, yes, I have verified that you at least showed up for that."

His tone was extremely accusatory, as if he expected nothing better from a troublemaker like me. He added crisply, "That is no excuse for abandoning your other duties."

I frowned. "What other duties? I've been on-board a month and had no other duties to date."

"Yes," he bit back. "I see that you have never attended passenger drill."

"Why would I do that? I'm not a passenger."

"You are in a passenger cabin."

"Charles is in a passenger cabin. I'm in the staff hallway."

He gave a dismissive wave. "I do not care about the Englishman. Department heads are exempt from passenger drill."

I tread very carefully when I said, "I *am* a department head. There is no contractual difference between an auctioneer and his associate."

"There is if you live in a staff cabin. Anyone residing in a staff cabin is staff."

"I see. OK," I agreed. "If that's the case, then why didn't anyone say anything? I've been here a long time and was never given a single memo. What exactly do you want me to do?"

He answered breezily, "You will go to the muster station assigned to the auctioneer's cabin and follow those procedures."

I had to ponder that a moment. "You mean, attend as a... as a passenger?"

"Yes. You will wear your life vest, of course. You are not above the rules."

"Let me understand this," I said, confused. "Instead of doing my job setting up an auction, I have to pay someone else to do it for me, because I have to stand in a passenger's muster station because someone else is living in a passenger cabin. Twice a week. *As well as* attend the crew drill."

"Yes."

"So, uh, if the alarm goes off, I am to now go to the passenger muster station? The whole point of passenger drill is to train you to mechanically go to your muster station. And that's not my muster station."

Hot Man's face wrinkled in annoyance. "Obviously not. That spot is designated for whoever resides in the passenger cabin."

"I'm sorry, sir, but this doesn't make any sense to me."

"You don't need to understand," he snapped. "You need to obey. Regulations are clear: staff must be active during passenger boat drill. Since your position as supernumerary has no actual duties, you will attend as a passenger."

"And Charles, who *lives* in the passenger cabin, does not have to attend passenger boat drill. I do it for him."

"And his wife," he agreed. "And furthermore, I find your begging for reprieve distasteful and ungrounded. You may leave now."

I left his office in a daze, but the hits just kept on coming. The next blow came from a visitor to *Majesty*, our fleet manager.

Mary Elizabeth was a very tall woman with long brown hair that hung past her shoulders in copious, tight curls. Her figure was broad of shoulder, yet flat-chested and flat-bottomed. Wearing a pair of somehow-designer brown coveralls with designer tears and patches, she looked like a walking sheet of plywood. Her face was gentle and more than a little tired, but her smile was broad and genuine.

Her visiting us in homeport at Miami was a surprise, but not unwelcome. Charles was thrilled for any opportunity to voice his grievances in onerous detail. Sure enough, over coffee in the Windjammer Café, Mary Elizabeth opened, "We need to talk about your emailed complaints about this ship."

"Hell, yes!" Charles wiggled excitedly in his seat, preparing to cut loose.

"Wait," she said, forestalling him with a raised hand. "I'm talking specifically about the officers removing you from the Champagne Bar."

Charles drooped, sensing things were not to go in a direction of his liking. He asked quietly, "Yes?"

"This issue is much bigger than you likely know. This isn't about you and the Champagne Bar. This is about the status of all auctioneers, on all ships, everywhere. Sundance has taken this up with the top tier of RCI."

Charles raised an inquiring brow. "Are you serious?"

"Very," Mary Elizabeth answered. "I suggest you watch your back while this is being tossed back and forth. I have no doubt that the hotel manager will be keeping close tabs on it."

"Now I get it!" I said. "That's why I just got ripped up by Hot Man!"

Both turned to me, surprised.

"You?" Mary Elizabeth asked. "This should be about the auctioneer, not the associate. What happened?"

I quickly explained the unlikely extra boat drill procedures I had been ordered into mere minutes before. Charles' face darkened, but Mary Elizabeth merely pursed her lips.

"I feared some backlash like this. Tread carefully, both of you, while this is worked out on higher levels. You will feel better knowing that Frederick himself is going to bat for you."

Charles nodded deeply, suitably impressed.

"Now," Mary Elizabeth said with a smile. "My presence here is not to be a cheerleader. We do have another issue that is more pressing."

"Dare I ask?" Charles deadpanned.

"I brought more than news. On the dock you'll find a shipment of empty D containers. There is to be an art swap…"

She trailed off and eyed Charles warily, biting her lip. Hesitantly she finished, "…this cruise."

"What?" Charles exploded. "*This* cruise? That's impossible. Those take weeks to arrange!"

"I've organized everything already," Mary Elizabeth said, "Except talked to the boson about extra storage in his area for 24 hours. The new art will be waiting for you in Nassau tomorrow. You're there all day, so you *should* have enough time."

Charles eyed her incredulously. "*Tomorrow?* Are you insane? You *are* aware that this is only a three day cruise?"

"Yes."

"And we are in port the whole time?"

"Yes."

"And that an art swap will take *at least* two full days?"

Mary Elizabeth leaned back and crossed her arms beneath her breasts. "Yes, Charles."

"I won't be able to do a single auction. I will not make goal."

"I am aware of this. I came in person, didn't I? I wanted to reassure you that Sundance knows your situation."

"But Sundance won't remove my goals for this cruise, will it?"

Her lips quivered into a near smirk. "Of course not. But rest assured; your failing goal will be accompanied by a note of explanation from me."

Charles snorted rudely. "Frederick won't care, and you know it. He'll see a big fat zero and I'll be fired."

Mary Elizabeth said nothing. That was a dangerous hint corroborating Charles' fear.

"Good!" he suddenly cried, rising and striding away. "I hate this goddamn ship anyway."

Charles' stomping off in a huff was probably a good thing, lest he say something truly regrettable. No doubt Mary Elizabeth had expected some anger because she just sighed.

"You'll understand soon enough," she explained to me. "Art swaps are a lot of work, but are definitely a good thing for a ship and its sales. Once a year on every ship we swap out all the old artwork and replace it with the latest and greatest. So tonight you'll have to box up all the art on-board."

"Wait a minute," I cried, suddenly realizing what this meant. "*All* the art is being swapped out? You mean tonight we have to box all one thousand works?"

She nodded grimly and explained, "Tomorrow it will be offloaded in Nassau, and a whole new set will be waiting to replace it. I hope you are on better terms with the boson than you are with the chief officer, because you'll be entirely dependent upon him. He'll be the one craning out boxes of old art and craning in the new. Then you'll have to unpack and inventory it."

I stared at her, stunned as realization sunk in. "An inventory alone takes a full day."

"This is a good thing. Trust me."

Presumably the look on my face was not reassuring, because Mary Elizabeth immediately tried to coax an ally out of my by buttering me up. "Charles tells me that you did an entire auction last night."

"I did," I said proudly. "I had already finished a number of auctions for Shawn when he was here, but this was the first one I organized from start to finish. The first twenty minutes were a bit rough, but after that I got smooth, baby."

"Yes," she agreed. "More than Charles sold the previous auction, if I recall correctly."

"Well, yeah," I demurred, "But it was raining during my auction. His was during a gorgeous port of call. Hard to sell to people on the beach, you know?"

"Oh, I know," she said with a smile. "Even though I answer to Gene, I am on your side. Art swapping situations to the contrary. You seem to be doing well, so take credit for it. Shawn had great things to say about you, and so does Charles."

"Thank you," I said earnestly.

"So what are your ambitions? Do you want your own ship or to be an associate on a big ship? Both are highly profitable."

"I absolutely want my own ship," I answered. "My girlfriend is waiting to join me. She'll be brilliant at this."

"I didn't know that," Mary Elizabeth said happily. "I like auctioneering couples. They are far more stable than the single ones who get sidetracked by booze and sex. You were in the March training class, weren't you?"

"April. I was hoping to have a short vacation in September or October because my girlfriend is on vacation then."

"Six months is usual for auctioneers," she agreed. "If I can make arrangements to pencil you both in the October advanced training class, you could both go directly from there to your next ship. How would that work?"

"I think that would work marvelously! That way she won't start another contract as a waitress."

"She already knows ships? Even better. Just make sure she resigns properly, because we don't want Sundance accused of poaching talent. Anyway, don't hesitate to keep me informed about your schedule and desires. I'm here to do what I can. In the meantime, you may need to go feed oxygen to Charles."

That Miami afternoon Charles and I examined the D containers that had been craned into the bow storage area. They were ingeniously packed boxes of intricately folded sheets of 245 pound corrugated cardboard and a clean, new pallet. The whole tidy package sprang forth into a box of large dimensions capable of hauling 1200 pounds. The walls rose a cumbersome 45 inches, but were designed to slide open for easy front access and still sturdy when in place. It was a great example of how a little thought could elevate something as simple as a box into a masterpiece of engineering.

Charles demonstrated how to unpack and assemble a D container. It was dirty work, and he folded his hands together awkwardly before him in order prevent soiling his clothing. He looked like a praying mantis.

"After we pack up all the boxes, we will wrap them in plastic wrap, nice and snug. I want it waterproof. Once I was on a ship where the containers were left on the dock during a rainstorm. Can you believe that? That was in Barbados, which doesn't have a hanger for such things. It was a pure goddamn miracle I didn't lose millions that day."

"Let's hope we don't need a miracle like that," I said quietly, daunted at the thought.

"I would prefer to start in the morning. I'm going to bed early because it will be a long, long day of humping boxes. We can't sell anything tonight anyway, because we won't get credit for it. The new art data is for the oncoming work. So tomorrow morning, when you're ready, *'call me so I can get it juicy for ya.'*"

I blinked a moment, then asked, "Did you just say, *'call me so I can get it juicy for ya?'*"

"I did," he replied smugly.

"I think you're barking up the wrong tree," I said, laughing. "Congrats, I have no idea what song that is."

"Me neither," he admitted with a shrug of his skinny shoulders. The gesture combined with his folded hands reinforced his mantis look. "I just heard it the other day, but it sounded suitably naughty and hip-hoppy."

"Hip hop-*like*," I corrected with a smile.

Because there was no auction, I went to bed way too early. A few hours before dawn I was already wide awake, so reluctantly decided to start on the packing. Though I knew the boson's area was always stiflingly hot, perhaps I could get a big chunk of the work done before it got really *really* hot. I wore only shorts and sandals, leaving my tank top in the art locker.

The hallway leading from the art locker to the boson's area scared me. It was dark, long, and the high ceilings made the walls squeeze inward. Creepy claw marks marred the linoleum walls, as if crewmen were hauled against their will to the strange door at the end. Indeed, the only source of light escaped from around that thick metal door, hammered outward as it was, presumably from a demon locked behind pounding to escape. The stifling heat added to the impression.

Perspiration already beaded upon my forehead from the heat, but as I crept to the metal door, rivulets of cold sweat trickled down my neck. Heat poured from the cracks of that scarred, battered door as if it held back the Inferno. Indeed, the boson's area was directly beneath the bow, and several feet of steel under the torrid Caribbean sun inevitably creates a furnace. Even the relatively cool hours of night were not enough for it to dissipate.

Ever-so-cautiously I opened the door, and was immediately assaulted by the heat. A huge chamber stretched far, far into the steaming dark. Countless chains hung above; heavy, motionless, sharp hooks dripping with moisture. A path meandered beneath the hulking shapes of everything needed to fix a ship at sea. I was pretty sure this was the set for *Hellraiser*, where condemned souls waited to be torn apart. Something dripped somewhere in the blackness. At any moment I expected to encounter a topless blonde bound for sacrifice and screaming in terror.

Nearby was the boson's tiny office, currently empty, of course. I peered inside and gasped at the stack of burnt ledgers. Despite myself, I opened a leather book, awed by its seared edges and ash-smeared entries in a tiny, foreign script. Only then did I notice that the ashtray, overflowing with bent and smashed cigarette butts, was currently in use. A fresh cigarette emitted a delicate line of smoke ramrod straight into the hot, unmoving air.

Surely the boson wasn't here in the middle of the night? There was only one way in or out, so he was in the shadows somewhere, presumably watching me. Perhaps he was summoning a demon. Perhaps he *was* a demon, busy devouring a bikini babe in this labyrinth. None of these thoughts were particularly helpful.

Now more nervous than ever, I shivered at the sight of some odd black smear snaking across the floor into the confused depths. Was that ichor from the otherworldly beast within, or just engine grease? Then I heard something that made my blood run cold.

A giggle.

I froze into a crouch. Only my eyes moved, frantically searching among the hulking shapes for whoever made that noise. That was *not* my imagination, but a child, perhaps an adolescent, giggling in the labyrinth. But how could that be? Yet it obviously wasn't a grown man I just heard. Who—or *what*—would play among the machinery in the middle of the night?

The giggle sounded again, followed by a sharp, pained gasp, as if someone was being hurt. It repeated over and over, as if a ghostly reenactment of an untimely end echoing through time. My God, was this place actually haunted?

A faint glow smoldered in the hot distance, wavering and orange. I inched closer. Whispering voices now teased my ears with a velvety prickle, but I could not make out the words. I paused just around the corner to the light, and peeked.

Then I saw it. Aha! I *knew* it!

Candles blazed around a metal table streaked with blood, and there, upon it, squirmed a gorgeous blonde awaiting sacrifice. She was chained at the wrists and ankles, wearing only her bra and panties. Sweat mingled with red slashes crisscrossing her belly. A dark figure towered above her, preparing to finish her off with great ceremony of movement. Its back was to me, and as I strained to get a look at his face, I tripped.

With a clatter I tumbled into the light, breath expelling in a great gasp upon striking the steaming metal deck. I frantically scrambled to my knees, but the specter had already vanished.

I gaped at the half-naked woman chained on the counter.

She gaped at the half-naked man panting on the deck.

She screamed at me.

I screamed at her.

It was not my finest moment. I fully intended to run like a little girl, but the victim's odd curses made me pause.

"Damn it, Erik!" she snarled into the void. "You're gonna leave me like this? Are you goddamn kidding me?"

"Wh-who?" I stammered.

"Erik, the limp-dick boson, that's who!" she snapped. "Erik! Come back here and unlock me, you stupid son of a bitch!"

But the boson was nowhere to be found. The only trace of him was another abandoned cigarette smoking itself absently near a flickering red candle. Finally the woman gave up on him and took her frustration out on me.

"You just gonna stand there like an idiot?" she yelled. "Get over here and unlock me!"

Approaching, I finally realized what was actually happening. Those weren't bloody gashes along her belly, but rivulets of hot wax dripped from a candle. Now this was *my* kind of foreplay!

"The key's on the table over there," she ordered, nodding behind me. I took up the key and reluctantly began releasing the padlocks that chained her down. The young woman was obviously one of the dancers, evident by her phenomenal physique. She never looked at me, but focused on plucking bits of wax from her belly as soon as her hands were free. Once fully loosed, she snatched her dress from the table and tugged it over her head.

She started to leave, but paused to look me up and down. With a mischievous smile she said,"Let's do this again some time."

Then she stormed out, leaving me with the D containers and the creepy, lurking boson.

So I began to assemble all the boxes. Space was a severe limitation and I had to ensure they all had a place, so each path meandering through the greasy equipment became filled with fresh cardboard boxes and their pristine pallets. Eventually the dread machinery of the chamber was supplanted with my own junk. Trepidation melted away. I continually banged my head against hanging chains, caught my hair in their dangling hooks, or slammed my shoulders into jutting metal things. But eventually the containers were unpacked and placed where I could get at them while hauling cumbersome artwork. Of the boson, there remained no sign.

Dawn came early and the tropical sun already blasted the metal deck mere feet above my head. In these conditions I had to box one thousand works of art. Swapping the art collection from a cruise ship should be outlawed by the Geneva Convention!

Everything that was in the art locker had to go into a box, so I just systematically worked my way to the back. While it was fortunately a short jaunt from the art locker to the boson's hell hole, I had to haul the laden cart over those damn lips in the hallway. Each trip sent a jolt of pain down my back until the ache overflowed into my loins.

Humping boxes was *not* the way I preferred to be soaked in sweat with sore loins.

D containers have high sides, so arranging frames inside was a chore. I had to bend all the way over the edge and heave and haul and push and arrange big frames while fully extended and bent in half. I would have preferred being drizzled with hot wax. Sweat burned my eyes and the many scrapes and burns that popped up from working with so much cardboard. After nearly four hours, all the locker's artwork had been arranged tightly in the boxes.

After this, I had to haul in the unframed artwork from my cabin. These prints were professionally matted and matched to a backing of foam board, then neatly shrink-wrapped in plastic. Thus, they were very light, very slippery, and exceptionally prone to static cling. Moving them was an electrically charged mess because corners slipped from my grasp and poked into my thighs or snagged walls. Everything I touched snapped at me, and it took all my patience to resist hurling the impish prints overboard. There were hundreds of the buggers, but I finally got to them all.

Finally Charles and Tatli joined me in late morning. They were shocked when they saw me, head-to-toe filthy and sweaty. I gave them a grin that was more than a little crazy from the heat.

"Why did you do this all yourself?" Charles demanded.

"I wanted to," I defended with strangely misplaced zeal. "It was a challenge."

"I'll say," Charles said, wonderingly. I suspected that he was more than a little pleased at not having to do the work himself.

Actually, there *was* a reason why I slaved through the heat alone. I couldn't say it, but I wanted to prove something to Charles and Tatli, and I want to prove something to myself. I loved hard work. That was the Iowan in me and I was damned proud of it. I had always worked harder than everyone around me, if admittedly not as smartly. So once I started this job, I wanted to claim it all as my own.

"This little bit of achievement," I explained, "is my birthday present for myself. No doubt this is the only birthday humping I'm gonna get today."

"It's your birthday?" Tatli asked. "Oh, Brian, you should have waited for us!"

"'tis nothing!" I boomed melodramatically.

"We'll gather the art from the few displays around the ship," Charles said. "I want to wait and make sure Hot Man is in his office when I take away the Rembrandt he's been enjoying."

After everything was packed, Charles and I began the process of plastic-wrapping the D containers. Sundance had provided a dozen mega-sized rolls of the stuff, and Charles expertly danced around the boxes with a long, clinging line of green. The shriek of the plastic pulling from its roll echoed strangely through every corner of the hot metal prison. We burned our fingers on the cardboard tube, so fast did we work.

Thus, after some six hours of insanely intense labor in brutal conditions, the packing was finished. That was step one.

While Charles arranged to crane all the boxes onto the dock, I returned to my cabin to relax my brutalized muscles. But recovery was not meant to be. Just as I was about to nap, the phone rang.

"Have you seen the boson?" Charles asked, fear in his voice.

"What do you mean, exactly?" I asked warily.

"He's not answering his phone or his pager."

Relief flooded through me. I hadn't wanted to explain that I had, indeed, seen the boson. But as awkward as that conversation would have been, the boson's disappearance was worse.

"We need him to work the crane!" Charles continued, voice cracking in concern. "You haven't done anything to piss him off, too, have you?"

"Uh... not exactly."

"Goddamn it, Brian!" he barked through the phone. "My new artwork is melting in the goddamn Bahamas, time is running out, and everyone on this ship has a problem with you."

"Not your wife," I offered cheerily, but Charles just snorted and hung up.

In fact, we never found the boson. An hour later the boson's mate was called in and, with the assistance of two able seamen and a skiff loader, the boxes were eventually offloaded. I thought it would be a good feeling to see the fruit of my labor resting upon the Bahamian dock, but I was wrong. Like the boxes baking in the sun, the drama was just heating up.

Just because the artwork was ashore did not mean our hands were washed of it. Until the local port authority signed for the artwork, Charles remained liable. The Bahamian refused to sign because, not surprisingly for such a major undertaking on short notice, there was a paperwork discrepancy. Until the port authority received an authorized bill of lading from Mary Elizabeth, he would not take financial responsibility for the artwork.

Hours passed, and Charles paced back and forth the whole time. His skin reddened with the sun, but the smoke coming from his ears was indignation, not burning. Charles ranted at the port authority on the dock, and raged at the fleet manager on the phone. While he fumed, I fretted, because baking beside our fifteen outgoing D containers were a whopping twenty-two waiting to come aboard. Until we signed off on the one, we could not accept the other.

The sun lowered in the sky, and our hour of departure grew imminent. Charles never once left the dock, and was dangerously close to watching *Majesty* leave from there. The worst part was that if the paperwork snafu did not clear, we would have to haul the fifteen boxes back aboard. Sundance would then have to send the twenty-two boxes to our *next* port, no doubt charging us for the expense, and the whole mess would repeat again. Missing auctions every step of the way, of course.

But finally the proper forms were faxed in, and as the sun dropped below the horizon, twenty-two crates of new art were craned into the boson's area. The few hairs on Charles not already grey had certainly gone over to the other side.

Deep into the Nassau night Charles, Tatli, and I unpacked and inventoried the new art. Alas, we could not actually remove the items from the D containers because we could not yet place them in our art locker. All one thousand frames wore protective cardboard corners, stapled firmly. This explained why twenty-two incoming containers equaled fifteen outgoing: the corners added tremendous bulk. There was no hope of removing them without umpteen hours of labor.

Finally becoming a blessing rather than a burden, the boson acquiesced to locking everything in his chamber for the night. No doubt because there would be no action with any dancers tonight!

So next morning saw three tired souls grappling with piles of cardboard corners. Each protective corner was secured by four staples, and of course there were four corners on each frame. Multiply that by one thousand works of art and you have a lot of damn staples. We were only mildly disappointed that the Calypso boys were performing in port this day, because we could only imagine the ways Kelvin would adopt for slowing us down. By noon, the three of us literally had 16,000 bent staples and 30 bloody fingers.

Numbed beyond belief, mentally and physically, we knew our day was just getting going. Guests were returning from port, and we had to get moving on our one and only auction in which to make goal. From bad to worse.

Very late that night we slumped over our table on the open deck. We were dead tired, and the hot, thick air caressed us into sleep. The moon, like our sales figures, was conspicuously absent. Few stars could compete with the light pollution of a modern cruise ship, so the sea below us was black as our disposition. This was a night to ponder fragility of situation, of floating atop a fractious surface above the immensity of the sea. Truly pondering those inky depths was intimidating indeed, and every man's nightmare would be to tread those dark, dark, vast waters alone.

After mechanically sipping our champagne for an hour, Charles loosed a long, deep sigh and stared at his watch.

"Only forty more minutes," he said. He sighed again.

Because this was the last night of the cruise, we had to meet with the ship's accountant to finalize our paperwork. It was a loathsome thing, this waiting. It was the salt in our wounded pride and bodies. We had been crushed by labor and then crushed by defeat: we made not one sale. So our 1:30 AM meeting was to sign off on a ledger full of zeros.

Another cruise ship crept in on the darkness, passing us in a far off tangent. Rarely in the Bahamian waters did you not see a ship in the distance somewhere. We all absently stared at it.

"Think that's another odious RCI ship?" Charles asked. "Think if I spit hard enough, I'll hit it?"

I squinted at the tiny dot of light so far away. As I leaned forward, my muscles reminded me smartly that they preferred identifying my bed. "I can't tell whose it is."

"Princess," Tatli said. "See the big thing rising over the back?"

Silently we all peered deeper into the night, saying little and feeling less. We were quite pathetic.

"Oh!" Tatli suddenly said, bringing everyone up with a start. She fished something out of her bag and shrugged apologetically. "I forgot."

She handed me a slender hardcover book. "While Charles argued with the port authority, I ran into town. I'm sorry I didn't have time to wrap it."

"What is this?"

"For your birthday, silly!" she said, stirring awake. Her round cheeks flushed with enthusiasm.

I flipped the book over in my hands and smiled as I read aloud, "*The Highly Selective Thesaurus for the Extraordinarily Literate.*"

"Perfect, no? It was my idea," Charles boasted, suddenly waking as well. Tatli's lips wiggled, but she said nothing.

"You found this… *in Nassau*?" I wondered aloud. "You have a magic touch. But then, as Carl Sagan said, 'A book is proof that humans are capable of working magic.'"

"That's what I always say," Charles agreed. Tatli stuck her tongue out at him.

"Really Tatli, this is amazing. I can't believe how kind you are. Both of you, thank you. I mean it. I never in a million years would have expected a birthday gift."

"I remember you said you want to be a writer someday, and this will come in handy," Charles explained. He plucked the book from my fingers and flipped through the pages randomly. Finally he stopped and said, "For example: *cup-shaped.* Adjective. Instead of saying cup-shaped, you can say poculiform or scyphate. Isn't that exciting?"

"Oh, yes," I agreed. "Readers appreciate that sort of thing."

Seeing the sarcasm on my face, he quickly slashed through the pages again. "Let me try again. Let's see, your birthday is the thirteenth, June... here we go. A better example: Page 13, line 6: *blockhead.* Is that worthy? It is a noun, synonymous with dolt, dullard, and loggerhead. Hey, I'll bet that's what O'Neil means when he calls Kelvin *'laggahead'.*"

Charles ribbed Tatli and said, "See? I told you I'd figure it out before Brian did."

7. SUNDANCE 101

Near the end of the next cruise, I wandered down to the Centrum for my errand of rotation. Whenever *Majesty* entered the port of Key West, some sort of cross current rocked the ship and caused our display easels to fall. This was more than a mere annoyance, because our art displays on the ship were so few and so key they held the most expensive artwork. When I arrived, I discovered that the artwork had not fallen over at all. That was not a good thing, though.

Some asshole had stolen my easels.

Crew members constantly pinched items and equipment when they needed them. Despite having two dozen extra easels folded neatly beneath the stairs of the Centrum, no one bothered to contact us and ask for them. Instead they stole those holding our huge and rare works of art, including a $40,000 original Salvador Dalí.

I bent down to wrestle out replacement easels when I was greeted by the hotel manager. Well, perhaps the word *greeted* was a bit misleading.

"I see the display of artwork is not being properly managed," an irritated voice called from behind me. I backed up and rose to see the hotel manager towering over me, stiff and formal. Before I could reply, he glanced off into the distance and said, "I don't think the Centrum is an appropriate location for you anymore."

"We have plenty of easels," I replied sourly. "Whoever took these could have simply asked us instead of stealing them in the early morning hours."

"You misunderstand," he continued. "Despite this obvious failure, I do not see fit to deny your use of this area to display your artwork. But further auctions here in the heart of the ship are out of the question."

I blinked in shock. "W-what? Did you take this up with Charles?"

He finally eyed me with an expression that made it clear he was not pleased to do so. "I am taking this up with you. You claim to be a co-department head, do you not? Your sales figures last cruise were zero. Certainly *that* cannot justify the intrusive presence of auctions here."

"This is our primary location," I protested. "And you know we had a surprise art swap last cruise. Denying us this lounge will cut our sales in half!"

"And I've noticed that you auctioneers have begun taking the day off while at Nassau," he continued blandly. He stared off to the wall again.

"We have *not*," I replied. "Every other cruise we take an *afternoon* off. Nothing more."

He almost sniffed. "If you aren't going to take advantage of every opportunity offered, then I will give such opportunities to others who will."

"No one else wants to use the Centrum," I defended. "Or they would have contacted us."

"Like those who needed your easels?" he countered mildly. "If no one else needs the Centrum, then it will remain empty. Clutter has no place on a ship, as all sailors know."

Hot Man strode off, and so did I. I went straight to Charles, who had just returned from the internet café. While I fumed, he was grinning from ear to ear. Before I could relate my bitter encounter with Hot Man, he launched into a happy dance.

"I just heard from Mary Elizabeth!" he cried. "Come to my cabin and I'll tell you and Tatli the good news."

Inside their cabin, I sat beside Tatli on the bed while Charles pranced about gaily.

"The official answer has come in!" he explained with a hop and a step. "Frederick himself bullied RCI, Carnival, and all the others at the highest levels. He hammered them with our enormous revenues and tiny expenses. Man, if you've ever met Frederick, you'll know how dangerous he is to mess with. He is the most ambitious and aggressive man I have ever met. So he was when establishing the rank of auctioneers on-board. We are three-stripe officers!"

Tatli's eyes bulged. Mine, too.

"*Three* stripes?" I repeated incredulously. "That would mean we are the same rank as Hot Man!"

"That's right," Charles gloated. "We are three-stripe motherfuckers. Three-stripe motherfuckers are we."

"So the Champagne Bar is now officially available to us," Tatli said, relieved.

"Yes!" Charles hooted. "We win!"

"I'm not so sure about that," I said, regretfully breaking the joyous mood. I quickly explained how we lost the Centrum. I needn't have worried about bursting the bubble of Charles' joy, however. The captain, being the only man able to supersede the corporate office, closed the curtain on the Champagne Bar drama by decreeing that no artwork could be displayed for safety reasons.

We lose.

One afternoon I stopped into the passenger's internet café. While the crew internet was easier on the wallet, with one terminal for every seventy crew it was exasperating to find one. This built in me a mania to check email at every possible opportunity, regardless of hour. Now that I was an officer, I had to learn to keep that in check.

But it was so difficult! Sending emails to Bianca had kept our romance alive through very long separations in the past. In writing love letters, my passion for Bianca was given an outlet and the prose flooded out like a burst levee. Alas, with Bianca slaving away as crew on *Carnival Miracle*, she could reply only every few days at best.

Before, when we were both in the restaurants, we had avoided discussing work because we did the same thing, day in and day out. But now I shared every detail of my odd, new life. Bianca was remarkably intelligent, but lacked the imagination to see that a different sort of ship life was possible. Knowing I was now a three-stripe motherfucker would surely help.

I was desperate to show her the perfection of our future life together as auctioneers, all things Widow Maker aside. But Bianca insisted on discussing important matters only in person, which was more than a little vexing when thousands of miles lay between us. I resisted the idea that this was stalling and signaled a possible fear of commitment. I was hard at work building, whereas she had merely to wait. Waiting was arguably more difficult.

Excitement pulsed through me when I saw Bianca's name on my inbox. Every time was as fresh and exhilarating as the first. Just two words from her, *any* two words, would be a balm for the worst burn life could offer. Or so I thought. The four words I received, typed in all capital letters, threw me for a loop. They were the only words of her email, and I read and reread them, perplexed and unnerved. Had she heard some rumor about me?

"WHY YOU HAVE CHICKS?"

That night the rain hammered the open deck mercilessly, dropping on the teak in crashing waves. Lightning flashed maniacally above, blindingly, as if the heavens were gleefully throwing electricity about like mashed potatoes in a food fight. Charles, Tatli and I relinquished our soaked table of choice, but refused to abandon our nightly drink outside. We sat beneath the overhanging deck, surrounded by the lumpy white bulkheads and lifejacket bins, wincing from the harsh bare bulbs directly above us.

I held up my glass of champagne and said, "I propose a toast. To Joan Miró, without whose fine artwork we would never have reached our second goal this cruise!"

"Hear hear!" Charles cried, and we all clinked glasses. "G2 in the bag!"

Thunder rumbled in agreement. I was delighted to find the weather had a taste for modern art.

"I, too, have a toast to propose," Charles said. He gave Tatli a searching look, but her round features offered no response. She seemed a bit sad, actually. I suddenly sensed he was going to announce their retirement.

"To the art associate on *Carnival Conquest!*"

I blinked. "Huh?"

Charles looked me in the eye. "I just received word from Mary Elizabeth. You are being transferred to *Conquest.* You leave on June 25th."

I stared at him in shock. "You are serious?"

"I am, indeed!" he said. He offered his hand, which I shook heartily.

"In just seven days? Who is replacing me?"

"They don't know yet, but I assume some kid from this month's training class. You, my friend, are on your way up. Congratulations."

"Do you know who the auctioneer is on *Conquest*?" I asked, my mind reeling. "Is it still out of New Orleans?"

"Yes, its homeport is New Orleans and no, I don't know who the auctioneer is. I'll find out for you. I have to tell you, Brian, we'll miss you. As sucky as this ship is, it *has* been fun working with you."

"Thank you, Charles. And I've enjoyed working with Tatli."

"Anyway," Charles said, clearing his throat. "Back to work. We sold that huge new Miró print we on-loaded and cleared G2, so I guess the art swap was worth it. Armed with this success, I want to work out some sort of deal with Hot Man to get our Centrum back. We sold almost nothing in the Spank Your Wagon Lounge."

"We need the Centrum," I agreed. "Shawn said he almost never made goal without it. The problem is that we *did* make goal without it. That doesn't help us. Ironic, eh?"

"Not necessarily," Charles replied. "We had our first auction there on embarkation night before we got kicked out. I'll change the date on the Miró invoice to show it was sold in the Centrum's auction. When Hot Man sees that, he may change his mind."

"Good idea Tatli," I said, looking past Charles to her. This earned me a satisfyingly sour look from him.

"I need to ask you something, Brian," Charles said slowly as he leaned back from his champagne. "And I want to do so with all the delicacy and restraint you showed in your reflection of my culture."

"Yes?" I asked, suddenly nervous.

He folded his arms across his thin chest. The harsh artificial light blasting down on him from above made him look like a corpse with a purpose.

"Are you a closet asshole?"

"Why, Charles," I replied, feigning surprise, "I thought you'd never ask."

"No, really. You seem like the nice guy pining for your long lost love and all, but both Hot Man *and* the chief officer have had problems with you. At least they both dump on you instead of me, which is nice, I must admit. Have you done something that I don't know about to earn their enmity?"

I frowned in thought, but had trouble focusing. I was going back to *Conquest* and the Big Easy!

"I don't think I've done anything. Now, while I was on *Conquest* as low level management I was targeted because of my nationality. And Shawn mentioned the

Dutch officers sometimes have a problem with Americans. They are both Dutch. But I don't sense that here."

Charles mused for a moment, then shook his head. "No, I don't think it's anything like that. If you haven't done anything specific, we'll be fine. I just wanted to know everything before I have my showdown."

"Maybe it's because he takes it," Tatli offered.

"What is that supposed to mean?" I asked, somewhat miffed. "Are you saying I'm just a big pushover?"

"Not at all," she clarified. "You take it without flinching. Charles lost his cool on the very first day, when he was ordered to cut off his hair."

Now it was Charles' turn to sniff.

"They haven't bothered him since. But they haven't broken you yet. They don't send the bad news to us in a memo. They target you. I think they want to see you squirm."

"So they know my ex-wife?"

The Jamaicans began appearing in small clusters. Our table was the largest protected from the rain, and we welcomed them to join us. We had three bottles of champagne, but the Jamaicans preferred to drink Red Stripe. Thus, Charles, Tatli, and I downed a full bottle of champagne each. Eventually Tatli retired, but Charles and I remained to smoke some cigars and feel the electric pulse of the night and the dominoes. We flashed some blood, and were wet. It was a good night.

⚓

During the month or so I was on *Majesty of the Seas,* I had yet to escape onto Royal Caribbean's private island of Coco Cay. This islet was a pearl from the broken strand scattered about the insanely picturesque Bahamian waters. Overhead copious palm trees gently swayed to the oceanic beat, while clean sand was always underfoot. As a resort island, numerous sandy paths neatly lined with rocks led to scattered tiki huts overflowing with fruity drinks, or barbecued goodies, or water toys of all descriptions.

I tendered to the island early in the morning on a small, noisy craft that lived at the island. Other than a few yawning employees toting equipment ashore, I was alone. Once ashore I immediately noticed that the air was particularly fresh after the thrashing rain of the last few days. Humid, but not yet hot, the palm fronds shuddered with the promise of torrid heat yet to come. It was strangely quiet, broken only by the cries of gulls.

My destination today was the big half-moon bay of shallow waters, blocked from the sea by a jagged reach of rocks whose black looked alien in this place of white and blue. The sand was just-right white, and the waters were perfectly aquamarine. The ubiquitous recliners were white and blue. So, too, was the big-ass cruise ship anchored nearby.

The beach was an empty opera house, with a semicircle of hundreds of recliners surrounding an amphitheater of sand and sea. All were neatly arranged, empty, waiting. Beyond them open space abounded in groomed sand, as yet unblemished by the garish colors of a thousand beach towels. Alone I strode up to the stage and slipped into the warm waters.

I had come to snorkel, and chose early morning in hopes of seeing the largest amount of fish before they retreated from the heat and people. Coco Cay had a sunken airplane in a mere fifteen feet of water. How cool was that? The swim out to the plane was not long, and made easier by blocked swells. A platform had been erected near to the spot, and it unerringly led me to my underwater destination. Through the drunken, gentle morning light spearing into the turquoise waters, I could see amazing detail already. This was it!

Excitedly I plunged below and kicked further from the surface. I passed over the cadaverous aircraft, hardly believing my eyes. The small, propeller-driven plane was fully intact, but for the tail being shorn off. All rested snugly in a bed of sea grass, open and inviting. The doors had been removed to the cockpit, which reminded me of an old Volkswagen Beetle. The engine cavity was also exposed and empty.

I dove and dove again, crawling around it and searching its secrets in the mottled greenish hues of the sea. The encrustation of the metal was fascinating, and I wondered how long it had been here. I imagined a sunken ship would feel somewhat like this, silent with secrets and perhaps a dramatic end. Here, at least, no one had lost their life, for this plane had belonged to a drug smuggler who missed a runway on a small, neighboring island.

Though peaceful as a grave, there was life. Oh, was there life! Holding my breath longer and longer with the practice, I poked my nose ever deeper into the nooks and crannies and came face to face with fish of intense electric blues and fiery reds. Time passed as I explored the wreck, and the locals came to explore me.

All of a sudden I was immersed in a huge school of fish, each member six to eight inches long, fat and happy. Most were long and silver with bolts of vivid yellow shooting down their length that flared into sharply pronged tails. There were also some rounder silver fellows, whose back carried a mantle of brilliant yellow with vertical black stripes. I was barraged on all sides by fish mere inches from me, and they thumped me like tiny bumper cars. Every stroke of my hand and kick of my foot met a vibrant little body. I became mildly alarmed and felt smothered, but slowly began to realize that the situation wasn't wrong, but oh so right.

They thought I was a fish!

I had seen videos of vast schools of tropical fish swarming and swirling in one solid, shimmering mass, but had never realized what it would look like being one of their number. They pressed within an inch or two of my face and under my chest and between my legs. The crowding silver and yellow blinded me and I squirmed to get away. As a group they went with me until I fumbled up to the surface. Panting, I looked about and saw that I was in the middle of a massive cloud of yellow.

With a grin, I dove back in.

I became one of their school and, surprisingly, sometimes even the leader of it. We would lazily float with the waves for a bit, when I would suddenly turn ninety degrees and stroke in that direction. The whole group happily followed, their big eyes glancing me over, wondering what had prompted me but not particularly caring as long as it wasn't a shark. Time passed and it felt as if I had fins in my face all morning. In reality it was closer to an hour. Eventually a romping, splashing kid approached and tried to hit the fish. Within seconds the school was gone, recognizing the negative presence instantly.

I drifted elsewhere. I wanted to get away from that intrusive brat and continue my harmony with nature. Perhaps my euphoria was just overcompensation for living in the artificial environment of the ship, with literally every breath air-conditioned and every drink chemically dense, if not alcoholic! I stroked to connect with nature even as it strove to avoid humanity. I had to go further and further out and the sea's bottom dropped further and further away.

When the waters were perhaps twenty-five feet deep, I suddenly flowed through a huge mass of sea jellies. They were transparent, yet I could see shimmering red and yellow on the little folds of their bodies in the twinkling sunlight. As mesmerizingly bountiful and beautiful as they were, I was intimidated by possible stingers. Obviously these little five-inchers were not Portuguese man-of-war, but that didn't mean they weren't packing heat. Not that I could do anything about it, because I was already suspended in about 6,000 of them.

And then they were gone. I floated still further out, into water about thirty-five feet deep, and saw something that caught my breath. A sting ray! He was directly below me, casually sliding over the lumpy rocks of the bottom. For fun, I followed him about twelve feet away. We were going with the current, and were swept into deeper water. The temperature of the water chilled perceptively and the water changed to a darker, mesmerizing blue.

Then there were two more sting rays, both some four feet from wingtip to wingtip. They circled each other in a slow motion pirouette a mere twenty feet below me. Their sleek black bodies were clean and smooth and oh so gorgeous. Still, I had no desire to join their dance or enroll in *their* school!

After I had my fill of swimming with the fish, I wandered around the sun-drenched sands of the island. Signposts rising above sandy crossroads led me to a lunch buffet, where I snarfed down a couple cheeseburgers. With belly full, skin soaked in sun, and brain soaked in salt, I happily discovered a cluster of hammocks nestled among the palms. It was not long before I fell asleep.

Upon waking I found Charles and Tatli snuggled asleep in the neighboring hammock. Apparently they arrived and had not wanted to wake me. I returned the favor and quietly watched them sleep for a while. I was reminded of a hammock nap with Bianca in the Red Sea one year ago. An ache flashed through my gut.

Later I was given a special privilege by the jet ski tour operator, who arranged for me to be lead guest on the afternoon's tour. I was no stranger to jet skis, but had always been confined by riverbanks and shores. Not so today, and being the leader in a wild streak across the sea was intoxicating. We tore across the open water at full throttle, gleefully leaving the island behind. Glasslike was the word, for the water was that smooth and that transparent.

The shallows stretched from horizon to horizon, the clean white sand a mere three feet below. Imagine being *miles* out at sea, yet standing only waist deep! The vast sandbar was freckled with thousands upon thousands of bright orange starfish. We finally stopped when *Majesty of the Seas* was just a white blip where the sea met the sky.

The tour operator suggested we hop off the jet skis for a swim. So I did, slithering off the back of the seat and splashing in the turquoise waters. She also commented that it was good luck to kiss a starfish, so I did that, too. Starfish had always fascinated me because they appeared as solid as bone, yet were able to move. I picked up the nearest guy, scarlet red and about a foot long. He was amazingly heavy and didn't seem to mind my amorous advance.

Then, as if it were all a dream, I found myself back on the ship, sunburned and sad the day was through. But oh, what a time! A good way, indeed, to close the book on *Majesty of the Seas.*

⚓

Mere weeks ago, I was suffering slings and arrows of auctioneer training, but now I was assigned to one of the largest cruise ships on the planet. The timeline was staggering in analysis: in less than one month on the Widow Maker, I had changed auctioneers, changed art movers, and had a brutal art swap. Rather than being an unpaid trainee for a month, I was upgraded within days. After conducting my first full auction, I was upgraded again to a bigger ship with bigger money and bigger responsibilities. I did not feel ready at all, and was quite intimidated. I could already see that success at Sundance meant being set up to fail on a higher level. Look at poor Shawn!

But, again, this wasn't really about me. This was about Charles. He was failing, and they would probably give him a lower-ranked auctioneer trainee straight from training. Widow Maker was again set to feed. My departure left Charles floating in the wind, but that was the business. My future lay elsewhere, and I certainly wouldn't get to my Bianca on *Majesty of the Seas.*

I was going to miss Charles and Tatli. They were a lot of fun. More than that, though, it was the pressure-cooker environment of cruise ships. In a very short period of time they had become family. This was a world where you had to live for the moment, and tonight, my last night on *Majesty*, was the moment I had been working so hard for.

Yet we sat more or less in silence. Our table was brightened with silver moonlight, and the air was humid but fresh. The restless ocean surrounding us filled the night with a passive energy that was conducive to reflection. It was sinking in that I was to leave in the morning, and the reality that we hardly knew each other muscled in. For the first time, we had nothing to say to each other. So absently we sipped heavy, heady-sweet liquor from glass tumblers. I bought a bottle of Anguilla Pyrat XO Reserve, and, garnished with those gargantuan local limes with paper-thin skin, we absorbed all things Caribbean.

"Think they have roaches on *Conquest*?" Charles asked eventually, eyeing the scurrying flurry on the teak around us.

"I doubt it has roaches," I said honestly. "But I've worked there before and *know* the crew mess doesn't smell like shit."

He nodded and then returned to his drink.

"What time does your flight leave?" Tatli asked quietly.

"Very early. I was given early clearance and have to sign off at 5:15 in the morning. It's a pain in the ass worthy of invoking the Chicken."

"Is that voodoo or something?" Charles inquired in his deep baritone. "I presume this is not a reference to the proverbial choking of the chicken?"

"That's it!" I exclaimed.

"Then perhaps you should keep that to yourself," Charles deadpanned.

"No, no, that's a whole other sport. I have been wracking my brain over this weird email I got from Bianca, and it just struck me. She asked 'why you have chicks?', and I was worried she thought I was cheating on her. Now I remember I said I won't count my chicks before they hatch."

Charles nodded again and returned to his drink, unimpressed. Time drifted away from us, tossed by the waves. I wondered if I would ever see them again. They had been seriously discussing leaving Sundance, even before meeting the Widow Maker.

"Oh," Charles said finally. "Mary Elizabeth said something about Captain Kirk being the auctioneer on *Conquest.* I don't know what that's supposed to mean."

I knew exactly what it meant. I had met the man to whom she referred. In fact, it could easily be argued that it was Bill Shatner's lust that had launched my entire auctioneer career!

Part II: The Beginning of the End

"Nobody ever went broke underestimating humanity."
—P.T. Barnum

8. THE DEVIL TAKES A WIFE

Art is as much a lustful, chemical reaction as romance. A painting can call you like a Siren, capturing your eye from across a crowded gallery and luring you closer, perhaps even against your will. You look her over from every side and fantasize about her at your place even before you have the courage to ask her name. Hopefully you get lucky, sometimes you do, but so often she's way out of your league. But when a connection happens, oh, how your life brightens! And like a love affair, the best art grows more complex the longer you are with her, and more appreciated.

Or so I thought, before becoming an art dealer. Shows what I know.

Ship life is about far more than being on ships. First is the monumental task of being hired for the job. Gaining my first contract for the dining room meant flying to New Orleans for interviews with a very high level of Carnival Cruise Lines management. Though insanely overqualified, I was nearly denied because the international cruise community had learned the hard way that Americans did not adapt well to ship life. Yes, the sweatship conditions were brutal and impersonal and low paying and all that, but the hardest part was the transience.

Once hired, I had four weeks before my sign-on date, though it could just as easily have been six weeks, or ten. After each contract was an unpaid vacation anywhere from four to ten weeks. This type of unpredictability was tough on Americans entrenched in mortgage or rent, car payments, unsecured debt, or any other number of monthly expenses.

When I finally did get aboard, jealous ship management torpedoed my career. They did not want a precedent for other Americans to follow, as if that would ever happen. So how to return to sea, to my Bianca? Hope came from my discovery of Sundance.

But alas, the auctioneer hiring process made Carnival's methods look all soft and squishy. To get into the seven-day auctioneer screening, I had to lie, cheat, and steal. Perhaps this was intentional. I was going to be an art dealer, after all.

Thus, even while slaving literally 100 hours a week on *Carnival Legend*, I hammered every level of Carnival and Sundance hierarchy. Once again, I was perfectly qualified for the job and even had a degree in art history, but only after a gift of a duty-free $100 bottle of cognac was my resume passed up to the Sundance fleet manager. She reviewed it and grudgingly agreed to grant me five minutes with coffee on her next visit to *Legend*, which was weeks away. After schmoozing her successfully, which did *not* involve shagging her as I had been advised, she recommended me for a phone interview with her boss. This came just days before for my signing off *Legend.*

In fact, Sundance's big dog Gene and I had *two* separate phone interviews. After the second grilling he instructed me to videotape myself in action. Choose any two artists on the Sundance website, he ordered, and create a five minute history on both. Deliver the presentation, memorized, in a designer suit and have the tape *in his hands* in three days!

So that Sunday night I wrote and memorized all ten minutes by practicing in front of a mirror. On Monday I scrounged friends and family for a video camera, even as my best suit was tailored. Tuesday I picked up the suit at noon and delivered my lines like a maniac in order to finish the tape before the 3 p.m. deadline to overnight by Wednesday. Then I had to follow up with two more calls, wherein the second he asked me for an additional video tape. When I refused to do any more without some sort of guarantee of entry, he let me in.

Yes, being *at* sea was much easier than getting *to* sea!

So back in April 2004, my auctioneering career began with a flight to Pittsburgh. While gathering my luggage at the baggage carousel, I was shocked to see a man with a sign reading 'BRUNS'. I suffered a moment of pride, never having dreamed anyone would wait for me in such a manner, and certainly not a chauffeur in coattails! But such formality soon grew boring as I sat alone in the back of the stretched Lincoln Towncar, idly browsing the selection of reading material: the New York Times, the Washington Post, the San Francisco Chronicle, the Economist magazine. Sadly there were no Playboys, but at least Charles wasn't sitting next to me nakedly playing with his little wet baggy.

I was dropped off at the Garden Plaza Marriot. The front desk manager instructed me to be in the cocktail lounge at 9 p.m. for a meeting.

"I assume I share a room…?" I pried.

"Yes, Mr. Bruns," he answered smoothly. "A Mr. Stewart will be sharing your room. If that is not to your satisfaction, I could look into an upgrade. However, my records indicate you are not yet an auctioneer."

"Oh, no, it's fine," I answered. After a year at sea, a strange roommate was not an issue. I was just relieved to know *in advance* about it. Almost exactly thirteen months prior I had been put up in a hotel by Carnival Cruise Lines. While I blithely shampooed my hair, a Croatian man was having wild sex with his girlfriend in what I had thought was my bed. Even more shocking, the Croat had halted his activity to challenge me on 'my' military actions abroad. In a towel, shocked and dripping, I had to explain that I was not personally responsible for America's invasion of Iraq and the embarrassing 'Mission Accomplished' sign… all while trying not to stare at the naked woman in front of me. This time, at least, I would be prepared with a quick quip or at least a dirty limerick.

"Any idea how I will know Gene? We've only spoken on the phone."

The manager chuckled. "Oh, you'll know Gene. He's a patriot."

At the appointed hour the lounge was filled with some thirty men and women, predominantly beautiful. Most could have been models, and I suddenly became self-conscious of my big chin. Also noteworthy was the tremendous youth around me: few, if any, were even 25 years old. Though I was merely 31, I felt closer to the handful of older folks due to my high mileage. All the pretty children drank like fish. Figuring my first meeting with the boss would go more smoothly sober, I declined booze. A rare and painful decision, to be sure.

Fashionably late, a man arrived wearing the most outrageous outfit I had ever seen worn in public. His windbreaker was one giant American flag. His jogging pants neatly continued the pattern where his jacket left off, and even his tennis shoes were splashed in red, white, and blue. Only coattails and a stovepipe hat could have made him more patriotic. Also like Uncle Sam, his face was lined with age to look both tough and wise. His curly brown hair had all but lost the fight with gray and the goatee desperately clinging to his chin was almost entirely white.

"Hello, everyone!" he boomed, eyes sparkling with delight. "Everyone here for the auctioneer's training, gather round! Let's get the chairs into a circle and get going."

My neighbors were completely opposing types. To my left was a woman with dark skin, raspberry lips, and deep Brazilian eyes that sucked me in like a black hole. A tight orange dress accented her cocoa skin to perfection. On my right was a tired yet powerful middle-aged man best described as a strung-out William Shatner. Not the handsome, young Captain Kirk-type, but an older, thicker one with a ruddy complexion. Yet he seemed familiar to me.

"OK!" Uncle Sam continued. "I am Gene, and I'll be in charge of your training this week. Wow, what a big class! We usually number only a dozen, but there are thirty of you this time. That's exciting! Oh boy, is Sundance moving forward. I see a few auctioneers returning for advanced training, but most of you are *soon-to-be* auctioneers. Of course, not all of you will survive until the end. This will be a tough week, probably the toughest of your life for some, but it's nothing compared to the real thing and living on ships."

He paused and peered more closely at the circle. "Who here has ship experience?"

Perhaps half a dozen hands rose. Beside me Shatner raised high his double Jack Daniels. The Brazilian babe beside me, whom I dubbed Hot Cocoa, did not.

"This job is incredibly difficult, but also incredibly rewarding! Work seven days a week for many months in a row, on call at all hours, especially as associates. You will be in a different foreign country every week and have to organize and transport art for shipping through ports with alien names and people. You will have to find employees from the crew, which represents people from all over the earth. Then there's boat drill! You'll find out all about that soon enough.

"So tonight," Gene continued, "is informal. Classes begin tomorrow and we will meet every morning at 8AM to shuttle you to the gallery. If you are late, you are out. We break for an hour's working lunch, and then leave the gallery about six or seven or so. Save your receipts from lunch and any dinners because we'll cover it. We'll pay for a drink or two, but we won't cover the restaurant sharing the hotel's parking lot. The funny-looking modern one with no name on it? That's one of the ten most expensive restaurants in the Unites States. Literally. We won't cover that one."

Gene looked us all over intently. "Seriously, folks, you will *not* all make it. I cannot stress that enough. Even if you make it through our training, there is a real chance the ships will devour you. I have seen the best student of a class fail horribly at sea."

He paused to let the words sink in. Having worked at sea, I was aware of and unfazed by the horrible truth of ship life. Around the circle, most of the kids just grinned stupidly, not really listening. They were in for a world of hurt. In truth, just a year ago I was the same. After those thirteen months slaving for Carnival, however, my soul was thin and nearly broken.

"But!" Gene continued, "Some of the worst students proved to be fantastic auctioneers out at sea. You'll be alone out there, no one to help you... or hinder you. Isn't that right, returning auctioneers?"

"Thank God for that!" Shatner slurred with emphasis.

"The auctioneers will come and go for their advanced training, so new guys: don't count on their help. At the end of the week, if you survive it, the new guys will conduct an auction to be supervised by all auctioneers and trainers."

The circle shivered in anticipation and dread. Gene grinned wolfishly.

"Every day everyone should dress in auction attire. That means gavels. Who has the gavel I asked you to bring?"

About half the hands rose around the circle. I frowned at that. We had been specifically instructed to bring gavels with us and I had busted my butt to find one. One doesn't just hop down to K-mart for an auctioneer's gavel, after all, and I had to order one from a woodcutter in northern Minnesota, for cryin' out loud. How could all these kids ignore instructions before they even arrived? Did they think six-figure incomes, without a prerequisite education no less, were a dime a dozen?

"Auction attire also means suits and ties," Gene continued. "We want to see you all pretty."

"What, no American flags?" someone asked.

"Absolutely not!" A voice suddenly interjected. "I'm English!"

All eyes turned to see the approaching speaker. He was distinctly unimpressive in appearance, despite walking with a swagger to humble John Wayne. His height was a bit less than average, his waistline a bit more, and his clothing a sloppy, untucked mess. Sandy brown hair was delicately thinning and combed straight back to curl behind ears that jutted out to the sides. His smile was also unkempt, vaguely snaggletoothed and decidedly predatory.

"Aha!" Gene said. "Everyone, meet your trainer for the week. While I am in charge, I get one hundred emails a day, so this man will be leading most of it. Everyone, this is—"

"Lucifer," he interrupted again. "I assure you, by the end of the week you will *all* call me that, one way or the other."

"Which reminds me," Gene continued smoothly. "We might as well get started with the names. You're all in a circle, because we are going to play a game."

Groans rose around the room, my own heartily included. I hated name games. During Carnival's training I had been forced to remember people from some sixty nationalities. Strangely, I found it easier to remember names like Biljana, Egle, Yhasmina, and Rasa more so than Jims, Bobs, and most definitely Jim Bobs.

"No, not the usual name game," Gene consoled. "We will go around and find out what famous person you look like. For example, can anyone guess who I look the most like?"

"Colonel Sanders!" someone answered, bringing a sour look from Gene.

"Uncle Sam, obviously," a voice answered.

"Yes!" he agreed. "Most of you already know me as Gene, and that's fine. You already know Lucifer here."

"That's *Lord* Lucifer, to all you new kids," the Brit added smugly.

"You will have enough to remember this week, so I don't care if you know people's names or not. You can learn names on your own time. If you look like J. Edgar Hoover, then we will all learn you as J. Edgar Hoover. It's that simple."

"Who?" asked someone. Gene tried not to grimace.

"So, we'll start on my left." Gene eyed the tall, slender blonde man at his side. "You are a no brainer, Mr. Stewart, but I wonder… where's Harvey?"

The young man frowned in confusion and the circle was silent.

"Jimmy Stewart?"

"My name is Thomas."

"No, no, you look like him. You know, '*Mr. Smith Goes to Washington?*'"

"Smith? Will Smith is black!"

"No, you look like Jimmy Stewart," Gene pressed. "You've never been told that? I was only joking about Harvey."

"Who's Harvey?"

"An invisible six foot rabbit."

The boy stared at him in silence, then finally demanded, "What the hell are you talking about?"

"You look like the actor Jimmy Stewart," Gene explained, equally exasperated. "He did a movie in 1950 wherein his companion was an invisible six foot rabbit."

"Jeez," the kid bristled. "What kind of screwed up movies did you guys watch in those days?"

Obviously Gene was not prepared for the generational gap between himself and this group. Defeated, Gene glanced to Lucifer for support, muttering, "Maybe this wasn't such a good idea."

"Hey," Lucifer replied, "This was *your* idea. I wanted to label them pond scum one through twenty."

"But my last name *is* Stewart," the blonde defended. "That's why I was so confused."

"Oh," Gene amended lamely. "Fine, so the first one didn't work. We'll move on."

We continued to the next lady who bore a stunning resemblance to the actress Rebecca de Mornay. She was the spitting image, in fact, and had turned everyone's head upon entering the room. We moved down the line, past Jim Nabors and his wife Scarlett Johansen, Antonio Banderas, and finally William Shatner. My turn came.

"Oh, everyone, this guy already has a leg up on all of you. On the phone he offered me an autographed copy of his book about ghosts. He's already figured out an important component of ship life: bribery. It works. So, who do people say you look like?"

"For some reason that I cannot fathom, some people say I look like David Hasselhoff."

"Maybe," Gene grudgingly accepted. "You have the big hair and the big jaw, but not really the look."

"Bruce Campbell," I offered, swallowing my delusions of Ben Affleck. "From the *Evil Dead* movies. I hear that all the time, actually."

Murmurs of assent sounded, but Gene was still not satisfied. "I love movies, but I don't know him."

A voice called out, "He did *Xena: Warrior Princess*, too! With Lucy Lawless."

I frowned. "Wasn't that the porn star from *Deepthroat*?"

"That's Linda Lovelace," Bill Shatner smirked knowingly. "I'm proud of you."

"I know!" Gene suddenly burst in. "I know who you remind me of. From *Toy Story!* You're Buzz Lightyear!"

The Sundance Gallery of Fine Art was huge, modern, and simply brilliant in execution. It was the largest privately owned art gallery in the world. The neoclassical façade marched ever onward in boldly contrasting angles to allow dozens of art nooks, all stately presenting original works from such as Albrecht Dürer, Pablo Picasso, Salvador Dalí, and Marc Chagall. As large as the main gallery and gallerias were, however, the back-offices were equally impressive in scale and cutting-edge security. Here entire banks of employees worked the phones, supplying the latest artwork to avid fans all over earth. It was here, as well, that the overwhelming logistical nightmare of supplying 100 ships with millions of dollars in art was undertaken.

Once inside, the trainees gathered in the lower level of the gallery. This was a warren of little gallerias focusing on current impressionists, animators, and splatter-painters. Every direction held another series of rooms extending into the distance. Though I was grounded with a strong direction sense and had navigated 2000-year old streets in Romania with nary a misstep, even I nearly got lost in the labyrinth.

Lucifer allowed us no time to absorb the surroundings or, for that matter, breathe. He marched through galleria after galleria until we were in a far back corner of the building. We halted in a room barely large enough for the twenty-six new trainees, and were nearly blinded by the jumbled colors of dots and rough slashes on canvases all around.

As Lucifer reviewed us with dissatisfaction, I reciprocated. Today he had dressed in a very English manner. His suit was medium blue with a tight pattern of pin stripes, and beneath it he wore a shirt of baby blue with a second pattern of pinstripes. His extremely wide tie was orange with yet a third pattern of stripes, this time diagonal. His sleeves were white and French-cuffed.

"You are all pond scum," Lucifer began. His voice was not loud, but it sure was sharp. "You aspire to be more, this I know. Some of you may… *may*… achieve this. By the end of the week a few of you may actually evolve into tadpoles. It is my duty to help you crawl out of the primordial soup and become something greater. Once on a ship, those tadpoles who survive may someday become frogs. And please, nobody give me any crap about you being the Frog Prince. You're not.

"To be an auctioneer is not easy. You've all seen them on TV talking a mile a minute. We don't do that: we aren't selling cattle. We are selling art. So that means in one short week I have to teach you how to *advertise* for an auction, *organize* an auction, *run* an auction, close sales *during* the auction, finalize paperwork *after* the auction, and finally how to transport the sold art from ship to shore… in multiple nations. I won't even begin to discuss how every ship on every cruise line has an entirely different set of criteria for how to bill, pay taxes, bills of lading, port clearances, and so on."

Lucifer leered at us, letting the magnitude of our training sink in. The group shivered as one even before he dropped the bomb. "And that's not even talking about the art!

"We have hundreds of artists from all over the earth," Lucifer continued. "You won't just learn about Picasso, but all the modern masters as well. You will learn who they are, where they live or when they died, what they are known for, their style, their medium, all of it. If you are not yet scared, you should be. Gene was being nice when he said this will be the hardest week of your life for some of you. That's crap. It will be the hardest week of your life for *all* of you. I am here to ensure that."

So Lucifer now officially had the role of bad cop.

"So, little sea urchin-wannabes," Lucifer said. "This morning I am going to teach you the very, very basics of selling artwork. To begin, let's see who knows anything about art. Hands?"

My hand rose, as did a few others.

"Anyone here work for an art gallery before, or have art education?"

Only two hands remained up, mine and Rebecca de Mornay's.

"You, then!" Lucifer declared, pointing at me. "Buzz Lightyear, you are to be my bitch. Come to the front. What is your background, little man?" He seemed unaware of the irony of his insult, considering I was four inches taller and thirty pounds stronger than he.

"I have a Bachelor's degree in Art History and worked as an art historian for a gallery with locations in Reno, L.A., and London."

"So you think you're smart, then?"

"Oh, no," I demurred. "My ex-wife and my cat shattered those delusions long ago."

"Good. Had they not done so before, I would have now. So, genius, sell me this art."

"What, this one here?"

"No, the one on the floor beneath your feet," he snapped. "Come on, make me want to buy it. I'm a tough sell, so do your worst."

"I don't know who this is, or what it is," I protested, looking up at the trite image before me. "Obviously it's one of those ubiquitous French street-café scenes, a knockoff of a Van Gogh but with Day-Glo colors. But that's all I know, I'm sorry."

"You *should* be sorry," he needled, "For failing so miserably. See? Your knowledge is useless! You may return to the back of the class where you belong. Now, listen to me, you little people. You don't need to know about art to sell art! You just need to know about what's in front of you. Selling art can be ephemeral or it can be tangible. Until you idiots learn about our artists and some art history, we are going to teach you the tangibles."

Lucifer pointed to a corner of the canvas. Hidden among the jumbles of color were a signature and a number.

"This reveals it as a limited edition," he instructed. "Number 25 of 200, signed by the artist. This is from a Frenchman named Picot. I hate Picot. I mean, come on, he's French! But he has made a name for himself and Sundance would not carry his work if he hadn't. This is all you need to know to sell."

"How so?" Cindy Lou Who asked.

"Think of the rarity!" Lucifer exclaimed, gesturing broadly.

"But there are 200 of them!"

"Oh, and that is a lot?" Lucifer jibed. "McDonalds has sold *billions* of hamburgers, but you Americans lap them up as if they are going out of business. You are telling me that 200 sounds like a lot? People are stupid. They think there is only one original. That's crap. Do you know how many versions and copies Michelangelo did of the Sistine ceiling? One original my ass!"

"Now wait a minute," she retorted, shifting her stance into a solid, yet curvy, model of obstinacy. "Original means one of a kind. Like a painting."

"No, it doesn't," Lucifer retorted. "*Non*-artists get that in their heads from somewhere. I presume Americans are taught that in school or something, because you all say the same thing and no one else in the world knows why. Original is anything made *by hand* by the artist. If you found a drawing by Picasso of one of his 'original' paintings, would you throw it away as a mere copy? Get this into your pointy little heads now, people. If something is handmade by the original master artist, it's not a copy. A copy is a Xerox or a poster."

He pointed to all the works surrounding him. "You think we sell posters? Posters are done by machine lithography and have no artist contact at all. They can crank them out in the millions. These are handmade, printed painstakingly by the artist and the atelier in concert. This is the way fine art has been done for centuries, people. *Centuries!*

"Why does the average, uneducated American think he knows more than Rembrandt, for example, who was a master printmaker? He was the greatest etcher in history! Apparently you get taught in your schools that only paintings are worth anything, but I beg to differ. Pablo Picasso produced more artwork than any other artist in history; he worked ten hours a day, seven days a week into his nineties. If he didn't have a woman on his johnson he had a brush in his hand. You think his handmade prints are cheap copies? Hell no!

"And here, in the tradition of such greats as Rembrandt and Picasso, we have Picot and his iconic Parisian street cafés. Only 200 ever made, each and every one by hand, signed by this *internationally renowned* artist. How do we know he's nationally renowned, you might ask? We're not in France are we?

"This was just released a few months ago and is available for X dollars. Now, that's the *opening* price, folks. But think about it: Sundance at Sea is the largest arm of the largest fine art gallery in the world! We are on 100 ships having over 200 auctions a week. How long do you think this will remain available? Not long! Once half of them are gone, and with the demand higher than ever, the price will only go up. How could it not? Within one short month these 200 handmade prints will seem like an awfully small number. Within two months this price will double or more, due to overwhelming demand and tiny availability. A lithograph a mere copy? Hah!"

Suddenly I realized what he reminded me of: a hyena. He was far more intelligent than people gave him credit for, as well as far more predatory. Most mistook him as a lowly scavenger because of his unimpressive features: his smile was toothy and crooked, his body misshapen, and his ears jutted out all funny. Unlike a hyena he never laughed, but his mannerisms were just as unpredictable and creepy.

"What's a lithograph?" someone asked.

For the first time, Lucifer was speechless. He gazed over the crowd of big, frightened eyes, but could not identify who asked the question.

"What? Did one of you really just ask me what a lithograph is? What the Hell? I was horrified last night when some of you morons admitted you didn't have gavels. So how many of you losers don't have the books I put on the list?"

About half the hands went up. Lucifer looked at all of them incredulously.

"Are you stupid bastards serious? You are making it *so* easy for me. We gave you a list of books to read *before* you come to class, and half of you haven't even bothered to buy them? What is wrong with you? Did you geniuses think you could waltz in here and we would pay you huge sums of money because you're pretty?"

With a sigh, Lucifer composed himself. "All right, those of you who actually have the books can make photocopies of them or whatever. I don't care. But by tomorrow morning, all of you must know the difference between a painting, lithograph, serigraph, cell, seri-cell, linoleum cut, etching, aquatint, mezzotint, and a giclée. I will test you in the first five minutes of class."

His voice softened to an intimate, lover's level. "If you don't think you can learn it by the morning, don't bother. Just pack."

9. THE EMBARRASSMENT GENE

Two days in and I was already mentally exhausted. Lucifer's teaching technique was abusive and by the end of a ten-hour day my brain was crammed. We were required to regurgitate entire lists of information learned merely minutes before to a large, highly critical audience. Once we endured that, we learned a second list and had to repeat the lesson with the new information, this time heckled and interrogated mercilessly. Then, mere minutes after *that*, we had to weave both lists together into yet a higher level. Those first two days were more concentrated and intense than anything in my entire four years at the University.

Already four people had dropped out and I had no doubt that tomorrow the class would be even thinner from those who quit. There were also a fairly large number of students who would not make it through training because of poor performance.

I lay back on my bed and loosed a long, relaxing sigh. Unlike the first two days, tonight I opted out of hitting the gym right away. I was just too tired. Usually the physical workout helped me sort my thoughts and compartmentalize lessons into the dusty shelves of my brain, but tonight I just wanted a bacon double cheeseburger. Tell me *I'm* not a patriot!

The door opened and my roommate entered. Jimmy Stewart was the tall, handsome blonde who so vexed Gene on the first meeting. He was a nice guy, but I didn't think he would last the week. He didn't seem to think so, either.

"We are being taught by Satan and Uncle Sam," I lamented to the ceiling. "Doesn't that unnerve anyone but me?"

"I thought they were the same thing." Jimmy said cynically, tugging at his tie. "What a day! Lucifer is such a bastard!"

"I'm not religious," I commented drily, "Yet I strangely concur."

Jimmy removed his suit and regarded it with a mix of affection and disgust. He brushed off a stray string, but soon his brushing grew from a pat to a rough scrub and up to a beating. He began swearing and finally threw everything forcefully onto his bed. Surely it was illegal somewhere to so mistreat an Armani.

"I'm not going to make it!" he cried. "I'm not going to last this goddamn week!"

"I agree."

He regarded me with surprise. "What?"

"I agree," I repeated, rising from the bed. "Look, man. You go to the bar every night and don't come back until two in the morning. Have you picked up a book since you got here?"

"How can I study after getting my brain squeezed all day long? I need a beer to relax!"

"Well, sure, I understand that. But you aren't taking any responsibility. No one here is. You didn't buy *any* of the books you were told to. What, you thought buying a nice suit would get you the job?"

"I have a nice gavel, too."

"A gavel does not an auctioneer make."

"Hey," he defended. "I spent every penny I had for these suits. I borrowed money from my mom for the plane ticket here. I am risking everything in the world to come here!"

"So what? Oh, you think that makes you brave? Maybe your friends think it's ballsy, but I don't. It just means you're a gambler. You're going all in, hoping the magic card will turn up. You have no plan, no goals, just reckless hope. You showed up and wanted some miracle to make your life work better."

"When did you get so holier than thou?" Jimmy retorted. "You are Lucifer's bitch. He smacks you down every day. You think you're so smart?"

"Of course I do," I replied with a grin. "Unfortunately, no one *else* ever thinks so. But I'm going to pass this week and I'm going to get a ship of my own. I'm going to get it because I listen and do what I'm told. I mean, come on, man! They put it all down on paper and handed it out to us: buy this, learn this, say that. We have *written instructions* on how to make six figures a year. *That's* the miracle! All you have to do is follow it, but you won't."

"Maybe you're right," he admitted. "I have to make this happen. You think not drinking will help?"

"Whoa!" I protested. "Now I would *never* say that! You don't think I hit the booze after Lucifer shoves his horns up my… well, you know what I mean."

"What did you do to him, anyway? He seems to hate you most of all."

"I have that effect on assholes," I commented. "They gravitate towards me."

"Birds of feather, perhaps?" Jimmy asked, with surprising eloquence.

The gymnasium at the hotel was small but nice, boasting multiple treadmills, stationary bikes, and weight-systems that catered to the entire range of musculature. Yet the best feature was surely the view. Directly before my treadmill, where I sweated and panted for many a reason, Hot Cocoa performed yoga. During the name game, no one had known any Brazilian celebrities, so when I suggested Hot Cocoa, Gene surprisingly concurred.

Though running was my refuge after a hard day, Cocoa doing the Down Dog in tights made my heart race even faster. We had exchanged a number of smiles while observing each other and already found harmless fun in flirtation. My disappointment at her leaving the Down Dog position, and thusly losing an unparalleled view of her bottom, was relieved when she moved into Cobra Pose. She slithered towards me, arching her head back high to offer me an open view of her magnificent cleavage.

"How fast are you running?" she asked me with an intentional heave of her bosom.

"Eight miles an hour," I called back over the pounding of my steps. "I usually run four to six miles a day. It gives my mind a chance to shelve the information gathered during the day."

"So much mental focus," she teased as her large, black eyes met mine. "Thinking about … *shelves*… big Buzz?"

"I'll show you shelves you'll never forget."

How pathetic could I possibly be? That comment even sounded lame to me. I was completely outclassed and had to change the subject before my melting knees dropped me onto the treadmill to tumble end over end like laundry. "I used to do yoga, but it's too hard for me now. Watching is good for me, though."

"Oh, I love being watched," she replied, mercifully opting out of any obvious 'hard' jokes.

Cocoa bounded into a Triangle Pose. She faced away and sank low as if to do the splits, but slid to the side and hugged her calf. Her tights pulled low enough for me to follow the beads of sweat rolling down the small of her back. I lovingly watched each drop disappear into the hint of her crevice. My eyes flew wide when I saw ink.

"You have a tattoo!" I exclaimed. "This I have to see: you have no option."

Still in pose, she reached over to pull her tights down even further, revealing a red chili pepper snuggling mischievously between her cheeks. I stared too long and suddenly stumbled on the treadmill. I lurched onto the side rail just before being torpedoed into the wall, and my free arm hammered the console to stop the thing.

So much for our flirtations being harmless!

Panting desperately, I proclaimed, "That's the hottest pepper I have *ever* seen!"

Wheezing, I limped off the treadmill and plopped heavily onto the weight bench. The door opened, saving me any further embarrassment. Or so I thought. Rebecca de Mornay poked her head in and scanned the room. "Ah,

Cocoa, there you are. We have thirty minutes before the group gets together and the possible Frederick sighting."

Though we had slaved for nine horrendous hours already today, a few more hours of labor yet awaited us. Our homework was to gather in groups and prepare long presentations on a cluster of artists. There was a rumor that the gallery's legendary owner may make an appearance.

"Jeez, Buzz," Rebecca said, eyeing me up and down with approval. "You look like you're going to die."

"Is that why I am surrounded by angels?"

"I love a man who's already sweaty and beaten," Rebecca observed with a twinkle in her eye. Suddenly I was overwhelmed by a flash of recall about one of the most trying aspects of my ship life on Carnival. There was a dizzying surplus of beauty, and I wasn't talking about the sunsets. I had always maintained focus on Bianca in my heart and mind, but my eyes couldn't help but wander. I was a lifelong student of art, after all, how could I not appreciate living beauty when awash in it?

"Tomorrow," Cocoa teased, "Try to stay on your feet."

"You've swept me off them," I replied. "You should be proud of yourself, you know. I can handle a treadmill at high speed with the ship rocking and outrunning a hurricane… but your tattoo humbled me!"

Both women stopped. "You've been on ships? What are the gyms like there?"

"I've only been allowed to use crew gyms in the past. Every ship has a gym and spa and all that good stuff, and most have a running track around the top, too. They tend to be small, of course. On one ship it was perhaps fourteen laps per mile, so that'll make you dizzy."

"They have separate gyms for the crew?"

"Ships have separated everything for the crew," I answered. "You think they want a thousand crew members to push out the guests from a gym with a capacity of fifty? In reality, of course, none of the crew works out except the entertainers."

"Why is that?"

"Who has the time? Almost everyone works 80 hours a week or more. Remember, there aren't any Americans there trying to work off Big Mac fat. Half the crew only eats a plate of rice with a ladle of fish soup on top, for cryin' out loud. They don't want to work out."

"I would still work out," insisted Rebecca. "I have to or I go nuts."

"Crew gyms are crazy, though. No windows, no air, tripping over discarded dumbbells and plates. They stink of old sweat and the walls are filthy from, well, who knows? Age, tobacco, and lack of ventilation leaves them off white with streaks, as if the sweat flung from exercise had left its mark."

"Tobacco?"

"Yeah. On *Fantasy*, for example, the crew gym was in the crew bar. All nasty and sweaty and stinky. Upon reflection, however, that's exactly how I would like to see you."

Rebecca's nose wrinkled at the thought. "No alcohol napkins to swab the machine seats, or fresh towels?"

I snorted. "Yeah, right. To towel off they have toilet paper, man. Don't worry, though. Our experience will be orders of magnitude better than crew. Imagine living in a guest cabin... actually getting a full night's sleep! The food will be better, spa privileges, you name it."

"Assuming we get that far," Cocoa added, grounding us all.

That evening I sat at a round table beside my group member Alanis Morrisette. The third trainee in our group, Elvis, was nowhere to be found. He ignored our assignment in order to follow our assigned veteran auctioneer around like a groupie. So he and Bill Shatner ogled and jeered at everyone unfortunate enough to be nearby and have two X chromosomes.

Our assignment was to discover the commonalities of three disparate artists and find a way of using the credentials of one to sell the other. For example, one of our best selling artists, Marcel Mouly, at one time worked with Picasso himself. By selling Picasso's credentials, we could educate and excite people about Mouly. Though on our 'free time', we wore auction attire because of the rumor of a Frederick sighting. Such visits by the gallery owner were rare and cause for great speculation and more than a little fear. Frederick was famous for a raging, unpredictable temper. As sole owner, he could, and had, fired many for no apparent reason, including even his highest earners.

Alanis fidgeted nervously, chomping her fingernails with huge, perfect teeth. The only thing more generous than her smile and sheer talent was, unfortunately, her self-induced frustration. She continually stressed that her best was not enough.

"Well," I eventually said with a sigh and rising from the table, "I think that's pretty good. We have several pages of material approaching it from three different angles."

"What?" Alanis squawked. "What are you doing? Are you leaving me? You're giving up! Oh my God!"

"Whoa, slow down there, tiger," I soothed. "I'm just getting a beer."

Alanis nearly trembled with nerves whenever I even set my book down. I gently took up her hand to calm her. Though her mouth was so large and pretty, watching it tear human flesh freaked me out. Her obsessive nature and fears of abandonment did have one immediate, practical benefit however: Bill gave her a wide berth.

"Relax, we're doing well," I said, intentionally interrupting her cuticle dinner. "May I buy you a drink?"

"How can you drink now? What about Frederick? Frederick is coming!"

"Look, we are technically on our own time. I am having *one* beer because we are all but finished. Chill, baby doll."

"Pardon me," a young lady beside me interrupted, "Did I overhear that Frederick is coming? Do you mean the owner of the Sundance Gallery of Fine Art?"

I looked in surprise at the stunningly attractive woman who had been sitting beside us at a computer. Because we sat in the business center, two banks of computers competed for limited space with our table such that we all overheard each others' business.

"Indeed," I replied. "How did you guess that?"

"You have a big voice, you know," the brunette chided. "I love art and am watching the Picasso auction even now. Everyone in town knows of the owner of the Sundance Gallery. I have not yet met him and would delight in doing so."

"Well, if he's pointed out to me, I'll let you know. I'm Brian, by the way."

"Lisa," she replied, taking my hand.

"Brian?" Alanis chirped. "Your name is Brian? I'm still calling you Buzz."

Lisa frowned. "Buzz? What, are you a soldier or something?"

"It's a long story," I explained. "I have been accused of looking like the character from *Toy Story*."

Lisa laughed. "Buzz Lightyear! Now *that* is funny! You do raise the one eyebrow like him a lot and seem to think everything you say is worthy of melodramatic oration."

"And you're so animated," Alanis added, laughing uproariously at her own joke.

"Ha ha," I replied drily. If I was going to be teased, I preferred what had happened in the gym!

Mercifully the business center abutted the bar which, of course, was packed with auctioneers. Free from the pummeling of Lucifer that squeezed the trainees into all sorts of funny shapes, the auctioneers were apparently only here to drink. As I ordered I listened to Lucifer entertain Bill Shatner and Don Rickles. Hovering nearby, but obviously not part of the conversation, was Elvis.

"And so the bitch left!" Lucifer was saying. "Can you believe she said, 'money isn't everything?' Ha! What a stupid bint."

They all chortled arrogantly, like a cluster of corpulent masters of industry dangling society by the strings on their fingertips.

"Money *isn't* everything," I instigated, eager to rile Lucifer outside of class. "Who said art dealers cannot appreciate beauty?"

"*I* did," Lucifer retorted cockily.

"The only people who say money isn't everything," Rickles added while stroking his pink tie, "Are people who don't have any."

"You and your goddamn art loving," Lucifer added condescendingly. "I hate that. We aren't museum curators, we are dealers. It's about the money. When you learn that, maybe I'll start to like you."

"Perish the thought," I retorted drily.

"Just like my associate," Shatner chimed in. "You love art. You pay attention to composition and shit like that. Who cares?"

"You mean like the proper use of color?"

I had noticed that like Don Rickles, both Lucifer and Bill were wearing a pink tie. In fact, all three men before me wore pink ties over pink shirts. They looked ludicrous. "Oh, I get it. GQ just had that article on pink being the new 'power color'. Yeah, really hip, guys. Trend setters you are. I hope Frederick likes pink."

I left, and surprisingly Shatner followed. Elvis trailed behind like a fallen leaf swirling after a passing car. Catching up, Bill said, "You're right. Frederick only likes the green we make him. That's why we walk on water."

"Funny thing to say near *Lucifer*," I taunted, emphasizing the name.

"I like you," Bill said. "I like you because Lucifer hates you. You don't take his shit without a fight."

"Yet I still lose every time."

"Who cares? Once you make the money, you'll be king for a day, too. You look familiar. On ships already?"

"Yes. I was a restaurant manager on *Carnival Conquest* last year."

"That's my ship! No wonder, we probably met in the crew bar. Man, I wish you were my associate. My current guy is horrible."

"Doesn't do his job, eh?"

"It's not that. He's good looking and dresses sharp, but he never drinks and never helps me get laid. What kind of a wingman is that? I don't need help getting money, only getting pussy!"

"You are truly a gentleman. But really, even on ships?" I asked incredulously. "I've had to beat them off with a stick and I'm nothing special."

"Bah, you're still young. At least here I've got Elvis as my wingman!"

Elvis was a beefy California surfer dude. His thick build was larger than that of his namesake and he was not nearly as handsome, but there was something distinctly Elvis-like about his sideburns and hair. Though a mere 20 years old, the pull from his auctioneer parents had gained him entry into the training. It obviously explained why he had not already been cut from class, as well. His efforts were devoted to following Bill around like a puppy, awed by the man's insistence of success with money and women. Naively Elvis needed no proof of either, and fairly humped Shatner's leg in his effort to get attention.

At the table Alanis waited impatiently, munching on fingertips fairly ruined from this behavior. Before any of us returned to work, Elvis leapt forward to take my chair. He pulled it away from the table and up to Lisa's computer. His excitement melted when he realized she was not watching sports.

"You are watching Sotheby's online?" he asked her, disappointed.

"What, you thought she was looking up porn in the hotel lobby?" I said to him. Then I added as if he were a child, "Leave the nice lady alone."

I couldn't blame Elvis for being intrigued by Lisa. Her ice blue eyes were accented by a lustrous ebony ponytail that curled lovingly around her shoulder. Her snug dress matched her hair and was obviously of a designer cut. She was clearly well off.

"A Picasso painting is being auctioned," Lisa replied honestly before giving a feigned pout, "Oh, you aren't familiar with his work? What a shame."

Elvis brightened, taking the bait. "Oh, do I know Picasso! He's just the greatest artist who ever lived!"

She gave us a wink. The hunted had chosen to become the hunter.

"Oh, I quite agree. But why do *you* think so?"

I stifled a groan as Elvis launched into the most amateurish explanation of modern art I could possibly imagine. Because we had just studied Picasso this morning, Elvis regurgitated every bit of miscellaneous information he could recall: incorrectly. He blathered without rhyme or reason, mixing his inaccurate history with plenty of pipe dreams about his future wealth as a soon-to-be auctioneer.

Lisa pretended to listen carefully, while actually focusing on the monitor. With each imaginary point he believed he scored, Elvis leaned in closer. He didn't give her a chance to respond at all for a whopping thirty minutes straight. I had never seen such a sonnet before.

Even Hamlet had less to say upon debating his very mortality.

"My father-in-law has a Picasso," Lisa finally mentioned after Elvis finally exhausted his brain. At long last, the youth seemed speechless. "Two, actually. One is a painting he bought decades ago, but we recently purchased an original etching from Sundance."

"Wow, what's it worth?"

Lisa smiled kindly. "That's none of your business."

"What's he do for a living?"

"Oh, he owns a few steel mills. Well, more than a few, actually."

"Cool. Well, you wanna Bud or somethin'?" He eyed her trim figure appreciatively. "I guess you want Bud Light, yeah?"

"Oh, no, thank you," she gushed overtly. "I have a bottle of wine decanting. Would you be a dear and ask the bartender to serve us? It should be ideal by now."

"Uh, OK," Elvis said. He was evidently unsure of how to handle a woman who chose wine over beer. He trudged off, leaving Bill and I to hide our amusement. Alanis, however, was completely unimpressed.

"Doesn't anyone here ever work?" she lamented. "My God, time is ticking away! Ticking away and so much to do! And what if Frederick comes? He's going to come, they said he would come!"

A moment later Elvis and the bartender arrived. An expensive bottle of vintage Opus One was soon expertly serviced. Lisa offered her young suitor a glass, who reluctantly accepted. Within moments he was expounding upon Californian wines, a subject about which he knew far less than he did Picasso.

Eventually Lucifer informed us that Frederick cancelled and we were all dismissed. Just in time, I thought, eyeing Alanis's heaving chest. She was nearly hyperventilating from self-induced stress. As I departed, I wondered what kind of stories Elvis would have to tell in the morning.

Over coffee Elvis boasted to me that he had returned to his room at 3 a.m. Though his roommate, Antonio Banderas, sat beside us quietly shaking his head at the fallacy, the surfer just bounded along enthusiastically about his scoring with Lisa. On the drive to the gallery I overheard him bragging to Bill that he got home at 3:30. By the time we walked into the gallery, his return had been at 5 a.m.

For class this day, Uncle Sam had us begin with our seats in a circle. As always, Hot Cocoa sat to my left. She had learned that here, in the lee of Buzz, was protection from the storm of Lucifer. To my right was an auctioneer, John Goodman.

"So!" Gene boomed to start us off, "Today we are going to do a lot. Much more than usual."

A groan swept the room.

"Are we all here?" he counted the chairs and frowned. "Someone is missing. Well, we can't hold up the class. We are doing two things today. This morning we will teach you Sundance's custom auctioneering program. You'll even have a chance to meet the programmers who designed it. They will be taking questions and comments from the returning auctioneers, so this will give you trainees an excellent opportunity to hear some of the real issues.

"This afternoon we will learn how to drip. Dripping, you see, is the constant dripping of little bits of artist information, like a leaky faucet. Through the viewing before the auction you'll be talking and dripping a few lines here and there, then moving on. By the start of the auction the guests will have learned a lot about the artist without having slogged through a tiring sales pitch.

"But before we begin I want everyone to list, in order from best to worst, their ranking for all the trainees, including yourselves in the list. Auctioneers, you don't have to, just the trainees."

We spent a few minutes in silence, contemplating. As far as I was concerned, labeling the best trainees was easy: Cindy Lou Who and her husband Sammy Hagar were the best. I figured I was about number five. But who should I judge as the worst? That was a toss-up between Jimmy Stewart and Elvis, but I couldn't decide which had the dubious honor.

Suddenly the door opened up and Elvis burst in. His eyes were wild and hair disarrayed. I promptly filled in the last line.

"Elvis! Thanks for joining us this morning," Gene said. "I trust you have a good reason for being late?"

"Uh, yeah!" he replied, haphazardly thinking on his feet. "I had to take a cab here because I got in so late. I had to entertain a guest at the hotel until late this morning, if you know what I mean. She's the daughter of a high powered industrialist and I gave her a lesson on Picasso."

Chuckles rose from those of us who knew he had been smoking outside and merely lost track of the time.

"Well then," Gene said. "This seems like an excellent time to do something important, but fun, before the tough stuff later. I want to make sure none of you have the embarrassment gene. Elvis here obviously does not. Now we'll see about the rest of you."

"The embarrassment gene?" someone asked.

"Yes, we want to make sure none of you are nervous getting up in front of a large group of people. As auctioneers you will control groups of several hundred people. When you make presentations at the beginning of the cruise, however, you will be on stage before *thousands*. We want to know you can handle it.

"So, I want everyone to stand up in the center and tell us in detail about your most embarrassing moment. Whoever goes first will have to top Elvis's BS story about scoring with Lisa that we all heard at breakfast ad nauseum. So if your story does not involve a beautiful woman, or at least some sex, I think we'll all be very disappointed. You are going to ships, after all. So, who volunteers?"

The room plunged into silence. Beside me Hot Cocoa squirmed. Alanis practically fainted.

"Buzz volunteers," Lucifer shouted. "Buzz! Get up there and show us all how lame you are."

Reluctantly I rose and walked to the center of the circle of some twenty chairs. I glanced around at all the trainees and auctioneers and instructors, desperate to recall something embarrassing.

"Well, I can't think of anything at the moment," I said slowly, stalling. "I haven't been embarrassed since I discovered what girls were, it was all downhill from there."

Lucifer gloated. "That's crap! You've never even kissed a girl. Your mummy doesn't count."

"All right, then," I said, rising to the challenge. "I have a phobia of lobsters that came about from my near-death experience in the desert wastes of Nevada."

The circle fell silent, no one even guessing where this was leading.

"My ex-wife and I had foolishly driven from our hometown in Iowa straight through to Reno, but taking a long route through Colorado so we could see a town called Crested Butte. So I had already driven some twenty hours more or less straight at this point. I was thoroughly exhausted, and the unending desert was not stimulating enough to keep me awake. So we, uh, added some stimulation.

"We decided to have sex while driving. We hadn't seen anyone else on the road for hours and hours and hundreds and hundreds of miles. The cruise control was set to 80mph, and she pulled off her pants and got on me as we sped along. It was kinda awkward, but exciting, you know? Fortunately I was very young at the time and knew the whole thing would last only a minute or two at the most.

"Anyway, right as I was about to climax we passed a sign by the road that warned, 'Lobster Crossing.' I didn't think anything of it, of course, but through my haze of intense fatigue, desert boredom, and sexual ecstasy I *actually saw* a small herd of lobsters moving onto the road.

"I lost control… of the car, I mean. My Saturn careened out of control and I had a Hell of a time staying on top of it with her on me. We ran off the shoulder, spiraling on the flat desert and plowing through scrub and sage. The soft sand grabbed the tires and threatened to flip us sideways at that speed, but I jerked the wheel to the side with all my strength. I overcompensated for a moment and it seemed like we would tumble end over end the other way, but finally we straightened back on the road.

"I remember us panting and shouting as having gone through a great ordeal, but the massive desert just ignored us, the sun kept blasting down, and everything was as if nothing had happened. It turns out that some bored locals had posted the sign and nailed a bunch of rubber lobsters by the road as a joke. I thought we were going to die, man. I've never been to Red Lobster since."

The circle was silent for a long, long time.

Gene then mused quietly, "Why, Buzz, I had no idea."

10. BITTER BUTTER

Thursday night I sucked lovingly on my cigar and watched the smoke rise up until the bar's funky sideways fans shredded it. I sat at the polished wooden bar of Teddy's Grill across the street from the hotel. It was a deceptively large and quality establishment hiding in an otherwise ugly strip mall. All week I had avoided coming here, focusing instead on my work. But today had been very rough, and we were nearly finished so I indulged myself.

Tomorrow we had the test auction, but my only concern was that we would skip the auction preview part and focus only on the auction itself. I had learned that my best talent was dripping, and had hoped to strut my stuff for Lucifer.

That morning we slogged through hours of learning the auctioneering software. The customized program was impressive, to be sure. The art-related sections were straightforward enough: a biography on the artist, description of the artwork, sometimes a picture. You could toggle through all works from that artist, and even see the highest price paid for one, were it a limited edition. We learned about how each ship's art data, or POS, depended on the cruise line. Carnival buyers were generally different than Radisson buyers, for example.

What made the day so fatiguing, however, was the nightmare jumble of numbers on the screen. It was designed so that a passing glance would not reveal the lowest allowable price. Therefore a freakishly large, complex chart of numbers dominated the screen to overwhelm curiosity seekers and, unfortunately, new auctioneers.

Commissions paid for selling the work in question varied based on tiers of overall cruise sales, so that each work had five different numbers listed vertically. This was cross-referenced with a horizontal row of numbers corresponding to the higher commission based upon the higher price sold. As if this chart were not enough numbers, along the side ran a vertical row with suggested bidding increments.

All afternoon we practiced using small groups. This made the pressure less than that of real life, but Lucifer's horns were sharp as ever. His rebukes echoed in my head, criticizing my typing while holding a gavel and a microphone simultaneously, even as I searched the group for bids and input them. I needed four hands to look as smooth as the pros.

The dark recesses of Teddy's opened to reveal Rebecca de Mornay, stunning as always in painted-on jeans and a frilly, lacy pink halter top. She could legitimately wear anything fashionable on a young woman, yet exuded an aura of mature self confidence in her own femininity. Rebecca was more commonly seen in a dress, for example, than most American women I knew. No pant suits for her, and certainly no baggy men's jeans and T-shirts. She leaned against the bar and settled into a wonderfully wiggly pose.

"Buy me a drink, sailor?" she asked, getting a sniff from me as a response. "Just kidding. I need to borrow your body for a minute."

"I fear at my age a minute is overly optimistic."

"Don't worry. After that story in class, you've already exceeded my expectations."

"Figures. My best efforts are completely inadequate, but my premature ejaculation story exceeds expectation."

"I need you to help me illustrate something. We are discussing the way women get protective of each other in groups, or on the defensive if they are alone and pretty, or single or whatever."

"Uh, OK. So what do you need me for? Please don't say I make an ideal stalker."

"Here," she said, hauling me before Alanis and another trainee named Laura Dern. Rebecca stepped in front of me and tugged my arms around her as women sometimes do. "This is what I was saying, ladies. This is how women stand when they claim 'ownership' of the man. You'll note that arms or not, I would never stand before a man like this if he was just a friend."

The others nodded, apparently understanding whatever point she was trying to make. All I could focus on was her firm bottom pressed against me. She proceeded to push and pull, yank me around and generally manipulate me to illustrate her various points, and I quietly acquiesced. What, like I would really protest?

"Thank you, Buzz," she finally said, releasing me. "You know, you have quite a strong grip. You work out a lot. I saw you in the gym today making those muscles *rock* hard."

I paused, nervous at the way she had emphasized 'rock'. I knew something was coming, but wasn't sure what. The word hung in the air awkwardly for a moment, but then came the coup de grace.

"*Rock lobster!*" all the women sang simultaneously.

"I knew it!" I exploded. "I wish I hadn't made up that damn story."

"Oh, no," Rebecca disagreed. "You didn't make that up. There were way too many little, inconsequential details for that to not have happened. You just might be the most eligible bachelor here."

"After Lucifer was done with you," Alanis added, "I would call you *grilled* lobster."

"Ha ha," I said bitterly as they mocked me. I must have been called red lobster a dozen times already, or steamed lobster, boiled lobster, grilled lobster, as well as lobster bisque, lobster newburg, and lobster thermidor. I felt like Forrest Gump's friend Bubba had taken a fancy to the coast of Maine instead of the Gulf.

"You remind me of my son," Rebecca commented. "That's what he always says and he wants to be a writer, too."

"I didn't know you were a mother."

"Grandmother," she corrected. "I have three children, the oldest is nineteen. And a grandson."

"Wh-what? I've been fantasizing about a grandma? No way, how old can you possibly be?"

"Buzz!" Alanis squawked. "Oh my God! What is wrong with you? You can't talk to a woman about her age!"

"I am 43," Rebecca admitted with a self-satisfied smirk. "It's OK. I am proud of my grandson."

I had to add this one to my list: flirting with a grandmother; check. She was so pretty, though, who wouldn't? I tingled with pride that she had thought I was an eligible bachelor.

"Oh, I'm not surprised he said that," Laura muttered with disdain. All eyes turned on her. "I'm talking about a lot more than your cocky attitude. It's the way you present. You are really intense and a little scary. You talk down to everybody."

"You mean I'm not charming and witty?" I joked.

"You are arrogant," Laura affirmed. "And I think you beat your girlfriend."

"Wow. I'm arrogant?" I protested, intentionally not responding to the domestic abuse barb. "Have you, like, met *any* auctioneers? And here I always thought I was a nice guy."

I did not take her seriously at all, but Alanis watched with big eyes, worried something big was brewing. She really needed to lighten up! Not surprisingly, she had read the moment better than I had.

"Oh, you pretend to be a nice guy," Laura continued. "You claim to be the innocent, Boy Scout type.

"I *was* a Boy Scout," I defended. "Troop 63. My father was a Scout Master, as was *his* father, who opened the first racially integrated scout lodge in Kansas City. And my big brother was an Eagle Scout."

"I think something is lurking under there," Laura scoffed. "I think it's all a façade. Is it?"

Now all the eyes focused on me. Laura was adamant enough that I realized she was sincere in her accusations. Rebecca observed curiously in silence, and Alanis's huge teeth nibbled her flesh absently, as if on hors d'oeuvres.

"No, it's not a façade. I *am* a nice guy, but I am under a lot of pressure. I *must* get a ship so I can be with my girlfriend. My strength is my knowledge and experience at sea, so I push that. I have fought harder than you can possibly imagine to be with my girlfriend and been shot down before. I won't let that happen again."

"Girlfriend, you say? Hardly. You flirt shamelessly," Laura pressed. "Besides, we are all under stress."

"Doesn't seem so bad," Alanis commented austerely, tasting her pinkie.

"You think you are better than everyone else," Laura maintained. "And think all the women want you. Why else would you flirt so shamelessly?"

"Flirting *with* shame defeats the purpose," I snapped. I kept waiting for Rebecca to stand in front of me protectively again, but it wasn't happening. I couldn't figure out where Laura's animosity stemmed from, but was getting tired of it.

"And yes, I do think I'm better than some here," I continued. "I don't want to be counted among the lazy kids and their lack of preparation. I think Sundance intentionally hires them young and impressionable so they can mold them. Have you noticed how different all the returning auctioneers are? They are all middle aged, unattractive, hard headed, and arrogant. I prefer to stand with them. Excuse me, I'm here to learn but I'm *not* a lump of clay."

Laura backed down before my outburst. Without a rebuttal, she suddenly leapt off to the protection of Lucifer as he walked by. Rebecca patted my arm in understanding, though I was more upset at Laura's observation than her adversarial manner of expressing it. I had always been a borderline egomaniac and took pains to temper it with genuine kindness and honesty. Unfortunately, under pressure my impatience sometimes surfaced as cutting remarks or, in this case, condescension. Whether I agreed wholly or not, I resolved to accept her rebuke.

But stop flirting? Never! At sea, flirting was sacrosanct.

Unlike anyone else present, I knew that on ships one was surrounded by exotic, foreign people who wanted nothing more than a one night stand with a new nationality. As the 'rare American,' below the waterline, I was the greatest prize. For a Green Card, some damn hot women offered to do things that made my head spin. With Bianca gone for months, I had somehow maintained a perfect record of resistance. I was proud of my willpower, though it surely cloaked a bit of insecurity. I had never considered myself a lady's man, despite my talk. But with all the rampant sexuality of ship life, I had learned that flirtation was a very justifiable and very necessary release valve.

Bill Shatner approached, having departed Lucifer's side. He oozed up to our group with enough slimy self-importance to make me look like a garden snail in comparison. "You gonna let a woman talk to you like that? Lift your skirt and grab your balls, man. And here I thought you were my main man."

"Your Maine lobster, you mean?" Alanis piped up, smiling hugely.

"You're just like my associate: a pussy among ladies. Enough talk! I saw you holding Rebecca. She's much closer to my age and I should have her. Start that silver tongue, why don't you, and convince her to sleep with me."

"I'm right here, Bill," Rebecca said drily, arms crossed beneath her breasts.

"Buzz, come on, man! You gonna help me get these bitches in bed, or what? We have two of em' right here, but a bush in hand is worth two at the bar."

"Or in your case," Rebecca retorted, "A jerk in hand is worth two in the bush."

"And Laura says *I* am arrogant?" I marveled.

"Come on, turn on that charm. I have none. Help me out."

"Oh, Buzz won't help you," Alanis said, chortling. "He's too shellfish."

"That's it!" I barked in defiance. "I am leaving!"

"You know why he's a *red* lobster?" Alanis shouted after me. "Because he's embarrassed that his seaweed!"

Friday morning the trainees bundled together like raw nerves: tense, temperamental, electric. Sprinkled throughout the classroom were yawning, bored auctioneers and several trainers.

"Today is your last day," Gene began with a grin. "You all remember what that means: auction day! Now, we started with twenty-six students, you'll note we are down to… let's see, how many now?"

"Fifteen," Lucifer called from the back of the class. "Two are here as permanent associates, though, *not* auctioneers."

"Yes, yes, that's right," Gene said. "I assume you all knew Rebecca and Cocoa were doing so? So, first: let me explain why you all rated yourselves the other day. Instructors cannot see all the habits of the trainees, some of which may blossom on the ships without any supervision. The temptations of ship life are *phenomenal*, after all, and if a trainee can't handle his liquor or whatever here, he'll never survive at sea. So if one of our favorites is repeatedly listed very low by his peers, we'll know something is being hidden from us. It's quite simple, really."

He cocked his head to the side and smiled. "Would you like to know who was rated the highest?"

Gene paused for dramatic effect, and I actually found myself tensing. Funny, I was likely to rank about five, yet there I was listening with bated breath. Maybe Laura was right. Was I really that arrogant?

"Cindy Lou Who!"

We all gave a soft round of applause. None of us were surprised, of course. She and her husband, Sammy Hagar, were a fantastic auctioneering team. Cindy Lou Who was petite, adorable, and focused. Upon reflection, her striking similarity to the child cartoon character from *How the Grinch Stole Christmas* made me a bit more forgiving about my own nickname.

"So, we have a champion of the class," Lucifer said, strutting to the front of the room. I watched Laura's eyes trailing his every move, her eyelids actually fluttering. No wonder she hated me so much, she was in love with Lucifer! How could anyone find that hyena attractive in appearance *or* manner? I guess Bill was right: women must *want* to be treated like dirt. The wonders of the world never cease.

"Would the champion of all things care to be first?"

Cindy Lou Who shook her head emphatically. To my surprise, Lucifer did not press it. "You have earned the right to wait," he said. "So we need a volunteer to go first. Anyone?"

He scanned the room, his predator's head tilting to listen for an answer. I swear I heard a cricket in the back.

"So Buzz volunteers then? I just *love* volunteers!"

I strode up to the front of the room, not surprised I had been called. Lucifer always sought those in the back of class to drag them into the light. I preferred to watch and learn from others first, calling myself cautious. He called it cowardly.

The room was crowded and loaded with books, bags, and computers. The auction laptop sat on a portable podium next to a pile of papers, and chairs wildly filled in the channels between the tables. There was no room for artwork at all, so this practice auction would only involve a fraction of the distractions in real life. I had no fear speaking in front of groups of strangers, but I found myself suddenly nervous to perform before Lucifer. This test auction had not stressed me all week, but suddenly standing in front of him, fear gripped my guts and started to squeeze.

Lucifer called out the first work to be auctioned. "CP 207. Go."

I punched in the number on the auction laptop and scanned the information: Emile Bellet, hand-embellished lithograph on canvas, limited edition of 200, opening bid of $450.

I regurgitated the description of artist Emile Bellet we had learned earlier in the week and gestured to phantom art behind me. I made it into a game of make-believe, imagining where my associates worked the crowds, where my art movers were, what work they would bring up next. I called out instructions to them, played at being in charge, and actually had fun. Auctioneers shouted bids and Lucifer called out new artwork. Time fairly flew, and I felt great.

Maybe I was cut out for this work after all!

"Last work," Lucifer called. "Number 82."

My joy screeched to a halt and my confidence melted into a puddle at my feet.

Despite punching in the code twice, there was no information at all. I blinked at the generic list of specifications: serigraph, 11" x 17", 2001, number 107/250. No artist name, no artwork name, not even a picture. I frowned at the computer, feeling somehow betrayed by it. Aware that silence kills an auction, I had to keep talking fast or Lucifer would crucify me.

But what to say to keep the momentum?

"This is a serigraph, ladies and gentlemen," I stumbled, pointing to the imaginary artwork behind me. "This is one of the most interesting forms of original, handmade artwork there is. When people think of original, of course, they think of a painting. Who here knows how to paint a picture? Come on, when you were a kid you painted, didn't you? Show me those hands!"

A few heads rose in surprise at the question, as did a large number of hands.

"Now, how many know how to silkscreen?"

All the hand went down.

"Exactly! Painting is easy. Monkeys can do it, after all, and even *elephants* can paint. I saw that on the Discovery Channel. But to create a serigraph limited edition requires the use of not just a handful, but *dozens* of handcrafted screens of silk to channel the colors. I'm talking one screen per color, folks! Can you possibly imagine the effort to create 250 works of the same, perfect quality *by hand*? Imagine the human error factor for lining up the paper each and every time just right. Damn near impossible, I say! That's why lithography was done by masters like Picasso and Toulouse-Lautrec. Not because it was easy, but because it's so hard!

"And this, right here behind me, look at it! This is one of the few that survived the agonies of creation. And look at this beauty! It's called, uh, *Playmate Seducing the Auctioneer.* Look at her, classically unashamed of her nudity, curves in sharply contrasting colors to show off her sexy figure, the hint of modern eroticism that makes it timeless! What a piece of work! Who wouldn't want a piece of *that* in their bedroom?"

"Hallelujah!" Bill shouted. He jumped to his feet, captured in the moment. The energy in the room perked up, and laughter gave me added impetus.

"Yes!" I cried. "Stand up, I say, and raise those hands! Miss June is right here, waiting."

I pointed my gavel at Bill and shouted, "Waiting for *you*, sir!"

"Damn right she is! And she's hot!"

"Hot for you!" I clarified with authority. "Now I want you to reach deep into your heart and your pocketbook, and take her hand. Save the faith for just $200! Aw, Hell, *I'll* take her for 200! She's ready and waiting for you at just 225. Can I get an amen?"

"Amen, brother!" John Goodman bellowed, getting into the moment.

"Can I get a 250?"

"Amen!" Bill shouted.

"Praised be!" I cried, slamming down the gavel. "She is yours, man. Take her for just $250!"

Panting with the exertion, I stood exultantly before the crowd of dumbstruck students. A long, stunned moment later, a roar of applause burst forth. Flattered, I tried to ignore it all and watched Lucifer warily. Shaking his head sorrowfully, he strode to the front. Silence once again swallowed the room, and I was more nervous than even before I started.

"Amen doesn't work," he quipped. "You need to say 'sold'."

He paused a moment to gather his thoughts, and I waited for the hammer blow.

"*Playmate Seducing the Auctioneer?*" he said with a toothy frown. "Yet again you reveal how much of a wimp you are. A real man would have said *Auctioneer Takes the Playmate.* But, really, what I want to know is why you Americans cannot count."

I blinked in surprise. I had no idea where he was going with this.

"Really, do they not teach math in your country? How many times did they count and recount *and recount* your last presidential election? You finally see who has more votes, and then the loser gets to be president anyway! I don't get that at all. And you, Buzz, your numbers were all over the place. You would open at $450, go up in twenty dollar increments, then drop to five or ten. You just made up numbers as you went along. Further, you seem incapable of saying numbers quickly and clearly. You, with your goddamn art history background, could expound all day on the subtle differences between the Rococo era and Romanticism, but you can't cleanly go from 0 to 100."

I shared a quick, nervous glance with Cocoa, whose black eyes were large and frightened. I could tell she thought my performance had gone well, as had many others. If Lucifer cut up my auction so thoroughly, what would he do to the others?

"It wasn't that bad, Buzz," Gene said, softening Lucifer's sharp words.

"Well," Lucifer grudgingly admitted. "It had potential, maybe. You did get people to raise their hands with your question, as I taught you. That was a good way to push serigraphs. Overall you suck horrendously, but you may yet achieve tadpole status. This is how I will help you, Buzz. Write this down:

"Betty Botter bought some butter,
But, she said, this butter's bitter.
If I put it in my batter
It will make my batter bitter.
But if I buy a bit of butter
Better than my bitter butter
That will make my batter better.
So Betty bought a bit of butter,
Better than her bitter butter,
And she put it in her batter.
So 'twas better Betty Botter
bought a bit of better butter."

"Now," Lucifer explained. "Memorize that by the end of the day. If you cannot say it *clearly* in less than twenty seconds, you will not pass this training. You may thank me for my help before returning to your primordial ooze."

The room dropped into silence, and I trudged back to my seat beside Alanis. A shorn fingernail dropped from her numb lips.

I skipped lunch, of course, to spend the time learning Betty Botter. As the rhyme revolved in my head and tumbled from my lips, I explored the Sundance Gallery of Fine Art. It was massive, modern, and off-limits. The entire downstairs labyrinth of gallerias was cordoned off for a private function, leaving me with only the mezzanine to wander. Fortunately it contained the largest display of original Picasso pottery I had ever seen.

Eventually I headed towards the break room for a coffee. One small but incredibly well-framed artwork caught my eye. It was perhaps the size of a sheet of regular paper and composed of rather bland browns and tans. It had some sort of bizarre, living blob of flesh that was vaguely face-like rending the tissue from a similar blob. The mouth was hideous and bloody and riveting. Visions of Alanis flashed through my mind.

"*Men Devouring Themselves*," I read the label aloud. "By Salvador Dalí, illustrating Dante's *Inferno*."

Like a guard dog, this greatly disturbing work protected the entrance to a long, empty hallway lined with a procession of exquisite paintings and etchings. The forbidden hall. The hall leading to Frederick's office. I felt like Charlie staring at the intimidating yet intoxicating entrance to Willy Wonka's Chocolate Factory. What hidden treasures lay down there? Would I ever meet the titanic and wholly original man who had created such wonders?

In the break room I sat tiredly at a table, alone among the vending machines. Sundance provided excellent coffee, though they surprisingly charged fifty cents per cup. I was mumbling Better Botter when Gene entered.

"Buzz! What, no lunch?"

"I wanted to see the gallery before training was over. Alas, it was not to be. Well, I saw the Picassos."

"Nice, are they not?" Gene beamed. "Tell me, Buzz, who's your favorite artist? And don't blindly say Picasso like everyone else."

"Well," I answered slowly. "Probably David Casper Friedrich, the 18th century German painter. He does these incredibly moody landscapes just oozing atmosphere and reflection and a hint of creepiness."

"Oh, I know his work. He's wonderful, but rather dark."

"Much like my personality," I agreed wryly. "His work inspired the cover of my ghost-hunting book."

"The master of drip speaks," Gene laughed. "You never miss a chance to drip your book, do you?"

"If I am the master dripper, then Lucifer's a master plumber."

Gene sat at the table beside me and said, "Don't worry about him. He's just doing his drill sergeant thing. This morning you did well on the final challenge. Without any clue what to do, you just blasted forward without a care. This is why we did the embarrassment test, you know. Even better, you got the crowd involved with your question and asking for hands in the air.

"I do have some advice for you, though. I have noticed that when you are speaking, you tend to preach. You are an eloquent and animated speaker, but you have this booming, Hellfire presentation. You think your art knowledge is an advantage, but it's actually not."

"But you've been cramming art knowledge down our throats all week!"

"Of course. You think someone is going to give $20,000 to a kid at a shopping mall kiosk who can't even pronounce Monet? Your expertise *is* important. My point is that under stress you may fall back on your art history knowledge and not your auctioneer training. That's plainly what you did in the test auction this morning before you got Bill all horny. You sell yourself very well, but you need to learn to sell art, too."

"Thanks for the advice, Gene," I said. "You are not the first to mention my, uh, preaching. I'll work on it while I am an associate on… what ship did you say again?"

"Why, Buzz, you assume much!"

"Yes."

"I guess it wouldn't hurt to tell you. You're going to work for last year's Rookie of the Year. Shawn was the third highest sales earner in the fleet. Assuming you learn Betty Botter, of course."

And so I passed the brutal auctioneer screening. I was extremely anxious to get to my first ship as an auctioneer trainee: the *Majesty of the Seas.* I was so anxious to put the mess of Pittsburgh behind me that I was almost derailed in Miami... permanently.

I fidgeted in line at the airport amid dripping and steaming bodies. Needless to say, most people did not enjoy Sundance's chauffeur service and had to walk from the parking lot through driving, chilly rain. Despite my luxurious ride, I was not unaffected by the rain because the slowed traffic had me running dangerously late. I bobbed up and down, compulsively checking and rechecking the little glowing dots above the desk that spelled my destination: MIAMI. After an eon my tickets were finally in hand and my luggage checked. I fought for reassuring glimpses of my plane through the windows as I rushed to security.

I was an experienced flyer and knew how to prepare for security. Any delay would seriously jeopardize my chances of catching the ship in Miami, so I neatly prepared my shoes and belt in the plastic tubs alongside all my metal objects.

Sailors were kindred to the flight industry and allowed certain privileges. Unfortunately for me, I did not yet have a seaman's book to prove I was a brother. Crew members carried huge arsenals of unusual items that slowed security because they had to bring their entire lives with them wherever they went. My backpack was a loaded thirty pounds of laptop, iPod, cell phone, and art books. But when hopping from continent to continent one must also tote heavy power converters, surge protectors, and sometimes even different cell phones for different countries.

Not surprisingly, I was selected for extra screening. Security pulled me away from the line of bodies streaming towards the plane. I gave one last, longing glimpse at the window and anxiety pulsed hot through me. I did not have time for this and had complied as much as humanly possible!

I was led to a plastic chair centered in a large, open area as security slogged through the tangle of complexities in my backpack. A surprisingly aged, white haired woman fingered roughly through my belongings. She was well over 60 years old and I pondered such a curious choice for security. The burly, bald Hispanic guard towering nearby seemed far more likely to keep me in line. Then again, the look of severe disapproval chiseled into her face made me feel like a naughty little boy caught cheating by a nun in a religious school. I think I was actually more frightened of *her*.

With a careless motion, the woman jerked my cell phone from the bag. It clattered on the table loudly, and I cringed as the battery case popped open from her rough handling. She then curiously prodded a small, alien black box and its power cord. It was very heavy and her small, tired hands had difficulty turning it over.

"That's a power converter for my trips to Romania," I offered helpfully.

"Looks like something else to me," she snapped, raising an accusing eyebrow.

I blinked stupidly, not understanding her inference. "Like what?"

"He fits the profile," she informed the guard. "And he's loaded with foreign hardware. Full search."

Worst-case scenarios of invasive personal searches flashed through my confused mind.

"All right," the Hispanic man said with a quick rub of his shaved head, "Stick out your feet."

I complied and managed to mask my escalating emotions by asking gently, "To what profile does she refer, may I ask?"

He waved a metal-detecting wand around each of my extended feet and answered with a grunt.

"Terrorist."

"Oh, come on!" I exploded. "What, do I look like an Al Qaida extremist to you? I'm from Iowa!"

He smirked in great amusement. "You scare the white folks, bro."

I snorted at the irony of those words coming from a Hispanic man with a tattooed neck. My mother would have fainted at the mere sight of him.

He explained further, "You travel *very* internationally, almost erratically, from continent to continent. You always fly with oneway tickets purchased without any advance notice, usually bought by someone else. *And* you have uncommon electronics with you."

I was surprised they had such a full profile on my traveling habits at their disposal, particularly how much lead time there was in buying my tickets and whether the cruise line or Sundance bought them. I resolved to use the Freedom of Information Act and see what else they knew.

A word of warning rose from the white haired witch, a single damning word to bring fire and brimstone from the heavens to crash down upon me with great fury and judgement.

"*ARABIC!*" she hissed, so sharply that she may as well have shrieked it.

Time slowed as everything around me froze. Hands twitched in slow-motion toward side arms and guards moved in silently. The air crackled with fear as dozens of passengers scanned me. The only sound I heard was a muffled, "Oh!" as a mother who shielded her toddler.

I sat there, socked feet extended into the air, reviled and feared and helpless and above all, confused. Only then did I see what the woman had found: my passport.

"Holy Cat!" I exclaimed by habit, almost immediately regretting it.

"He's not even Christian!" someone cried with dismay. Frowns deepened and leather holsters creaked.

"Didn't they used to worship cats in Egypt?" an anonymous voice asked in confusion.

"Idolator!" the old woman spat. "Tell me of your travels to the heathen lands."

"Did you just call me an idolator? You go to Hell, lady! This is America, and I'm free to practice whatever religion I want!"

"I think not!" she retorted sharply.

"I traveled to the Great Pyramid in Egypt," I snapped angrily. "You know, one of the Seven Wonders of the Ancient World? What, you've never heard of King Tut? *You* should be ashamed, not me."

The ice in the air melted. It was so fast, in fact, that I would have thought I imagined the whole thing had not the Hispanic guard yet been flanked by three others. They hurriedly finished searching me and left me to return my own belongings to my backpack. I stuffed them in frantically, snatching frenzied peeks at the line of boarders tapering to an end. I rushed onward, terrified I would miss my flight and, thusly, my ship and, thusly, my career. At least they hadn't bothered to weigh my obviously overburdened carry-on bag.

Once I crammed myself into my seat, I panted and marveled at how I looked on paper. A single white male, between 30 and 40, of above average intelligence and educated, who seems like a nice guy. That was the exact profile for a serial killer. Now, somehow, it was also the profile of a radical Muslim terrorist! What had happened to my country? Was there *anyone* we were not scared of? My vacation to Egypt was nearly enough to win me a permanent vacation in Cuba… at Guantanamo!

Part III: The Fun Ships

"Yes, art is dangerous. Where it is chaste, it is not art."
—Pablo Picasso

11. WHO'S THE BOSS?

Strangely, New Orleans somewhat reminded me of Bianca: French speaking, vibrant and sexy with a promise of sweaty, carnal, and even gastronomic pleasures. The Big Easy was also kind of a dirty hussy with a long history and no shame.

It was hard to quantify my fascination with Bianca. She was my first world traveling, cigarette smoking, semi-trashy European beauty. I was spellbound the very first night I met her, a chance date that was overwhelmed by chemistry. Bianca had made a surprise visit to the States to see her childhood friend Mihaela, who happened to be my colleague and friend. But Mihaela and her boyfriend already had tickets to a concert purchased many months prior, so they asked me to keep Bianca occupied. Did I ever. After three days Bianca left for Romania. After three weeks, I did, too.

So a head-spinning three days of Nevada September prompted a heart-blasting thirty days of Romania October. By November she signed onto *Conquest*, and, suffering already the pangs of separation from my wild and adventurous Bianca, I resolved to follow in whatever capacity I could. Mihaela was already flabbergasted that I followed her childhood friend home to Romania for a month. She was aghast when I told her I was selling everything to follow Bianca to sea for good. A restaurant management position on a cruise ship was a far cry from my graphic designer lifestyle, but after all that magic, how could I let it end without a fight? Bianca was responsible for her family and was unable to live in America. So why *not* follow her to sea?

My life was surprisingly ready for such a crazy leap. After three all-consuming and tireless years building a business with my partner, too many disagreements forced a nasty split. My wife chose this time to run off as well, but that split was actually quite delightful. But only a short three months later my partner had completely devalued our stock into penny shares, and my ex-wife had completely devalued my credit. So I woke up one morning broke, yet could no longer bear to freelance my graphic design skills because it was just too similar to my former business. I needed something different, and a life at sea certainly promised that!

Hence my flight to New Orleans in fall of 2002 for an interview on *Carnival Conquest.* My entire life, prior to the business, had been in fine dining, so I was more than qualified for a low level management position. Yet Mladen, the interviewer, was uncomfortable with my nationality. In Carnival's thirty years, there had not been a single American in the restaurants who had not quit, not one. I offered to prove my mettle by beginning at the bottom and to undergo a whirlwind assistant Maitre d' training. We agreed on school for a month on *Ecstasy*, to include washing dishes and bussing tables, and then I could join Bianca on *Conquest* for the remainder of training. All told, I was to train four months before they gave me my officer's stripe, after which Bianca would be free to follow me ship to ship.

I imagined the joy of sharing a tiny cabin with my favorite woman, Bianca, in my favorite city, New Orleans. The reality was quite different. Carnival's foreign employees enjoyed being paid in U.S. Dollars, and intended to keep it solely for themselves. When the time came for my officer's stripe, I was denied based *solely* upon my nationality. The man who scuttled my career, a Dutchman named Gunnar, actually said to my face that he 'would not have on his record the promotion of an American who would just quit.' His two cronies, the Maitre d's Ganesh and Ferrand, both offered to assist my appeal, but when the time came they scurried under a rock and were never heard from again.

So a mere thirteen months after I joined *Carnival*, the international politics ended my career before it began. This led me to pursue Sundance which, surprisingly, brought me back to New Orleans and the mighty *Conquest*. But this time my position was quite different. I was no longer a landlubber naively assuming things would go as promised, oh no; I was seasoned by the sea. *Conquest* was a big money ship for Sundance and I was sent here to make things happen. No more shenanigans for me!

The change was apparent from the very beginning, when my Bianca was not on the gangway to greet me in a tight pink sweater and knee-high leather boots. Instead I got Bill Shatner, beside whom stood a young man I presumed was the outgoing associate. Their postures resonated open hostility, though Shatner's arrogant stance clearly indicated who had the better of any disagreement.

"Buzz Lightyear!" Bill bellowed with enthusiasm. He powerfully shook my hand, and indicated with a curt nod his companion. "That's Doug, my associate."

I extended my hand to the sour-faced man with dark, curly hair, but he looked to the floor and muttered, "You're in for a ride."

"Buzz," Bill barked. "You got a cock, don't you?"

"Why, yes, Bill," I said sweetly, "I do, in fact, have a penis. Thanks for asking."

"Good! Doug's gonna take your luggage to your cabin, and we're going to Bourbon Street."

I blinked, realizing he was serious.

"But, Bill, I haven't even signed on yet!" I protested. "I need to meet with the crew purser to get my ID and all that stuff."

"Bah!" he scoffed, pushing me back down the gangway. "Doug will take care of it. I need to see some tits, and we're going to a strip club."

"But survival training is mandatory."

"I'll tell you what's mandatory," Bill pressed. "Tits. You do like tits, don't you?"

"Well, sure, but—"

"Then we're going. Welcome to *Conquest*."

So much for no more shenanigans.

The walk to Bourbon Street from *Carnival Conquest* was a good twenty minutes on a normal day. But then, how many things in my life are ever normal? Today was the Fourth of July. Drunken, riotous bodies of all ages, shapes, sizes, and colors crammed Canal Street in drunken revelry. Heat rose in waves off the bodies and steaming concrete as an ephemeral souvenir of summer in the South. Bill pushed through the throng like a man with a purpose which, of course, he was. I stumbled along behind, trying hard to keep up but trying harder to derail him entirely.

"We really don't have time for this," I pressed. "We have to be back by 3 p.m."

"How the Hell would you know?" Bill retorted over his shoulder. "You just got here."

"I was on this ship for an entire contract!" I called loudly over a group of raucous college kids swilling beer. Bill muttered something, but I could not hear above the noise. We passed the entrance to a bar and the doors suddenly burst open, apparently from the buildup of noise behind them. Zydeco music poured out like water from a burst dam, flooding over us.

"My previous associate was such a pussy!" Bill shouted as we moved onward. He roughly shouldered aside a belching, rat-tailed man in a sweat-soaked tank top. "You better not let me down!"

"I thought your associate was Antonio Banderas!"

"He was, but he's off studying to be a goddamn priest, so then I got Doug!"

We turned onto Bourbon Street and dove into deeper and more riotous crowds. The street was closed to autos, but it was a traffic mess nonetheless. Everyone stood sweating in the street with their go-cups, enjoying the rare privilege of drinking alcohol in a public street. As we neared the strip clubs, Bill plowed through the bodies with more fervor than ever. Finally we stepped out of the chaos and into Rick's Cabaret. Instantly it was dark and cool and mercifully quiet. Well, compared to outside, anyway: the bass from the hip-hop thumped jarringly.

"Now we're talkin'!" Bill shouted with glee. He gestured broadly towards several stages, each graced with a bronze pole. Amazingly, we had the place all to ourselves.

Why the thousands of drunken young men chose to remain outside in the heat was beyond me. Then again, the heavy cover charge may have explained that. Bill marched into a sea of little round tables and planted himself firmly in a low-backed, stuffed chair.

"Antonio Banderas," Bill continued with obvious contempt, "Wouldn't set foot in here. Too religious, he claimed. We all know he was a closet gay. But Doug? He was horrible. With all the money he's making, he's banging some fat Steiner. Can you believe that? I didn't even know they *allowed* fat chicks."

A slender and scantily clad waitress slunk up to the table. She stood above us with a seductive wiggle. Bill never looked at her face even once, but stared obsessively at her overtly enhanced breasts.

"Hi, guys!" she bubbled. "I'm Trixie."

"Why of course you are," I replied lightly.

"Two Heinekens!" Bill boomed. "And keep em' coming."

"Oh, I keep em' coming," she replied with a wink. As she strode away, Bill reached out as if to grab her ass.

"Jesus, Bill," I chided. "You're panting already. Don't get too far gone, because we don't have much time."

"Quit your whining. A few beers won't hurt you."

"It's not the beers I'm worried about."

"What, you scared of tits?" he barked. "You are so damn uptight, Buzz. Chill out."

"With this crowd we're not going to get back in time."

"I'll take care of it," he dismissed. "You look so goddamn nervous. I think you're scared of big tits. What, you never been in a titty bar before?"

"Actually," I replied. "I dated a stripper in Iowa."

"Bullshit!" he called. He eyed the empty stages, muttering, "Where are the women, anyway?"

"Maybe they are understaffed because the Fourth of July is like, a wholesome family day and stuff."

"I want tits!" he bellowed at the nearest empty stage. After a minute of no response, he finally turned to actually look at me. "You're serious, aren't you?"

"About what?"

"They have strippers in Iowa? What, the Pork Queen, or Miss Hog Wild? That's what Doug was into. He was really into screwing that fat middle-aged chick from the Spa. Bah! You never dated a stripper."

I held up my fingers in a Boy Scout salute. "Scout's honor: I dated a stripper. I went to the Fox Den for a friend's bachelor party. There was a gorgeous little thing there named Tyler. Well, her real name was Penny. At first, when she was on the stage, I tipped her well. So she followed me around after that. Everyone else thought I was going broke paying for lap dances, and wouldn't believe me when I said I got them for free."

"I wouldn't either," Bill retorted. "I still don't."

"They had one of those old-style photo booths in the corner, and we disappeared for a long time in there. By the end of the night I showed them plenty of pictures and her phone number. I still have them in storage somewhere."

Bill frowned at me. "You *are* serious!"

"I am. There are few things more satisfying for a twenty-one year old than having free access to the dressing room of a strip club. I hung out there for a couple of weeks. The girls shared some of their tricks to get more money from us stupid, boorish guys. It was fun."

"Well?" he demanded.

"Well what?"

"Did you do her?"

"Alas, it didn't get to that. There was a huge bar brawl one night that ended all the good times. Scared the Hell out of me, actually. The bartender was this huge three hundred pound redneck who just got out of jail. When I saw him leap over the bar with a club and start whaling on an *entire* biker gang, I felt it was time to leave. It may look cool in the movies, but seeing a glass beer mug smashed over a man's head is decidedly not cool. The cops showed up fast, and in force. I seriously think the whole thing was a set up to close the joint down. Half the girls quit on the spot. Tyler was one of them, and she moved back to Wisconsin."

Eventually the stages were peopled and, not surprisingly, time flew. I checked my watch fanatically and grew paler and paler by the hour, but Bill couldn't have cared less. He was happy as a clam at high tide when staring at artificially-inflated breasts. When we finally did leave, hours later, he was half drunk with beer and wholly pleased with himself. I was aghast at the lack of taxis, and even more so at the pandemonium on the streets. The crowds were dense with rollicking, beer-chugging animals of the human persuasion, of all ages, shapes, and sizes. We plowed through them resolutely, Bill in the lead. I pushed him ever onward, but he refused to hurry and refused to let me lead at a faster pace. By the time we reached *Conquest*, embarkation had closed nearly an hour earlier.

We trudged across the metal gangway under the glowering gaze of the chief of security. He was a late middle-aged Asian man surprisingly larger than both of us. He folded beefy arms across his chest and chided, "You are lucky we kept the gangway open."

Bill merely shrugged as he was patted down. I followed, guiltily explaining, "There were no taxis because of the holiday."

"Irrelevant," he replied crisply.

Bill was already leaving when the chief barked an order for us to stop. He picked up the phone even as he glared at us. Nervously I stared at the thick gold bracelet he wore. It fairly glowed against his chocolate skin, and he spoke with enough gestures to make it rattle on his wrist.

"They're here," he said into the phone. "Yes, sir, both of them. The one embarking has his papers in order, though I don't believe it was handled by himself. The purser mentioned the outgoing auctioneer handled it. Yes, sir. Right away, sir."

He hung up the phone and said to us, "Chief Officer wants to see you both immediately."

My heart sank, and Bill continued to lead, only this time to the office of the chief officer. Though I was intimately familiar with *Carnival Conquest*, I had not yet been to a few areas of the ship. The engine room and boson's area were terra incognita, as was the bridge deck. This was where you did *not* want to be, if you were crew, yet here we were.

Bill unerringly led us past the officer's cabins on deck four, where I had lived as restaurant manager, then above and beyond to the bridge deck. He obviously knew where he was going, which I found even more demoralizing. I knew we were in trouble when the usual medley of nationalities dropped off and suddenly everyone was Italian. Carnival preferred Italian officers on their ships, and they were the only ones with business here. Unless, of course, someone was in big, big trouble.

Like us.

The door to the chief's office was open and Bill entered without knocking. He strode over to a chair and seated himself, completely at ease and acting as if nothing in the world were wrong. I, on the other hand, was completely freaking out. Crew members are rarely fired for being so late, but it was a permanent blemish on their record, and two strikes was enough for firing. I had already had all sorts of management trouble on *Conquest* from my restaurant days, and before I had even started work I was going to get a black mark! I was furious at Bill, but wondered where along the way I could have derailed him.

I stood beside Bill's chair, awkward and obviously unsure if I was to sit as well or not. The chief gestured to the remaining chair, and I dropped obediently into it. Before us sat an Italian man: short, slender, and handsome. He set aside his paperwork and silently reviewed us. Bill leaned back and crossed his legs, utterly unperturbed before the chief. In fact, he looked bored.

"You wanted to see me?" Bill asked bluntly.

"You were an hour late," the chief said quietly, with a thick Italian accent. "You think I would not?"

"We both know the ship wasn't leaving for several hours," Bill replied offhandedly. "So that is not a concern. It is a national holiday and we couldn't find a cab. We had to walk."

"You should not have been out at all, then," the chief retorted. "Your being late is completely inexcusable. Every crew member is my responsibility, and your new assistant here missed safety training."

"He's been on *Conquest* before," Bill scoffed.

"That is irrelevant," the chief snapped, words growing warm. I stared in shock at Bill, whose posture made it very clear that the chief was completely wasting his time. "Everyone attends safety training, including myself."

"He'll go next week," Bill said simply.

"Unlike you," the chief replied with an arched eyebrow, "I cannot so cavalierly allow any crew member to be a safety liability, not even for a single cruise. I could, *and should*, deny him entry on the ship."

My stomach flipped. This was no idle threat. The chief officer was second only to the captain himself and most definitely had the authority to do so. With Bill's cocky stance, he had plenty of inclination, too. I tried to speak, but Bill cut me off.

"He's not a liability. He's already been here for an entire contract, and in an emergency he's obviously better suited to help than a dancer or a Steiner. His job is to handle drunk groups of hundreds. And look at him: would you rather depend on him or a 90 pound Filipina stewardess? Furthermore, he is only a supernumerary."

The chief officer regarded Bill in silence and the tension in the room chilled it until I nearly shivered. It was blatantly obvious that Bill had no intention of letting this man's authority affect him in any way. No doubt the chief officer was deciding whether to back up his words with action.

Amazingly, Bill took the initiative away from the chief.

"We had only an hour to get the proper attire for my new associate," Bill said gruffly. "You think I can continue to net almost *half a million dollars a month* with an assistant not wearing a proper suit? I generate more money than any other crew member on this ship, including the cruise director, and cost Carnival only the price of a cabin. The least you could do for me is not bother me when I am a mere hour late on a national holiday… *my* national holiday… all while knowing the ship isn't leaving for hours."

The chief's smooth, handsome face was the very study of an opposite of Bill's blunt and pockmarked features, and his continued silence gave no indication of what was going on in his mind. Both men were undoubtedly superb poker players. I, on the other hand, was nearly wetting myself.

"Besides," Bill finished tartly, "It's not like we were on Bourbon Street at a strip club. We had business to do."

Another long minute of icy silence gelled around us. I was completely motionless, but my wide eyes hopped back and forth between the two men as if watching a tennis match. They met each others' eyes and refused to blink. To my astonishment, it was the chief officer who backed down.

"In light of your… unique… position on board," he began softly, "I will allow this transgression. In ordinary circumstances you would both receive a strike on your permanent record. I will let it pass."

I nearly deflated into a puddle right there.

"Do understand," the chief continued. "That should there be any further misbehavior, you may not receive the benefit of three strikes before being ejected."

"That's fine," Bill replied, and was instantly out the door. I was clumsily left behind, and sheepishly nodded to the chief before hurrying after Bill.

As soon as we were off the bridge deck, I breathed a huge sigh of relief. "That was close!"

Bill shook his head. "That wasn't close. That wasn't anything. I make so much goddamn money on this ship I can do what I want. There are only two departments on board that bring in as much money as I do, and they both have dozens and dozens of employees. He can't touch me and he knows it."

"I don't know…"

"I do," Bill scoffed. Suddenly he barked a laugh. "Ha! Not getting the benefit of three strikes, my ass! If it's not on our record, we are clean. What you saw was pure bluster. Don't let it get to you, unless you are as much of a pussy as I already think you are."

As we walked to our cabins, I stared at the back of William Shatner in wonder. I was in awe of this man, who had humbled the chief officer despite being completely and utterly in the wrong. There was no doubt about it: I was embarking on a fundamentally different aspect of ship life. Bill led me down the guest hallway on Riviera deck towards the bow.

"You got any good suits?" he asked, eyes still straight ahead.

"I have one nice suit," I replied.

"Designer?"

"Yeah, it's Pronto Uomo."

"Where in the Hell did a farm boy from Iowa get a Pronto Uomo?"

"In Iowa."

"Get more."

"They cost a lot, you know. I haven't been paid in a long time. Why else wouldn't I be handing out dollars at Rick's Cabaret?"

"'cause you're a pussy," he answered. "But don't worry about money. I'll cover you until you get paid. We need good suits for you. New Orleans will have something. Our ports are Montego Bay, Jamaica, Grand Cayman, and Cozumel, Mexico. I don't think those are good options for you."

"Probably not," I agreed. "Where are we going, anyway?"

"We're not going anywhere," Bill replied without even a hint of a smile. "We're here. This is your cabin."

Bill swiped the electronic key and pushed open the door of guest cabin 1202. He marched in, then handed me the key. Wide eyed, I followed.

"*This* is my cabin?" I asked incredulously. I stepped inside and gazed about the huge awesomeness. There was about a ten foot walk from the two beds to the three full-sized closets. Yes, I had to *walk* over there. In crew cabins you merely turned around to get to the closet, or took two steps to enter the bathroom, which frequently had the toilet *in* the shower. More exciting than the sheer size of the room, however, was that it was actually decorated with warmth. Neutral and hotel room boring, to be sure, but it was a far cry from the cold white metal of a crew cabin. It even boasted a mini bar and a refrigerator. Now *this*, without a doubt, was the mother of all cabins.

I strode over to peek into the bathroom, which was obviously designed for a couple. It gleamed with mirrors and polished brass. Surely there was a catch.

"I thought I didn't have to share a cabin," I prompted. "Doug did sign off, right?"

"He did. This is all yours."

"The two beds…?"

"Oh, that's Doug. That fat cow from the Spa was big enough to put his dick into, but too big to share a bed with, I guess. Whatever. He had the beds pushed apart."

"This is a huge cabin. I can't believe it's all for the associate."

"We're important," he said, shrugging. "Actually, Carnival tried to screw the associate in the past with a staff cabin, but after I sold a shitload of artwork one cruise I had Sundance bully them into giving me *two* guest cabins instead of one. Payback's a bitch."

I noted my luggage in the corner. "Well, I can unpack whenever. We already saw the strip club, so what's next? What's our schedule like?"

"I have to do the embarkation talk tonight at eight and ten o'clock," Bill answered. "I'll drop you off in the art gallery at six and you can hang out there until I pick you up at ten. Then comes the important part."

"At ten? Surely there's not an auction at that hour?"

"Of course not," Bill answered irritably. "At ten we hit the crew bar."

The art gallery intrigued me to no end, and I was anxious to see what it was all about, and where. When I had worked *Conquest* before, there had not been one. Bill led me through the ship to the main deck, midship. To my surprise, we were heading towards the Renoir Dining room. I had figured the gallery would be on Promenade deck with all the shops. He gestured to the small bronze lettering by the door.

"The Picasso Art Gallery," he said.

"Pissarro," I corrected.

Bill paused before unlocking the glass fronted French doors. "What?"

"It says the Pissarro Art Gallery," I answered, indicating the sign before us.

"Well I'll be damned," he said in wonder. "All this time I thought it said Picasso. Who the Hell is Pissarro?"

"A French Impressionist," I explained. "Everything about *Conquest* is decorated with an Impressionist theme, no doubt because the homeport is the French Quarter of New Orleans. *Conquest* has the Degas Lounge, the Monet Dining Room, etc."

"Where's the Deg-ahh Lounge?" Bill asked, struggling to pronounce it correctly.

"It's the big lounge. You heard the cruise director pronounce the 's', like in Vegas. It's French, though, so it's supposed to be silent."

"You really are gay, aren't you?" Bill asked. "The only French a real man should know is *ménage à troi* and French tickler."

"Anyway," I continued stubbornly. "If you look at the wallpaper in the lobby you'll see a montage of all sorts of famous Impressionist works, including Georges Seurat and my personal favorite, Toulouse-Lautrec. You'd like him because he lived in brothels."

Bill just stared at me blankly, his hand still on the key. "Do we sell any of these guys?"

"In Pittsburgh," I replied. "But probably not on the ships, no."

"Then I don't give a crap."

The elaborate glass and wood doors opened into a modestly sized room jam-packed with artwork of excellent caliber. The Sundance collection on *Conquest* put that of *Majesty* to shame. A series of easels in the center divided the room in two, and deep stacks of canvases leaned against every wall. In the far corner was a wooden desk above which was a shelf burdened with books. Should *Conquest* hit a rough wave I would no doubt be crushed beneath an avalanche of heavy art tomes. There were worse ways to go.

"This is where you will be every sea day from five until ten," Bill said. "Also after embarkation. You can sell to wanderers and do the paperwork here. If an important client is coming, I'll be here, but otherwise it's all you. You can handle that, can't you?"

"Of course."

"Good, because it's boring as Hell. We have an art locker, too, and I'll show you that tomorrow. Here is where all the expensive and nice artwork is located. All the Jean-Claude Picot crap is in the locker."

Bill fiddled with paperwork while I wandered the gallery and got to know the artwork. The lighting was soft, but sufficient, and at one spot punctuated by a portable light box set up to illuminate one particular painting. This was an original Tomasz Rut; a gorgeous and lusty painting of a naked woman washing herself by squatting over a tiny washtub. This was about as close as Bill would ever get to *'Playmate Seducing the Auctioneer.'*

One whole wall of easels had a series of the gaudiest patriotic art I had ever seen. All six easels featured iconic American imagery, such as the Stars and Stripes or the Statue of Liberty, but the colors were so neon intense they burned my retinas. Each work was a 3 x 4 foot poster-sized print. In fact, they *were* posters, of obviously poor quality, but with gobs of intense reds, whites, and blues slathered on top.

"These are the ugliest things I've ever seen!" I gasped incredulously. "They are posters with paint on em'. Who would buy that?"

Bill wandered over to my side, chuckling.

"What, you're not a patriot?" he asked. "Oh, that's right: you're poking that Russian ho, aren't you? You Commie bastard."

"The only ho I'm poking is your mother," I snapped. "She asked me to remind you to put your coat on before you go out and play. My girlfriend is Romanian."

"OK, OK," Bill apologized. "These are Peter Max 9-11 series mixed media. These are my bread and butter, man. Didn't they have those on your last ship?"

"They did not," I answered, marveling over the audacious in-your-face imagery. "So these are from the great Peter Max. I've heard of him."

"These go for the mid 4000s," Bill said. "So if someone is interested, make sure you let me know. If I sell one, I usually can sell two."

My eyes widened. "Four grand for a poster? Don't try to bullshit me that this is a painting, because less than half of the poster is painted on."

"It's not a poster, chump," Bill said. "It's a paint-over. Some dealers will say they are paintings, but that's just stupid. Well, what's stupid is people buying them believing they are paintings."

"Are you serious? Someone would pay four grand for this, thinking it was an actual painting? These are obviously mixed media."

"Trust me, in this business people fool themselves a lot more than we fool them. Most people have already made up their mind before they even come into an auction whether the work is authentic or not. I can't tell you how many people have listened to me lecture about Peter Max for twenty minutes, then turn and buy a Thomas Kinkade print, only to later bitch that I lied to them about what they bought. I never talk about Kinkade at all."

"Now *that* I can believe," I agreed.

"People are stupid," Bill said in very much the same tone that Lucifer had in Pittsburgh. "Most people call anything a painting: just like everyone still calls an album a record, even though nobody makes records anymore. But the name sticks, and some auctioneers don't bother correcting people when they are wrong."

"This is not cool," I commented. "Please tell me you aren't one of those lying auctioneers I keep hearing about."

"I don't lie," Bill said simply. "I don't need to. If I catch you lying to a customer you can bet your ass will be out the door in a minute. This gig is too good to lose for something like that."

"Unfortunately I am honest to a fault," I admitted. "My life would be a lot easier if wasn't. Nobody really believes Boy Scouts exist."

"Yes," Bill continued, "Some auctioneers lie. It's funny what some people will believe. I knew an auctioneer who promised whoever bought a Max 9-11 would get to have lunch with Peter Max. Can you believe that? So he sold like twenty of them in one auction alone, and everyone lined up to provide their phone numbers so world-renowned Peter Max would personally call to set up lunch. See? People are stupid."

"You've got to be kidding me!"

"Listen and pay attention," Bill ordered. "This is about the only training I'm going to give you. You don't need to lie to people. The art is what it is. Just a year ago I was selling these paint-overs for two grand. Now they are four and a half. Max just keeps cranking them out, and people keep buying them. The demand isn't that they are rare. The demand is that Peter Max himself is putting a personal touch on his already famous posters. It's not some flunky doing it. See that signature?"

He gestured to the unique artist signature on the bottom: a swirl of four different colors artfully twirled into a semblance of the name MAX.

"That's what he's famous for. You're not buying the poster, you're buying that signature. It's worth a lot more than just a pencil autograph."

"What do you mean, 'he just keeps cranking them out?'"

"These aren't limited editions, so don't sell them that way. They are unique mixed media, meaning something in between a poster and a painting. Actual paintings from Peter Max at this size cost over thirty thousand dollars… and that's just his iconic images that he paints over and over and over. The business model is simple: you don't have to be rich to have a personal Peter Max in your house. Will the value go up? Absolutely. Should you buy it for that reason? No. Buy it because you like it."

"So mostly Americans buy them, then?"

"Not at all," Bill explained. "Lots of foreigners like what America stands for. Before all this Iraq shit, anyway.

But everybody likes the Statue of Liberty. Peter Max was instrumental in the refurbishing of the Statue of Liberty in the 80s. His artwork is in over one hundred museums around the world, including dozens of U.S. Embassies. It is estimated that *two billion* people saw his painting of a soccer player doing a scissor kick into the stars for the World Cup poster of 1994. He's a living legend and anyone can have an original mixed media of his in their house. End of story."

I mused over the artwork again.

Bill chuckled. "Can you believe someone stole one of these from my auction last month?"

"What?"I asked, shocked. "How do you hide these? They're so bright you can see them from orbit!"

"Tell me about it. It wasn't even one of these, but a full-sized Statue of Liberty that's six goddamn feet tall. In the middle of the auction, with a crowd of about a hundred and fifty, this ballsy bastard just picks it off an easel and casually walks out of the lounge with it. I guess he figured it was so ballsy that no one would ever dream he was a thief. We searched the ship, but only found the discarded frame."

"I had always wondered about such things. I guess you can roll up a canvas in your luggage, eh? Damn, I wish I was the insurance broker for Sundance. Now *that's* where the money is."

But Bill was ignoring me, lost in his thoughts and muttering, "Serious balls, man. More than you've got. *Way* more than Doug had."

"Bill? It's bad enough you keep talking about my cock. Can we leave my balls out this?"

"Anyone steals anything like that when you're on watch," Bill said. "And I'll feed your goddamn balls to the fish!"

He added with a mischievous grin, "Or worse; I'll make Doug's cow the official mistress of the *Conquest* associate."

12. GHOSTS AND ECHOES

After Bill departed, I wandered the art gallery. The art was fascinating, but of more potency were the memories the room evoked. For this room was once part of the Renoir Dining Room. There were two such rooms in the old days, this one starboard and the port-side Cassatt Room. It was there, less than a year ago, that I had been caught tasting a dish by my nemesis Gunnar. Seeing an opportunity to force me to quit, Gunnar had literally denied me food for a month by ensuring I worked through every meal time, and had numerous spies to enforce my compliance. Of course there was a moral to the story: only by starving can one be thin. I hated life, but I looked damn good.

I stepped before the main entrance of the Renoir and nearly swooned as the memories flooded over me; of countless hours protecting my silverware from prowling gangs of waiters; of mind-numbing fatigue from endless months without a day off; of irate and irrational guests devouring troughs of food without any pretense of manners whatsoever. I had consoled dozens of crying colleagues in those days, including my assistant having an actual emotional breakdown in the corner pantry of this very dining room. Oh, what a nightmare that had been!

The memory of her slender body wracked with sobs still haunts me.

At the Renoir's podium was a tall and superbly built man in a tuxedo, with blonde hair in a designer tussle. His handsome face looked bored and he fiddled with a pen on a map of the seating assignments. I knew him, and eagerly marched right up.

"Well I'll be damned!" I called. "Would that be Leo, the *Other* Sexy Bitch?"

"Brian!" he cried, shaking my hand vigorously. "*The* Sexy Bitch! As always, I give preference to your greater age."

He noted I wore a suit rather than a uniform and asked, "You taking a cruise?"

"Nope, I just signed on as art auctioneer." I gestured to the art gallery and said, "This is my new office."

"Right next to my office!" Leo laughed, gesturing to the Renoir. As always, he rolled his R's with a long Afrikaans accent and his generous laughter sounded like a boulder rolling down a mountain. Oh, it was good to see Leo again. He was my compatriot during the long, trying months of being an assistant Maitre d' trainee. We had shared many, many mutual horrors during those days. He handled it better than I, because he simply drank away his worries.

"Your office indeed," I agreed. "You look magnificent, I must say, and strangely sober."

"Don't look too closely."

"That stripe and a half looks good on you."

"Thank you. I'm sorry about what happened to you, my friend. You seem to be doing well, though. Isn't being an auctioneer pretty high level stuff?"

"I'm a three-stripe motherfucker," I agreed. He whistled in admiration, and I suffered a flash of pride.

"So you outrank Ferrand and even Ganesh!" he suddenly realized, referring to our two restaurant superiors who reneged on their promises to help me fight Gunnar. "Man, I want to be there when you meet them again."

"They're still on-board, then?" I wasn't sure how I felt about that.

"Not Gunnar. But Ganesh and Ferrand are still here. Gonna rub their noses in it?"

"Nah," I scoffed. "It's not about that. It's about getting Bianca with me. This is a great gig."

"Still chasing your Romanian girl?" he asked, impressed. "I don't know how you do it, man. There's so many hot bitches on ships and so little time. Oh, excuse me a moment."

As if on cue, Leo indicated the approach of two ladies. I stepped aside and watched as Leo flirted heavily with an attractive young blonde. Her companion stepped up beside me, also waiting for the bantering to end. She was nearly as pretty as her presumably younger sister. In fact, all three of them could have been siblings: tall, athletic, blonde and with a hint of freckles. It kind of freaked me out to watch Leo drooling over them.

The older babe gave me a sly smile and, just before leaving, a wink. Lost on planet *Majesty*, I had forgotten just how many beautiful women were on Carnival ships; employees and guests alike. Fun Ships, indeed.

"Man, would you look at that?" Leo said as the ladies waded into the dining room, walking their wiggly walk. "She is so hot! And can you believe that was her mother with her? Damn."

"Really? I thought they were sisters."

"Me too, but she's not. Her *mother*, man! Think I can get 'em both in bed at the same time?"

Same old Leo.

"Well, that would certainly be a slam dunk," I commented. "That's something I haven't done before."

When Leo and I were both management trainees, we had competed in all sorts of things female-related. While we never did anything so crass as to count 'conquests' or anything of that nature, we did compete over who got asked out by the most guests, or posed for more photos. He always bought the beer because for some reason I always had more women flashing me in guest areas. Ah, the good ol' days.

"Oh, there's no competition anymore, my friend," Leo dismissed with enough swagger to make it clear that he had progressed far indeed since I had been gone.

"Leo, behave. They are guests."

"Who cares?" Leo wondered aloud. "I'm gonna find her table. If I clear her plate maybe I can lick her fork!"

We promised to meet in the crew bar sometime, and I returned to the gallery. When Bill finished his business in the main lounge at ten o'clock, he came by to drag me to the crew bar. But I wasn't in the mood, and excused myself. He protested, of course, but relented after I reminded him that he had already forced me into a titty bar all afternoon. I marveled that Bill and Leo hadn't buddied up yet.

I had had an eventful day, to put it mildly. But there was one thing I wanted to do yet. I yearned to relive one of the few joys I had found on *Conquest* when things were tough: the open deck sailing on the Mississippi. *Conquest's* homeport of New Orleans was a good eight hour sail up the river, and few things were more relaxing than that sail at night. I strode up to deck four and walked past the officer's cabins, pausing outside my former cabin that I had shared with Bogo, the insomniac Reborn Christian. With a rueful chuckle, I then exited through a short side hall onto the open deck. Not surprisingly at this early evening hour, I was alone.

As an art auctioneer, I was free to roam the guest areas of the ship, but I didn't want to. Being directly below the bridge, this was the only spot on the entire ship that was dark and quiet. *Conquest* silently floated through the thick forests of the massive Mississippi delta. Deck four was just barely above the treetops, and in the far distance I could see the orange glow of oil refineries. Over the marshes and swamps and forests I could see the dazzling, if tiny, popping of Fourth of July fireworks. Bourbon Street would be rocking right about now, but I was happy for the clammy quiet. I lit a cigar and watched the dark lumps of trees silently pass.

We were heading to the Gulf of Mexico, and my future. I was excited, but had already come to the obvious conclusion that this moment was the only thing from my old days of *Conquest* that I would find the same.

The next day *Conquest* was at sea all day, which needless to say presented a glorious opportunity for an art auction. In fact, we had a whopping three sea days every cruise. This was orders of magnitude better than the Widow Maker. Still, I based my expectations upon what I knew, and anticipated the auction would have all the same chaos of *Majesty*, but on a huge scale. Was it chaotic? No. Huge? Oh, yes.

First of all, the art auction was in a huge lounge at the stern of the ship that was ours all day. With no worries of being booted in favor of karaoke, the amount of artwork displayed was astounding. The six-member Filipino cover band had been hired in its entirety for the labor, and they hauled countless art carts as smoothly and in sync as if they were, well, a band. They knew exactly where to place exactly which work of art, as they unleashed every work of art for every auction. Setting up the auction took hours.

While the band played on, Bill and I were free to go over our strategy for the day. Though tagged by guests and appearing random, artwork was by no means taken to the auction block arbitrarily. During the preview, the Filipinos brought tagged artwork up to the stage, but it was then my responsibility to filter and place them in appropriate groupings to maximize our sales strategies. Sometimes I clumped style, sometimes I clumped artists. Other times I had to execute a subtle segue to get guests away from Jean-Claude Picot and towards Peter Max.

The preview alone was huge. A full hour was allocated for the droves of guests arriving for the auction. Bill dripped art facts on the microphone, while a line of passengers extended out the door. Another half-dozen employees had arrived to process the guests; handing out bidder cards, sticky notes, and tickets for free champagne. I noted that *Conquest* had a whopping four checkout computers.

Just as I thought the inflow of tagged artwork would flood over me, Bill began the auction. Easily two hundred guests were in the lounge, and half again as many remained on the periphery to watch the excitement. And exciting it was: the energy in the room was intoxicating.

Bill started the auction with a huge work of art: the Tomasz Rut painting. While it was undeniably the work of a master artist, alas, a painting of a nude woman bathing her privates was not to everyone's taste. When Bill opened the bidding at $42,000, sticker shock rippled through the lounge. Bill waited a moment in silence, then calmly motioned for the work to be taken off the block, mumbling about 'the interested party said he may not make it to the first auction'.

Behind the stage, I worked with two Filipinos affectionately dubbed Wax On and Wax Off. Despite having worked with the Filipinos for months, Bill had only deigned to learn the name of the singer, who acted as sergeant. I was too busy to learn anything new and was happy to let function label the men. So Wax On put art on the block and Wax Off removed it. Their efficiency and devotion to form would have made Mr. Miyagi proud.

After two stressful hours, the auction came to an end. I had been so busy that only once had I been able to spare a glance at the far end to see if another Peter Max was 'wandering' off. With all things so huge, even that crime no longer seemed a wonder.

The bank of computers was positioned to flank the doorway to the lounge, and four employees, no doubt dancers all, fulfilled the paperwork duties smoothly. Bill strode back and forth in front of his computers, would speak to a guest for a few minutes, then shove a sticky note in my face to move that person to the front of the line. Each employee knew exactly what to do, and no doubt the Calypso boys would have fainted in the first minute. I was seriously thinking about it. Later in the cruise, when I discovered the horror of inputting all those numbers into the accountant's computer, I nearly did.

The change of the crew bar on *Conquest* was obvious before even entering. The hallway outside had always been a moderately trafficked area of moderately thick cigarette smoke; escape enough from the chaos of the bar yet close enough to still enjoy it. But now I had to wade through thick clusters of revelers and their oppressive smoking because, shockingly, it was now a smoke-free bar.

To be sure, there were plenty of people inside still drinking themselves silly, or hooking up for a wild, noncommittal romp in the sack. Usually both. But the energy of the bar was, well, like a normal bar for normal people. The vibe of the past, of diving into a den replete with all manner of sin, was completely ruined by the loss of just one vice. I recalled many nights when I literally had not seen the ceiling due to the cigarette smoke; the canned lights merely blurry circles in the haze. Now half the tables were empty.

I scanned the isolated clumps of men and women, finding Leo easily. He was so tall as to be head and shoulders above most crew members, especially the Asians. He would have been easy to spot anyway, what with the crowd of fawning ladies gazing up at him with fluttering lashes. I pushed through the throng of babes and jokingly called, "Back off, ladies, he's mine."

"Brian!" he greeted, shaking my hand with an iron grip. "Get me a beer, will you?"

"Sure," I agreed with a smile, working back through the pleasantly curvaceous crowd. I pushed up to the bar and ordered a couple Red Stripes.

An attractive young lady sitting alone at the bar harrumphed at me. From my standing vantage, her ample bosom was impossible to ignore because she barely covered it. Blonde, bobbed hair bounced as she shook her head in disgust. "So he's got you doing his bidding now, eh?"

"I beg your pardon?"

"Him," she replied, nodding towards Leo. "Look at that line of harlots, will you? It's good to know that he has men wrapped around his finger, too."

"Wow," I said sarcastically. "I didn't know my crush was so apparent. He happens to be an old friend of mine who I haven't seen in a while."

"I was his friend, too," she bit back. "For a night, anyway. 'Nice shoes, wanna fuck?' I still can't believe I fell for that line."

I started laughing, despite my best efforts not to.

"You think that's funny?" she challenged.

"No, no," I defended. "It's just that I told him that line as a joke. I guess it's not so funny now."

"You're goddamn right it's not. Go take your beer to Mr. Forget-me-not, asshole."

Sensing a further reply was unwise, I worked my way through the crowds back towards Leo, but he was already sitting in the darkest corner getting close to a brunette in her bartender uniform. I stopped amid the throng of admirers, and glanced around with amusement. There were no less than six women staring with envy at the brunette.

"Don't panic, ladies" I joked. "I have beer! Who wants one?"

"Ooh," one said. "Red Stripe is what Leo drinks!"

"I'll take it!" another called. Suddenly everyone was clamoring for my Red Stripes.

"Are you a friend of Leo's? What's his cabin number?"

"Does he prefer brunettes, then?"

"I have hair color!" shouted another.

"Whoa," I cried, "What am I, chopped liver?"

Overwhelmed, I released the two beers as decoys so I could make my exit. From the sidelines I watched the ravenous women clamor over each other for a less obstructed view of Leo kissing the bartender. While I would no doubt behave similarly if Angelina Jolie happened by, it was pretty disgusting to watch.

Leo had always been a crew bar fiend. Like most South Africans, he loved to drink and was extremely sociable. When working with him just six months prior, he had been torn between fidelity to his girl back home and exploring the immense bounty of the sea. He marveled at my being faithful, but was unsure if it was worth it. Like most people, he was not really impressed with my being a Boy Scout in a candy store, but thought that I was, at best, a weak man or, at worst, a hypocrite.

Like so many who lie to themselves, Leo had played the field aggressively while trying to move forward with his girl back home. It was none of my business, and I withheld judgment. Leo had thought he was on the fence, but I knew better. There was no fence. So it was a surprise a few months later when he emailed me that he and his homegirl had gotten engaged, and I was invited to their wedding in the Turks and Caicos Islands. I was *not* surprised when the details never came and the whole thing was never mentioned again.

So now Leo was a crew bar ghost, lurking in the dark and making victim after victim scream. But he was tall, strong, handsome and fun, with a dash of authority, so he got plenty of action. After all, on a ship a fifty year old, overweight Indonesian could score with a hot twenty-something Slovakian. Still, watching Leo at work was an uncomfortable reminder of just how hard it had been to be faithful to Bianca on *Conquest*. I loved her to death, but knew there was no credit for saying no fifty times if I had said yes even just once.

If there was any doubt in my mind about Leo's priorities, it was settled when I met him by chance a few days later in Cozumel. The favorite crew hangout had no walls, but merely a thatched roof, and in that sweaty shade was always a party of MTV proportions. Literally. MTV once featured this location for a dance party and, keeping the spirit alive, the music pumped deafeningly and people flailed madly. There was no dance floor, so every aisle between tables pulsed with bodies contorting to the rhythm of the jungle beat. Brown-skinned waiters slipped in and out amongst the revelers with trays of perspiring beer or sizzling fajitas. Occasionally someone would bark when snapping oil burned them.

I found a small table beneath a sweat-streaked bronze stripper pole being worked by a drunken, middle-aged American woman in requisite blue jeans, T-shirt, and tennis shoes. She was no doubt a guest of the *Conquest*, and there was even less doubt that she would come to regret the photos her friends were taking of her.

Leo was dancing with the gorgeous guest he had lusted after all week. Again I was struck by how similar they looked, and watching apparent siblings grinding erotically was a little odd. Both were nearly naked: she in only a string bikini and he in shorts. Their tanned bodies traded perspiration while pressing into each other or sliding hands and lips across bare skin. Everyone in the crowd spared a glance of envy towards them: both was sexier than the other. Leo's impressive muscles pulsed with the dance, and he was all but oozing testosterone. And she, simply put, was goddamn hot. Mom was nowhere to be seen, which was probably a good thing.

I ordered a Negro Modela and was happy to be alone and lost in the past. Cozumel held many memories for me, and my brain was getting frazzled from too much rapid change. Indulging in something familiar was important. My reverie was broken when Leo slammed down into the chair opposite me. His grin was silly with alcohol and his eyes glinted.

"I shagged her mother this morning," he boasted, puffing up.

"Oh, no, Leo," I began, shaking my head. "Do you have any idea—"

"Mucho thrusting going on!" he interrupted with a thunderous roll of his r's. Leo rose, staggering a bit due to obvious intoxication, and slicked back his sweat-soaked hair. He took the Negro Modela from my hand and helped himself to a deep slug.

"Is she a princess or what?" he asked smugly, nodding to his half-naked female look-alike.

"*She is the queen,*" I agreed in my best iambic pentameter. "*Your other lover's daughter. And, would it were not so! —you did her mother.*"

"Huh?"

"Nothing," I replied, rising. "*Now cracks a noble heart. Good night, sweet prince.*"

As I departed, Leo called out over the thumping bass, "I'll give you a report after I show this girl the time of her life!"

Stepping into the hot sun, I whistled quietly to myself. Leo was playing a dangerous and childish game. Sleeping with guests was the ultimate consensual taboo on ships. If caught, he would be sent home immediately. It simply wasn't worth it. Not even for *that* mother and daughter. Probably.

I was less impressed than ever with Leo's behavior. We had been very close just six months prior, yet now I was not even on his radar screen. How many times did he need to get laid this week before he would give an old friend ten minutes to catch up? Out of sight, out of mind, I guess. Long distance relationships were hard enough as friends, and even harder on couples.

This, of course, is why I so obsessively avoided sleeping around on *Conquest*. Turning into a crew bar ghost is what I feared would happen if I dipped my toe in the waters: I would probably drown. Every cruise was a guaranteed fresh buffet of beauty both above and below the waterline. There had been many, many times when I wondered if I had been stupid for passing up such an opportunity. To taste the world, as it were. I had waited so very, very long for Bianca that I wondered if a nibble would have kept me from starving to death. But would I really have been strong enough to have a taste and not feast? Surely what happened to Leo would not happen with me and Bianca... would it?

⚓

Our first auction clinched more in sales than an entire cruise on *Majesty of the Seas,* and the second auction jumped a good thirty percent higher than the first one! Despite my pestering all cruise, I was not allowed to input our sales into the ship's accounting until the evening before our final auction. Bill dropped me off in the dismal accounting office with only rudimentary explanations of what I was to do. He was shocked that *Majesty's* accountant entered the sales into the ship's computer for us, yet still assumed I would know how. I was shocked that Carnival's modern mega-ship required me to punch numbers into an old-fashioned DOS-like green screen terminal. The interface made Pac Man look like a Nintendo Wii.

For hours I sat hunched over the tiny screen with an adding machine, swearing and scratching my head. The sole, bored Indonesian accountant on duty at this hour made it a point to ignore my repeated requests for assistance. The lighting was pale yellow and made the entire narrow chamber sickly and cramped. It was an awful experience. When I crunched the numbers and realized how much I was going to earn, however, I perked right up. This was huge money!

My excitement melted the next afternoon, when I received Bill's call while working in the art gallery.

"Brian!" he furiously screamed into the phone. "I just got woken up by the goddamn purser!"

"Awakened?" I asked. "It's noon."

"You screwed up the numbers last night and he's pissed as Hell. So am I. Get down to the accountant's office and fix it."

"OK," I said. "Sorry, Bill. Now I'll have all the accountants available to help me input the numbers right."

"Good luck with that. They're all assholes, you know. Get it right, because tonight they'll all be busy closing guest accounts for the debarkation tomorrow."

"You know, you could have taught me this stuff earlier in the cruise like I asked."

"Just shut up and fix it. Oh, and since you're in the gallery," Bill continued. "See a fat blue file on the desk? In there are all the fines I have to pay to Sundance every cruise. They expect us to do so without complaint because we make enough money to not whine. Fair enough, but make sure you do better than Doug. He was so busy playing Mr. Whipple squeezing the Charmin that he couldn't get anything right. I was so pissed at him that I didn't even speak to him the entire last cruise."

"You... you mean that literally, don't you?"

"You didn't see us speaking when you arrived, did you? Once he found out that I requested a new associate, he stopped talking to me. It was the happiest day of my life. So do better with those fines. They are starting to chap my ass, and I think Doug was intentionally doing things wrong to screw me. Of course, it came out of his cut, too, but he was too stupid to notice that."

Bill hung up the phone, leaving me to handle the blue file. The number of fines that Sundance leveled at the auctioneers was staggering. I had about as much chance of defeating those numbers as a Confederate soldier charging a Union cannon.

Some fines made sense, such as fees for incomplete shipping details, but were a surprising $25 a pop. Others were nuisance fees, such as another $25 for a husband signing for a wife's purchase. Fines that defined asshole behavior were being charged $25 for each client who chose not to include an email address or, astoundingly, fining the auctioneer for any Sundance credit card opened without any sales put on it.

The fines ascended the scale from asshole to insane, such as fines for not sending in paperwork within seven days... even if their ship was at sea the entire time! Further, Bill routinely paid $100 a month for use of gallery catalogues not even on board, and an additional $50 monthly for scanners nowhere to be found. Bill paid Sundance over $1000 a month for this minutia.

Punching the sales into the ship's computer the final night was the worst numbers nightmare ever. Each number entered on the green screen disappeared like going down the drain. Any typo ruined the entire sequence, but with no way to check entries, I had to slog to the end and hope all was correct. It never was. Worse, during the cruise changes were made to passengers' accounts without my knowledge.

After three consecutive failures, I finally called an accountant for help. I was denied. Using an adding machine in tandem with the green screen, Bill and I slaved for hours. I began at 7 p.m., right after the last, exhausting auction. By midnight the numbers still did not gel. The accountant kicked us out, so we lugged reams of receipts to our gallery. We did the numbers again and again, then redid them again and again. Our 3 a.m. deadline loomed, numbers blurred and bowels bulged. Bill denied me even a bathroom break.

3 a.m. passed, and we had to explain ourselves to the chief accountant. Beneath the sickly yellow light, we feverishly slugged away at the numbers. The only thing worse than Bill's belligerence was the Indian chief accountant pacing back and forth behind us like a prison guard, dragging his pen across the counter like a billy club on the bars. He denied us even a sip of water, which was

OK because I had been denied a bathroom break for fifteen hours!

Finally at 10 a.m. we had to give up and hand the whole mess over to the accountants to fix. The glare of the chief accountant will forever haunt me. And Bill? What was he thinking about his new associate now? Sure, he was happy that I had a penis, but now it appeared I did not have a brain. While that may describe most men, it certainly didn't help my chances at becoming an auctioneer!

13. DISAGREEABLE SALSA

I walked the overcast streets of New Orleans's French Quarter and ruminated. I hopped over puddles in the uneven, aged brick walkways and watched the last of the rain drip off centuries-old masonry. These buildings had seen many epidemics of yellow fever and malaria, and many hurricanes and many battles, from piracy in the century before America's Revolution, to slave revolts, to the War of 1812, and finally to the Civil War. And let us not forget the annual carnage of Mardi Gras! This was a place to put the puniness of my troubles in their proper place.

I was struggling to keep up with the swirl of all things new in my life. This was the first time I ever really worried that I may have taken on too much too fast. After so many quick moves from ship to ship, and overwhelming paperwork dropped on my lap, and meeting more and more stranger and stranger auctioneers who held my fate in their fist, my nerves were becoming taught. I was deeply disturbed by my failure on my very first cruise on *Conquest.*

Was I in danger of ruining my life's plans? Sundance had a very low tolerance for failure, and one bad word from Bill and I would be gone. Now, more than ever in my past, life with Bianca was within my grasp... yet I felt like I just dropped it.

Was I losing my long-term plans because the present was so challenging? But wasn't I *living* my long-term plans? I just had to keep my head down and plow through the newness and the numbers and the numbness. If it was just stress, well, I could handle that. But also in the back of my mind was the uncomfortable knowledge that I was broke. Now I needed new suits, and good ones. Bill made it clear that if my tie was less than $100, he would boot my ass off the ship. I was starting to believe him. Since I only had ten bucks in my pocket, my *last* ten bucks, I decided to blow it on a locally rolled cigar at my favorite cigar shop in the Quarter, the Cigar Factory on Decatur Street. At least Bill would approve of that.

Directly opposite the front door of the Cigar Factory was a small triangular park. This little spot of green was flanked on three sides by the streets Decatur, Conti, and North Peters. Each was hurried with cars and beyond them flowed the Mississippi. The little park was lined with shrubs that directed my gaze to a towering public statue. Resting upon tiers of marble were three bronze figures: the lowest a morose Native American, above a Bible-toting Capuchin monk, and boldly strutting above both was the founder of New Orleans, Jean-Baptiste Bienville. The sun peeked out from behind the heavy clouds, and suddenly everything glistened and steamed with renewed heat.

This spot was a favorite of mine in New Orleans, one that I would always remember. For here I would always kiss Bianca. Each and every time we passed here, we were compelled to stop and kiss. Every city we visited regularly had such a spot. I smiled as I recalled the best kissing spot of them all: in Sighişoara, Romania. A long brick road ascended up to the old citadel built in the 1200s. On our right was a huge stone wall that had literally held back the Huns, and on our left was a dense row of age-old trees. That first trip up the brick lane, walking hand in hand, I had pulled her to a stop in the speckled shade. In the middle of the road we kissed long and deep. I don't know why. From that moment on, we had always stopped at that very spot and kissed; sunny, snowy, always.

But Bianca was not in my arms today. Instead I had a Vieux Carre Lonsdale with a Cameroon wrapper. I wondered if my fixation with Bianca was because she was the only woman I ever met who didn't give me a guilt trip over cigars. I lost myself in the ritual of properly lighting a good cigar: punching open the receiving end, burning the business end until it charred, then puffing at it for a nice flare. I blew smoke up into the moist air. It wasn't nearly as satisfying as Bianca's lips, but would have to do.

I missed my Bianca something fierce, and watching Bill and Leo was a glaring reminder of just how different ship life would eventually make someone. Holy Cat, only one week with them and I had forgotten what real romance was! But it would all work out. I would not be fired for trashing the numbers on my first try, and I would not turn into a crew bar ghost. Right? If I lost Bianca because I couldn't add, well, I would jump overboard.

Then something happened that reminded me of the old days on the ships: I returned to my cabin to find an unknown, naked man.

I have a recurring problem with foreign, naked men in my room. When I first came to ships and was put up in the Miami Marriott by Carnival, I stumbled upon that foreign couple having sex in my bed. When I signed onto *Fantasy*, I opened the door of my cabin to find my Thai roommate sprawled spread-eagled across the cabin, naked. Even the reborn Christian roommate from India, Bogo, paraded around naked when we first met, without a care in the world... beyond the redemption of my atheistic soul, that is.

So I should not have been surprised to see before my bed an anonymous man bereft of britches. He was a very tall caucasian with with some extra weight high on his belly hugging his ribs, as happens with middle-aged men. His wavy, dirty blonde hair was parted down the middle. Unlike any of the other naked strangers I had encountered, however, he seemed as surprised as me. Quickly wrapping a towel around his waist, he sheepishly approached and offered his hand.

"Sorry!" he cried. "You surprised me!"

"The feeling is quite mutual," I assured him.

"I'm Dusty, the new art auctioneer," he quickly explained. "I'm taking over next cruise and came early for an easier handover."

I raised an eyebrow. "*New* auctioneer? I was not aware that Bill was leaving."

Dusty explained, "Bill's a buddy of mine, and took over *Conquest* from me a while back. He inherited Doug from me, in fact. I retired from auctioneering, but Sundance asked me to come back. They said Bill requested a transfer and no one else was making goal here but me. So here I am."

"Naked," I added, stalling to take it all in. As if things weren't already spinning too fast for me, I was already getting a new auctioneer? Talk about the Sundance Shuffle!

"So, uh, Dusty," I stammered. "Why are you in *my* cabin?"

"They couldn't find a free cabin for me, and I'm not staying in some crew shit hole. Bill won't take any cabin mate, of course."

While Dusty dressed, I sat on my bed to chat. "So you know both Doug and Bill, eh? So you maybe even know the elusive Frederick himself?"

"Of course," Dusty replied with a smug grin. "I know Frederick *very* well. And I know someone else, too. Mariana."

I searched my aching brain, but couldn't think of who he meant. "Who is that?"

"I believe you were the one who started her nickname 'Hot Cocoa'. You gotta be Buzz Lightyear, right?"

I laughed. "How do you know about all that?"

"She lives in Vancouver by me," Dusty explained. "I suggested she become an associate and work for me."

"But I thought she was Brazilian."

"She is, but lives in Vancouver. Your nickname from training stuck, so now everyone calls her Hot Cocoa. Gene thought it was so funny that he even got Frederick saying it. If you knew Frederick, you would be shocked."

Dusty glanced around the cabin briefly. Finally he said, "Man, do I wish *she* was the associate living here this week."

I chuckled. "There are indeed worse things than sharing a cabin with Hot Cocoa."

Dusty shook himself back to reality. "No, what I meant is that my timing is off by just one week."

I frowned, sensing a bomb was about to be dropped. I asked carefully, "What do you mean?"

"This cabin will be hers next cruise," he explained.

Boom.

My history with Sundance swirled furiously in my head as I marched to Bill's cabin. First I had to endure a week of training Hell; subjected to crushing stress and the ridicule of Lucifer himself. He made half the trainees cry and the other half quit. I survived that only to be sent to the Widow Maker. Two weeks on that beast and my ulcerated, impotent, and alcoholic auctioneer gets screwed by Sundance and denied vacation. In order to squeeze more life out of the poor bastard, I get promoted by default and they bring in a new auctioneering couple, likable but again alcoholic and dysfunctional. Then I get promoted again, making me the first of us trainees to become associate *and* the first associate to be given a big ship. But then comes Bill, the strangest auctioneer yet, who gleefully adds perversion to his alcoholism. Just one week with him and I am demoted to another ship?

So let's see: that's six weeks, three alcoholics, two sex addicts, one ulcer, and Tatli. No paycheck in there anywhere, and certainly no Bianca. What the Hell was I doing this for, then?

Bill was in the doorway of his cabin when I stormed up to him, but I paused because of the loud vacuum running inside. He stood with his arms crossed over his beefy chest, staring openly at the derriere of the Filipina room steward cleaning under his bed.

"Bill!" I called, "We need to talk!"

He nodded for me to enjoy the view as well, grinning just like a kid.

"What's this crap about Hot Cocoa coming here next week?"

"Oh," he said blandly. "You met Dusty, then."

"He's only living in my goddamn cabin," I retorted over the noise. I mustered all my anger consciously because, to be honest, Bill intimidated me. Of all the people I had ever met in my life, including the loathsome Lucifer, only Bill had ever done so.

"Only for a week," Bill said. The vacuum shut down and the room plunged into silence. The stewardess gave Bill a meek, pretty smile as she gathered up her equipment.

"Bill?" I pressed, but he ignored me to smile back at the Filipina like the Big Bad Wolf eyeing Little Red Riding Hood.

"Bill, where the Hell am I going next week?"

"You're going to *Ecstasy*," he answered easily. He stepped aside for his stewardess and said, dripping honey, "Thank you, sweetie. Good bye, now."

"You could have helped a Hell of a lot more with the paperwork, you know," I muttered accusingly.

"I helped all goddamn night!" he roared back. My shoulders drooped in defeat, but Bill continued onward with an explanation. "Look, Buzz, lighten up, will you? I asked to be transferred off of *Conquest* months ago. They're sending me to *Ecstasy*, and you're going with me."

I paused. "You mean I'm not being demoted to a smaller ship because of the paperwork snafu?"

"What, you think Sundance is that fast? No, we're going to my hometown of L.A., my friend. We're gonna make a killing."

"But it's so much harder to sell on smaller ships," I said.

"Not for me," Bill scoffed. "We're gonna make out like bandits, amigo. Sundance asked if I wanted Antonio Banderas back, or if I wanted to keep you."

"So you wanted to keep me?"

"We'll overnight in Mexico twice a week," Bill explained. "Antonio never helped me get laid, and the pansy even speaks Spanish! I need a wingman, don't I?"

Was it really so unrealistic to just want to settle in and maybe have a laugh with some friends I was lucky enough to work with again? It seemed like a simple desire, something easier to achieve than, say, architecting a life with an eastern European woman. But what did I get? A week of mind-shattering newness, unbalanced numbers, and libertines, followed by another week of the same, followed by still another ship where I get to do the whole mess again. Things were moving faster and faster, with no end in sight. How could I ever be in control when everything was so drastically new and different all the time? Jeez, at this point all I wanted was the *illusion* of control!

Yet the auctions went smoother the following week, especially with Dusty hanging around and helping through sheer boredom. Surprisingly, it was the ports that became annoying. Our first port of call was Montego Bay, Jamaica, where Leo and I planned to visit our old hang out at Sunset Beach Resort. There we had enjoyed many good memories, including a magical afternoon of snorkeling, water-gun fights, and partying during a tropical storm.

At about 9 a.m. I got a call from Leo.

"10:30's too early," he mumbled groggily into the phone.

"You woke up early to tell me you need more sleep?"

"I had a chase last night that kept me up way too late."

"What was her name?"

"No, not that. Some asshole stole my underwear from the laundry room. Can you believe that shit? Groupies are nice, but those Calvin Kleins were worth $40 a piece."

"Just page me when you're ready to go out," I said, then strolled up to the top deck with a steaming mug of coffee. I wanted to honor the beautiful, nearby Blue Mountains and their noble coffee plantations that made life so much better for us all. From on high I watched the dock and the comings and goings of all the little people below. The comings were all taxis, but who did I see going? Why, Leo, of course.

I swallowed my anger while watching him trudge off with a beach bag and today's hottie. Well, that was that. I was done with him. Sure, I understood that I was the 'new guy' on *Conquest* now, but I wasn't some groupie begging for his time. I was tempted to steal his underwear and throw it overboard. My disappointment funk smoldered low but hot. I had held out one last hope to relive some of the old days, but you never can. Instead I used the afternoon to shop for a nice box of chocolates as thank-you to the poor accountant who handled our mess from last cruise.

But the real port of call drama came in Cozumel, where Bill and Dusty bullied me into joining them for a downright uncomfortable afternoon of play.

The sky was thick with clouds pregnant with moisture, but Bill insisted we rent scooters and tour the island. We quickly passed through the cluster of tourist-centric shops to the edge of 'real' Mexico, where our destination was an old gas station-turned-scooter rental. The windows were gone, replaced by hurricane-proof plywood with a hand-painted scooter menu.

Just as we arrived, the clouds opened into a piddling, warm rain. The portly and mustachioed man sitting beside the available scooters jumped up and ran inside, as if that was the cue he was waiting for. He slammed the door shut in our faces, followed by the clicking of the lock.

"So much for that," Dusty said sourly, glancing at the door's sun-faded map of Cozumel. "What now?"

"There's still lots of places in Cozumel that are fun," I offered. "We could party as Carlos & Charlie's, for example, though I don't want to get too drunk. I still have a ton of paperwork to enter tonight. Or there's Chankanaab."

"No, I want a drink," Bill said. "And services."

"Yes, *services*," Dusty agreed with an emphasis that brought a grin from Bill.

"I'd imagine there is someplace to drink at Chankanaab," I said. "I think we can swim with dolphins at Chankanaab."

"How far is it, do you think?" Bill asked Dusty, ignoring me.

"Can't be too far," Dusty answered. "The island is only ten miles across at its widest."

"Chankanaab is only about ten minutes by taxi," I said, wiping rainwater from my face. "I think we should go to Chankanaab."

"Will you shut the Hell up?" Bill finally bellowed in my face.

"I just like saying Chankanaab," I explained calmly.

"Let's walk, then," Bill ordered. Even though Dusty had seniority in both age and the company, Bill was the natural leader here. As soon as he began marching, Dusty high-stepped to keep stride and I tagged along behind. We soon left the thin strip of civilization along the coast and entered the steaming wild. The jungles of Cozumel had trees on par with a two-story building. They reminded me of the Mayan men who lived here: solid and strong and short. The stroll in the warm Mexican rain through the jungle was actually quite pleasant.

"You remember Germaine?" Dusty asked Bill. "He got booted from *Navigator of the Seas*. Can you believe that?"

"No shit?" Bill asked, surprised. "Germaine was the biggest earner I ever met!"

"Get this," Dusty said, "They up and raised the goals by thirty thousand dollars per cruise. Germaine only made G1 three cruises in a row, so he demanded they lower the goals back to where they used to be. One week after he mouths off, he misses G1 and they boot him. *Once!* His associate stepped up and is already the biggest earner at sea. He's got *three* associates and still makes a killing."

"Three goddamn associates? Things are changing," Bill said. "No more lone wolf days."

I just shook my head in wonder. So ship nightmares weren't relegated to crappy old ships like the Widow Maker. Even the big boys can lose.

"You ever been on one of those monster RCI ships?" Dusty asked Bill.

"Nope. Just Norwegian Cruise Lines and Carnival."

"Don't get me started on NCL!" Dusty lamented to the rain. "Those Norwegians are stiff sons of bitches. On my first NCL ship, half of my art storage was blocked by this big, locked closet. I asked them to remove the lock every cruise for two months straight, because I really needed that space. They never got around to it, so I finally cut the lock off myself. You'll never guess what was in it.

"Jimmy Hoffa?"

"Enough weapons to supply a guerilla army."

"Like the one in Chankanaab?" I asked. They ignored me.

"I called security right away, of course," Dusty continued. "They had all sorts of assault rifles and shotguns and stuff. Don't think they aren't prepared for pirates, my friend."

"Did they have one of those sonic weapons?" Bill asked. "Like they used on the Seabourn ship against the pirates in Somalia?"

"How would I know?" Dusty asked. "I'm from Canada, what do I know about assault weapons? You're the American. Anyway, Chief of Security ran down at Mach Three to chastise me like I was some meddlesome child. They did a complete inventory on the spot to make sure I didn't take anything, and kept searching my cabin every cruise for a month. What, they thought I was going to sneak a stolen assault rifle into America after 9/11?"

We were now a long way out of town, but to my surprise a staggered line of people disappeared before us into the distance. There were small clumps of Asians and random Caribbeans. No Mexicans walked along the road, and there were no cars at all. Not that Cozumel had many of those, anyway.

"I sense we aren't heading towards the Mayan ruins of El Cedral," I finally said. "Where are we going?"

As answer Bill and Dusty shared a glance and sniggered. Eventually we arrived at a low compound extending into the mist-shrouded forest. The buildings were low, forming left and right wings reaching out from a central bar. The bar was built of thick wooden beams, with no walls front or back, but covered by a tin roof that clattered with the rain. Mexican bolero music blared from speakers perched beside Corona-drinking parrots. Rainwater poured down the gutter-less roof, creating a shimmering view of the rainforest as if looking through a waterfall. Only one car occupied the lumpy, rivulet-streaked dirt parking lot.

"Say, this license plate is not from Quintana Roo," I commented.

Bill stared at the empty bar room with a gleam in his eye, and Dusty licked his chops like, well, Bill eyeing his room stewardess.

"Quintana Roo is the state of Mexico that Cozumel is in," I added just to be annoying. "Someone drove from Quintana Roo in the Yucatan and ferried over to this shithole."

They continued to ignore me.

"I just like to say Quintana Roo," I finished quietly to myself. Something was up, but they weren't talking. We had followed a long line of men here, yet not a single person sat in the bar, nor played at either pool table. Only then did I realize that the long line of pedestrians were *only* men. Understanding washed over me with the warm rain.

"Oh no," I lamented into the drizzling heavens. "We're not at Salsa, are we?"

Both men burst out laughing.

"Why not?" Bill asked. "You got a cock, don't you?"

"I find it distressing that I have to answer that again," I snapped back, but Bill and Dusty shared more vulgar laughter at my expense.

Salsa. *The* Salsa. We were at the most notorious brothel on Cozumel!

We passed through the waterfall to gain entry to the bar, and Dusty nodded to the small, powerful, Mayan bartender. His features looked incredibly noble, with a bold, wide and proud nose and stern forehead. If he had been wearing jade and a quetzal feather instead of a beer-stained T-shirt, I could have pictured him leading Mayan warriors in fending off Conquistadores. I called him 16 Rabbit.

Dusty's silent order was for three Coronas and a rack of balls for the pool table. Soon we were standing around the decidedly off-balance table, and numerous women materialized from behind curtains and doorways. Like the bartender, they were also all Mayan, but mostly overweight. I didn't want to contemplate the stains on *their* clothing. Bill temporarily ignored the women and racked the balls, but Dusty was already perusing the wares.

"Don't panic, Buzz," Bill said as he chalked his cue. "I've never been to a brothel before, either."

"Oh, I never said I haven't been to a brothel before," I replied somewhat smugly.

"Bullshit," he quietly scoffed.

I was a little displeased at his lack of reaction, but not surprised.

"No, really. I lived in Reno for years. Believe it or not, a friend of mine who owned an apartment building in Vegas was considering purchasing a brothel. He was big on thinking outside the box. He flew up for a few days and we toured them in the deserts outside Reno, Carson City, and Fallon. There's a big Air Force base out there, so there's lots of brothels: the Kit Kat Ranch, the Moonlight Bunny Ranch, Sage Ranch."

"Let me guess," Bill said blandly, "You didn't screw anyone, but just looked."

"You sound disappointed."

"Not as disappointed as the hooker you would have hired," he jibed. "You're such a pussy. I actually do believe you because you're too stupid to lie. For most guys, the hard part is getting through the front door. But you, Buzz, you even date a goddamn stripper and don't screw her. What a waste of time."

Bill and I played a game of pool, or tried to. While the periphery filled with women of all ages, they kept their distance. It was actually Dusty who kept pestering us. He would grab Bill's shoulder when he was taking a shot, just to point out another chubby Mayan who caught his fancy.

"Look at that one," he would say, or, "Oh, look at her!"

"Just pick one, will you?" Bill snapped.

"I think I just did," Dusty said with a grin. "See the one over there?"

"You mean that girl by the Negra Modelo sign?" I asked. "What, is she even legal?"

"I'll just pretend you didn't say that," Dusty replied blandly. "Last time she said she's twenty. I doubt it, but as long as she's less than half my age, it's all good."

"Looks like she eats a barrel of pork everyday," Bill commented, sizing her up. "Am I missing out on something here? Everyone around me porks the fat ones. She does have big tits, though."

But Dusty was already wandering away as if in a trance, muttering absently about her smooth skin. Bill and I just shrugged and returned to pool. Every shot rolled into the same corner because the table was so off-kilter, but we didn't care. I actually enjoyed shooting pool and listening to the rain. Listening to Bill's perspective? Not so much.

"Dusty suggested this place," Bill marveled. "What a great idea. You don't have to deal with any of the bullshit women put you through and you get what you want."

"If all you want is sex," I answered. "But you have to pay for it."

"So what? Otherwise you pay for dinner and drinks, and you still have to beg for it. Cut to the chase, man."

After the second game, Bill motioned for two of the girls to join us. He specifically pointed to the most and least beautiful women in the room.

"I've no doubt you selected Bonita for you," I said sarcastically to Bill, "But did you have to choose Fea for me?"

"How do you know their names?"

"*Bonita* means 'pretty' and *fea* means 'ugly'," I explained. "Come on, Bill, you know I'm not going there."

"You scared to play some pool?" he asked. Then, to the ladies, "Shall we play a game of doubles, ladies?"

"What you have in mind?" asked Fea in fair English. She was without a doubt the least attractive prostitute I had ever seen. Not that I really felt qualified to make such a judgment, but I *was* being honest about having toured half a dozen Nevada brothels. Fea was perhaps thirty and perhaps five and a half feet tall, and definitely two hundred pounds. While her nose was Mayan broad, it was turned up in an ungainly, almost snout-like way. Her nose alone had more moles than I cared to count. It looked like a domino.

"Just pool for now," Bill answered her. "Since you are taller, you can partner with my friend Brian here."

Fea slid up close to me, but I fended her off by handing her my pool cue.

We played a game of doubles, but Bill was obviously much more interested in sizing up Bonita than anything else. She never said a word, but smiled suggestively and giggled at every comment he made. About halfway through the game, I went back to the bar to bring another round of beer. When I returned, Bill and Bonita were gone. Fea was leaning back against the pool table, fondling the pool cue suggestively.

Fea smiled at me.

I politely smiled at her.

"Game is over," she said. "You want... more?"

I sipped my beer slowly, stalling for time. "Another game of pool sounds great!"

So another game passed tensely, while Fea thoroughly trounced me. No doubt her looks provided her ample time to play pool. After a while, Dusty reappeared from behind the curtain. His long, sandy hair was a mass of disarray, and a line of sweat ran down his cheek. He wore a stupefied grin while ordering two shots of tequila from the bar. With a new limp he returned with the drinks to his companion.

"You want *different* game?" Fea asked after a second one-sided game.

"How about some food?" I replied.

"We have best salsa on island," she said with a twinkle in her eye.

"I didn't come here for salsa," I said pointedly.

"Oh," she replied, disappointed. As she left me, she gestured to the trees beyond the wall of rainwater. "We have best salsa on island. Avocados from those trees."

And so I was mercifully left to myself for a while. I returned to the bar and ordered some salsa and a fresh mango juice from 16 Rabbit. I enjoyed watching the rain pound harder and harder. The salsa came in a bowl the size of a cantaloupe and was, without a doubt, the best I had ever had in my life. The tomatoes were neither diced nor smashed into mush, but piled in a mound of meaty chunks the size of ice cubes. Mixed in equal proportion with the hearty tomatoes were chunks of rich, creamy avocado. The whole was covered with a veritable salad of cilantro. The snappy cilantro and ground garlic made it flavorful, but not spicy. It was so good, in fact, that a full hour passed before I knew it.

In all that time I never saw any of the men we followed here leaving. Apparently Bill and Dusty were not the only ones planning on maximizing their time here. I, on the other hand, was not at all interesting in doing so. I was getting impatient to move on, but walking back to the ship was not at all desirable. I was finally dry, and outside was raining dogs, cats, and all manner of farm animals, as Bianca liked to say. I asked the bartender to call me a taxi.

After a long while, the rain came down so hard the metal roof shuddered and shook. I seriously wondered if the building could handle it. There was still no sign of the taxi, so I inquired.

"*Taxi no aquí?*" 16 Rabbit said with obviously fake surprise. He wiped his hands on his nasty T-shirt and suggested, "Salsa while you wait?"

In the end, I had to walk back to *Conquest* in the rain or endure another few hours being accosted by Fea and her cohorts. Of course, I wasn't allowed to leave before paying everyone's tab.

14. ECSTASY

The final evening of my second, and final, cruise on *Conquest* presented me with an opportunity I had been secretly hoping for. While on my way to the art gallery in the Pissarro Room, I noticed two men conversing behind the podium of the Renoir restaurant. With nothing much to do before dinner on the last night of the cruise, the ship's two Maitre d's were chatting idly before the guests arrived. The short, solidly built man with very dark skin and gray hair ringing his balding head was Ganesh, the Maitre d' of the Monet Dining Room. Ferrand, the handsome Frenchman in charge of Renoir, was the junior in rank.

Just two months ago these men had stabbed me in the back. During Gunnar's thinly disguised case of prejudice in denying me my stripe and, thusly, my Bianca, these men had offered to assist me in my defense. They recognized Gunnar for what he was: a prejudiced coward. Alas, I did not recognize them for what they were: *lying* cowards. When I presented my case to Carnival's executives, both men claimed ignorance of everything.

I smoothed my suit, arranged my tie and approached them with a neutral expression. Part of me wanted to grin like an idiot and another part wanted to tell them both to kiss my ass.

"Brian!" Ferrand greeted with his usual obsequious smile. He glanced at my Pronto Uomo suit and commented, "You are looking sharp."

"Thank you," I replied blandly. "My new career demands a certain... panache."

Ganesh gave me a quick smile and held out his hand. "Hello, Brian."

I paused a second before shaking his hand.

"Leo mentioned that you are an art auctioneer," Ganesh continued, nodding with approval. "You seem to have done very well for yourself in a very short time."

"I have," I agreed. "No thanks to either of you."

"Well," Ganesh said, turning to Ferrand. "I think we both knew Brian would find success. Don't you agree, Ferrand?"

"Oh, I do," the curly-haired Frenchman replied, nodding a moment longer than he should.

The awkwardness of the moment extended as they faced each other behind the protection of the podium. Their body language clearly indicated they could care less about what happened.

Surprisingly, I suddenly felt the same. Though I had told Leo I was not interested in confronting these men with my superior rank, I secretly wanted to. At first I worried that I was just backing out of a confrontation, but then realized how pointless the whole thing was. These small-minded men had not been attacking me, but merely protecting their own little world. There was no grand melodrama. There was nothing.

I turned my back on them and walked away, never to see them again.

Unfortunately, I *did* see the chief accountant again. Astoundingly, the paperwork was worse than the previous week. All week I thought I was on top of it, but apparently some gremlins had moved all my numbers around. Once again I began alone at 7 p.m. and churned out list after list of misaligned numbers. Again I was frustrated, angry, and a little scared. Again I had to call in Bill at midnight for assistance. Again he was furious, but far more so than the previous week. Again our combined efforts amounted to nothing, and by 3 a.m. we were again booted from the accounting office. But this week there was one big, nasty difference.

I was stricken by food poisoning.

"What's your goddamn problem?" Bill snapped. "You've been to the bathroom three times and you're shaking like the goddamn coward you are. You stink."

"I don't know," I replied. "I can hardly see straight and have chills."

"What, salsa coming back to haunt you?" he chortled.

"Not nearly as bad as what's gonna come back to haunt you," I bit back. "Tomorrow I'll be fine, but you'll have that shit for life."

"Next time just follow my lead and hump some hos," Bill ordered. "See? Abstinence gives you cramps."

For twelve straight hours I worked through chills, sweats, vomiting, and diarrhea. At 3 a.m. we broke to take our luggage to the security chief for clearance, but immediately thereafter we were back at the accounting office. I began shaking so badly that Bill had to input the numbers. Worse, I became dyslexic in calling out the numbers and found myself having difficulty alphabetizing names. I know he would have hit me if he didn't think I would pass out.

Behind us paced the chief accountant, as ever in drill-sergeant mode. Each tap of his pen on the desk was a stab into the delicate sphere of agony that was my head. I was actually glad when diarrhea forced me to run to the toilet, because it eased the headache so sharply exacerbated by the Indian.

After three or four millennia, 7 a.m. arrived, and with it our last chance to accomplish the gargantuan numbers task before the chief accountant took over: twice in as many weeks. Signing off *Conquest* with unfinished paperwork would have surely meant my firing and probably thousands in fines from Sundance. But by an absolute miracle, the numbers gelled at the last moment. It was such amazing timing, *literally* the last five minutes, that it felt staged. Bill kicked back his chair forcefully when we finished and stormed out. I, on the other hand, shakily pushed myself up from the table and fell into the wall.

Fifteen minutes was all we had to gather our carry-on luggage and go. My entire body ached and reeked, and I was desperate for a shower, but there simply was no more time. Stinking and wretched, I labored with my backpack to the gangway, where Bill impatiently waited for me.

"Jesus, Brian," he chided. "You smell like shit."

"Thank you."

"You aren't gonna throw up on the plane, are you? Just sitting next to you for the flight and smelling you will probably make me barf. Or are you gonna crap your pants waiting for the taxi? Or in line at the airport? I am still having some raw oysters at Acme before we get on the plane, you know. Jesus, you are making my life hell."

"Yes, Bill," I simply said, fighting a shiver. The thought of raw oysters at that moment was not a good one. And the pressure on my bowels when the jet took off? Ugh.

But *Conquest* was being left once and for all and I had complete closure with her. Though looking and smelling of filth, I was leaving vindicated. That said, I was very pleased to slink out without anyone I knew witnessing that last, parting image of me sickly and sullen. But really, who did I know that would even be up at 7AM, after all?

Why Hot Cocoa, of course.

"Buzz!" she shouted, rushing up the gangway to me with arms wide. Suddenly she reared back on the narrow metal stairs and regarded me skeptically.

"He's got the shits," Bill explained helpfully.

"Oh, too bad," she said with a ravishing, mischievous smile. "I was going to give you a big hug and a kiss."

Unlike Shakespeare's Juliet, I have found names to be very important. She decried rhetorically 'What's in a name?' and was willing to cast aside her and her forbidden lover Romeo's family names as being irrelevant. Though certainly not in love with them, I, on the other hand, have found Carnival names to be singularly appropriate. My restaurant training on *Carnival Fantasy* was living the dream of going to sea and being surrounded by hordes of hot foreign women. On *Conquest* I was brutally conquered by the ship's management, while my trials and tribulations on *Legend* were indeed epic.

And *Carnival Ecstasy*? It was all that and a bag of chips. I marveled how the ship could live up to it's name while lacking the sublime presence of my Bianca. But it did, and then some.

Ecstasy ran three and four day cruises out of Long Beach, California. These would involve a stop at Catalina Island and the Mexican port of Ensenada, or both. Each cruise offered a day at sea, but no other opportunity in any way for art sales events. This made me nervous, but Bill was confident of reaching goal with a single auction per cruise.

"Aren't you a little concerned about this proverbial placement of all our eggs in one basket?" I had asked.

"I know L.A. people," he replied simply. "I will clear G2 easily."

Not convinced, I ominously warned, "As you no doubt recall, it was Abraham Lincoln who said, "The chicken is the wisest creature in all creation, for she doesn't cackle until *after* she lays her egg."

"What is it with you and fucking chickens?" Bill snapped.

"I've never fucked a chicken, Bill," I deadpanned.

"Well, do it and quit your damn whining. You don't even have to do the accounting on this ship, so just follow my lead and we'll be fine."

Bill's bravado was hardly reassuring, but his performance at the first auction more than made up for. Oh, did it! We far and away surpassed our entire cruise goals in those two hours. Within two weeks of arriving on *Ecstasy* we had shattered all its previous sales records and were the highest revenue earners on-board, surpassing the casino and, astoundingly, competing even with the total bar sales! When Carnival saw that merely two men were challenging the revenues of one of their largest departments, we were given carte blanche privileges on board. We strut like peacocks. We rolled in money. Women flocked to us.

We were rock stars.

The majority of my time on *Ecstasy* was spent on the Promenade deck at the Rolls Royce Café. This was the only source of cappuccino on the ship, making it highly important in this era of being defined by ones coffee habit. This gem of a spot doubled as our art gallery, with its two walls angling into the coffee counter displaying our best artwork, floor to ceiling.

If that wasn't enough to catch someone's eye, out in the main walkway was parked an actual vintage Rolls Royce, presumably with one helluva parking brake to refrain from rolling on the high seas. Beside its back bumper sat an easel proclaiming our auction hours to all who passed by on their way to coffee or to the lounge. Bill and I parked there ourselves, before the hood, throughout the evenings distributing free raffle tickets for the auction. This had less to do with advertising and more to do with a lack of anything else to do.

Bill would come and go from the Promenade deck, usually only remaining in the evening to ogle those silicone-laden L.A. women as they strolled past in their nightclub attire. I was tasked with actually remaining in the area for hours at a time, which was pretty much where I would want to be anyway. I was very much a coffee shop kind of guy, despite a lack of any coffee affectation. Besides, my cabin was about as bland as one would expect of a room walled by steel bulkheads. Sure, it was gloriously mine and mine alone, but I have never encountered a chamber in such dire need of feng shui in my life.

Ecstasy had not started on such a high note, however. Our first day, in hindsight, was a laughable example of Bill's and my auctioneer/apprentice relationship. It was also a metaphor for how much training, or lack thereof, he deigned to bestow upon me.

Beginning on *Ecstasy* necessarily involves the ending on *Conquest*. That final day on *Conquest*, of course, was a nightmare of all-evening auction, followed by that all-night battle with intense accounting. This, while fighting vomiting, diarrhea, and convulsions, was followed immediately by flying halfway across the country and the pressures of signing onto a new ship. I nearly passed out during the survival training, for which I was roundly reprimanded, followed promptly by the further draining stresses of the auctioneer handover.

After all that, a solid thirty hours of uninterrupted Hell, with great compassion Bill demanded I join him in the crew bar!

I replied that, perhaps considering that only minutes ago had I finally ceased vomiting, this would not be a good time for copious amounts of noise, alcohol, and cigarette smoke. He called me a pussy. I promised to join him every night for the next week, but he wouldn't let up. His persistence was only topped by his selfishness.

Bill was never wrong, despite being frequently so, and he smoothly pushed blame onto those around him. Usually these unfortunate souls were too intimidated to push back. True, at that first night on *Ecstasy* I had plenty to account for because of my second failure on *Conquest*, but his petty insults on top of everything else were hard to swallow. No wonder Doug hated him with such passion. Antonio Banderas had felt the same, but was too composed to say so. It took all of my cool not to rear up as Bill habitually, and falsely, accused me of all manner of little mistakes that simply did not matter. But tolerance is strength, and so long as I was not being truly trod upon I could handle it. That was just Bill's way of remaining leader of the pack. Though I was learning nothing from Bill, he was paying me large sums of money for it. So I bit my tongue at the trivial.

Bill had a dynamic, powerful temperament indeed. His was one of those personalities that made you defensive because you are not like him, even though you don't want to be like him. He is at home on the ships, happy in the transience of the life and the lack of social accountability it provides. He had no desire to build anything or care for anyone. His only hobby was looking for another pair of tits. Other than money, he simply could not fathom anything beyond seeing a bigger pair than the last time. Except, perhaps, groping them.

Yet, strangely, this audacity made him fun to hang around with. Bill needed an audience and a follower. While I was happy to occasionally be the former, I refused to be the latter. I chose when I wanted to retire for the night, something which Bill seemed unable or unwilling to do. He raged at my departures and refusals every single time. But I held my own through his every questioning of my libido. How he could consider me, of all people, prudish, is a marvel. No wonder he gave up on Antonio Banderas and Doug with open contempt.

On one small thing, however, Bill and I were in agreement over: my need of a new suit. It's all very well to be treated like a rock star, of course, but if you know you don't look it, your mojo remains askew. Can't have that, now. My current suit was excellent, to be sure, but it was lonely and worn seven days a week. I had been trying unsuccessfully to purchase a partner for it for months, but opportunity had been lacking, not to mention funds. But now, finally, my first paycheck from Sundance had trickled through the red tape to me.

Alas, my first funds, as exciting as they were to receive, were limited to only being an associate on the

Widow Maker for a few weeks. Cataloguing huge commissions on *Ecstasy* was nice and all, but they were yet months away from being received. Bill offered to loan me plenty of money, but I was loathe to owe *him* anything. I opted to take a peek at our new port in Mexico for my suits, hoping to stretch a buck.

My first trip ashore in Ensenada was hours wasted wandering the streets for a suit shop. It was not a pretty town, and the shabby buildings were close enough together to make me feel sweaty and dirty. That could be a nice feeling, such as in a wonderfully nasty bar or with a wonderfully nasty woman, but I was here for neither. I scraped the sweat from my neck, puffed impatiently at my cigar, and scrutinized the windows for evidence of formal attire. In hindsight, I should have scrutinized my path a bit more.

I stumbled into a suit shop quite suddenly. Literally. Ensenada's sidewalks were a jumble of broken concrete slabs as choppy as the sea itself, jutting up at every sort of angle imaginable. Pythagoras himself would have balked at identifying all those angles. I tripped and smacked face-first into a glass storefront, then slid squeakily to the ground.

What a smack it was! I rubbed my forehead in mild shock, but it was my cheek that smarted in a most peculiar manner. Dazed and with wobbly vision, I watched my cigar smolder hotly on the sidewalk, its blackened end splayed out like a trick cigar Bugs Bunny gave to Elmer Fudd. Wincing, I rubbed the seared flesh of my cheek and suddenly a jolt of concern flashed through me as I realized just how badly I could have burned my face. I leapt up with a further embarrassing little dance to avoid a dizzied fall again, and stared at my reflection in the window. Fortunately the glass had not shattered. Unfortunately I realized that I was staring into the gaze of two mannequins in white suits and two wide-eyed employees.

Too mortified to worry about my face any longer, I dusted myself off and entered with what little dignity I could muster. Both attendants were small, handsome men with pencil-thin mustaches. They wore the fruits of their trade smartly, at ease in white suits one frequently associates with Latin America. I glanced around the wares, but was disappointed to not find what I was looking for. While almost every jacket was several sizes too small for me, my main concern was the lack of my preferred double breasted suits.

Sensing my frustration, one of the attendants smoothly approached. His trim mustache was accompanied by a line of beard that defined his jawline with delicate precision. Communication was an issue when he asked, "*¿Le puedo ayudar, señor? ¿Qué busca usted?*"

"*¿Habla inglés?*" I asked in Spanish. When he shook his head, I had already exhausted my language skills beyond 'where is the shoe store?'.

Very slowly I asked, "Do you have any double breasted suits?" He frowned and glanced at his companion, who shrugged. I wondered how to say 'breasted' in Spanish. I had a bit of experience in international pantomime, and thought I could surely figure this one out.

"Uh, chi chis," I stammered. Back home was a restaurant by that name and I vaguely recalled someone saying it meant 'breasts'.

He raised an eyebrow at me.

"*¿Mendigo su perdón?*"

I enacted a woman as best I could and cupped my pretend breasts. "Dos chi chis...?"

"*¿Desea el burdel?*" he asked slowly, fighting a smile. His companion chortled from afar. "*¿El sexo?*"

I sensed that 'el sexo' was more up Bill's alley than mine. It suddenly struck me that *burdel* meant 'bordello'.

"No, no," I replied, frustrated. I wracked my brain for every Spanish slang I could think of. After a few moments of standing there like a moron, I finally blurted, "Tits!"

The man now raised both eyebrows, and gave his partner an amused glance. "*¿Tetas?*"

"*Si, tetas!*" I cried. "*Dos tetas*... suit... for me. Oh, uh, *para mi. Comprende?*"

He shook his head, but I blithely blundered along. I knew that clothing was *ropa*, so I tried throwing that in there. "*Dos chi chis... ropa... para mi.*"

"*¿El brasier?*" he said. "*¡No brasieres aquí!*"

"No, no, I don't want a bra. Double breasted... oh, forget it!"

I stalked off, disappointed, while the two men openly mocked me on my way out. I should have stayed, because I could have learned some fun, if not particularly useful, Spanish slang. One man pretended to cup huge breasts and shouted to his companion, "*Guanabanas.*" The other corrected him by illustrating small breasts and saying, "*Oh, no, limoncitos...*"

Finally as I exited, I heard them muttering, "*Gringo loco.*"

Communication problems were not limited to foreign cultures, however. Connecting with Bill was equally vexing, like dealing with an unruly child. While Bill demanded I get new suits, he denied me much free time to obtain them in favor of his relentless pursuit of T&A. Finally I put my foot down while in home port on our third week, absolutely and irrevocably refusing to find a strip club. He was shocked, despite even the fact we were receiving an important art delivery this day. Thus I forced Bill to remain on board while I went shopping, which he sulkily agreed to. My little victory came with a high price, however, and I'm not just talking about the mess he left me in the art locker.

Ecstasy's art locker was an unused mustering chamber inside the ship's surplus shell door. This was a second access through the ship's hull, several decks higher than the waterline, for the occasional port facility that required such. It was rarely, if ever, used, and so the area intended for traffic flow was given to us. We filled it to the max. Rows of leaning canvases snaked across the floor right up to the bulkheads in every direction, leaving only a small floor space in the center of the room. I kept this area clear and, for the most part, clean. But this day Bill was punishing me for not letting him play.

Scattered everywhere were shreds of cardboard and unruly coils of bubble wrap. Bill had gleefully torn open all the boxes of our art delivery and tossed aside the wrappings like a child on Christmas morning. I whimpered when I saw all the little bits and pieces dropped into the hydraulics of the shell door. It would take hours to get that cleaned up and back to safety code. I waded through dozens of torn protective corners and over literally hundreds of staples which dug themselves into the carpet as snug as a bug in a rug.

The paintings and prints that Bill liked had been torn free of their packaging and piled haphazardly against one another. Those he did not care for, such as anything from Jean-Claude Picot, were left nestled in their boxes for me to dig out.

Bill's excitement was understandable, however, as our art collection was already getting slim of the good stuff and new material would keep our glory days rolling. A glance through the bill of lading gave me a thrill when I saw not one, but two Picasso etchings from the 1970s. I disregarded everything else and exuberantly hunted for the treasures amid the detritus of Bill's frenzy. With a cry of triumph I pulled from the mess a large, gorgeously-framed original etching from the greatest artist of all time.

I flipped the work over and greedily ate up the description on the back. *Le minotaure séduit la fille endormie*, it read: 'Minotaur seduces the sleeping girl.' How perfect! This was an iconic image for Picasso, and would fetch us many, many thousands in commission. Despite my burning curiosity, I couldn't find the second Picasso, which the bill of lading listed as *La femme avec le bracelet reçoit chouette et un chat.* There was no translation on the bill, and after my dubious chi chi fiasco I was scared to guess what it meant. I recognized the words for 'woman' and 'bracelet', of course, and vaguely recalled that in French '*chat*' meant 'cat'. I surmised it was a portrait of a woman with her cat.

Now why would Bill only take one Picasso for display in the Rolls Royce, and why a portrait instead of the hugely iconic minotaur? True, Bill's art history knowledge was pathetic and he may not even know the treasure he had overlooked. More likely the portrait showed some tits.

I grabbed the minotaur and happily rushed up to the Promenade. Beaming with excitement, I turned into the café with my treasure and nearly ran into a mother with her two children. They were as eager to leave as I was to enter.

"Oh!" I cried, "Excuse me, ma'am!"

She backed away and glared at me with tremendous contempt. I blinked under her furious, accusatory frown and leaned back. The woman gripped her little daughter's hand so tightly as to make her cry, while her older brother smirked mischievously.

"You should be ashamed of yourself!" the woman roared. "My word, showing off smut like that! I'm going straight to the purser to report you, you... you pervert!"

After spewing her vitriolic volley at me, she roughly dragged her children away, leaving me stunned even more so than when I had hit the glass window at the suit shop.

"What the Hell was that all about?" I asked Petra, the barista working the coffee counter.

Petra, a Slovakian so slender as to be a perfect runway model, crossed her arms beneath her breasts and leveled a potent stare my way.

"Can't you control your dog?" she asked sarcastically.

"Oh, no," I moaned. "What did he do now?"

Petra pointed to a new easel proudly standing front and center in the café. There, at eye level for children, was the most pornographic Picasso I could have possibly imagined. Stifling a cry, I leapt over to it and flipped it around before anyone else would see it. The label on the back read *La femme avec le bracelet reçoit chouette et un chat.* I had presumed that meant a portrait, but oh was I wrong.

"*Woman with bracelet receives gentleman,*" I translated out loud.

Petra, who spoke French, nodded sarcastically at the savvy use of the word 'receives', then corrected mockingly, *"With a cat."*

"With a cat," I repeated, stunned.

Picasso had masterly used criss-crossing lines to depict in stunning detail a couple engaged in oral sex. With all her curling pubic hair etched using the cross-hatching technique, the fat, squatting woman's vagina looked like a honey-baked ham. The 'gentleman' wore a dandy's hat and a jacket, but was naked below the waist and his outrageously erect penis looked like a polish sausage with a head of garlic on top. Suddenly I understood why my ex-wife was a vegetarian. Above them a cat indifferently observed.

My shock led to a long, lingering moment of silence. I was jarred back to reality when the phone rang and Petra announced that the purser wanted to talk to me immediately.

Four days later and finally sporting a sharp new suit, I was a bit excited to hit the Promenade and hand out raffle tickets. Though not double-breasted, I loved my khaki jacket with a trim sport cut and its obvious Spanish overtones. I bought it from Romeo's in Lakewood, California, after all, where I was the only white guy shopping. I folded the collar of my bold yellow shirt over the jacket collar, and strut over to the Rolls.

Bill and Petra stood beside each other, but were not speaking. This was not particularly unusual, as Petra's breasts were decidedly of the A cup variety and therefore beneath Bill's attention. When I arrived, Petra looked me up and down approvingly. Bill, too, immediately reacted.

"What's with the collar, rico suave? Trying to make me look bad?"

"Like that's hard to do," I said. "After getting yelled at by the purser on your behalf, I would think you would grant me a reprieve from your grossly incompetent observations."

Bill harrumphed and returned to his occupation. This was not the handing out of raffle tickets, of course, but leering at passing women. Despite Petra's presence, he immediately smacked me on the arm to openly point at a young woman walking by.

"My God, will you look at that!"

A petite Asian continued on her merry way as if she had somehow not noticed Bill's blatantly boorish behavior. She was extremely beautiful, barely five feet tall and surely less than one hundred pounds, with black hair streaked in blonde. Her large dark eyes were boldly outlined in purple, which matched her snug dress. Despite her extreme natural beauty, however, both Bill and I were unable to look away from her most overt feature... for entirely different reasons.

"Those are the biggest tits I have ever seen!" Bill exclaimed approvingly. "They're perfect!"

Petra rolled her eyes, but had no need to elbow me in order to repudiate Bill's sentiment.

"Are you serious?" I protested. "She's made of more plastic than a Barbie doll. Those have to be at least, what, double D cup? They stick out like a shelf and look just as stiff. Why, I could put my drink on those! It's ludicrous."

"I'd put something more than a drink on those," he chortled. Seeing that I did not share his train of thought, Bill regarded me with disdain. "What, you don't like tits now?"

"I like real women," I replied. "Anyone can buy tits like those."

"What is it," Petra interrupted, "About you men? We really are just pretty toys to you, aren't we?"

"Bill wishes," I quipped.

Yet Petra continued with enough volume and scorn to capture our undivided attention.

"Just the other day in Catalina," she began, "I was on the pay phone in port. Some stranger *took a photograph* of my behind when I was not paying attention! Animals, I say!"

On cue, Bill and I both leaned over to regard her bottom. We were well aware of Petra's penchant for wearing skin-tight mini skirts. Most European chicks did, for which I was eternally grateful. How she could be shocked that men wouldn't respond, dignified or otherwise, was surprising.

"Well," I offered carefully, "It really is exquisite, after all. I've fought the urge to do the same myself."

"It probably *was* you, wasn't it Brian?" Bill asked. "You've been sucking up to Petra since she backed up your story that I put the Picasso up and not you. It makes sense though, because Petra has no tits. No wonder you like her."

Petra fired back with an icy reply, "I'll have you know that I was a lingerie model in Czech Republic."

But Petra's cold look washed off Bill like water off a duck's back. Surprisingly, however, he retreated from this battle, sensing he would not win. Instead he ignored her and returned to bashing me, which he no doubt thought easier. He observed my shirt collar folded over my suit jacket and said, "I get it now. You're gay. Just like goddamn Antonio Banderas, who denied it, too. I don't know which is worse: Doug and his fat, old Steiner or you and your 'no fake tits' crap. You really are gay, aren't you?"

Petra squeaked in alarm, then came to my defense. "I think he looks handsome."

"Thank you, Petra." Then I added with a sigh, "You know, Bill, being fashionable and heterosexual are not mutually exclusive. It merely means you want to look good."

"You don't need to look good when your cock's the size of a Chevy."

"It's just so much better if I pretend I didn't hear that," Petra said, rolling her eyes.

I muttered quietly to myself, "*Post hoc, ergo proptor hoc.*"

"*Gesundheit,*" Bill said. "What the Hell are you babbling now?"

"It's Latin," I explained. "It means 'after it, therefore because of it'. It's a Roman-era attempt at logic, but it's almost always wrong. Just because you first see me fashionable and then, later, not appreciating fake tits is not proof that I am gay."

"Latin?" Bill roared. "Just like goddamn Antonio Banderas. What, are you studying to be a priest now, too?"

"The irony of that statement is more galling than you know."

"I think," Bill added with a look of profound reflection scrunched onto his face, "We need to have you bang that Steiner boss."

Petra gave Bill a surprised look, then turned to gauge my reaction to the suggestion.

"What are you talking about?" I asked, not really wanting to know.

"The manager of the spa. The Bulgarian one. She's kinda pretty, though she has small tits, too. She was in the auctioneer's cabin during the handover. She wasn't supposed to still be there, and had to endure the walk of shame on her way out. You were busy shitting, as I recall."

15. MY NOT-SO-PRIVATE DANCER

Ensenada was what I expected from a small port town in Mexico close to the U.S. border. Happily it was not Americanized, but sadly the locals could have benefited from some of the entrepreneurial spirit that comes with it. This part of the Baja Peninsula was bereft of industry and completely unsuited to growing anything, and as such the city historically relied on its port. This meant either fishing or catering to cruisers. Most locals focused on the ease of the latter. It was a dirty, poor town, but full of vibrant life.

On a hot afternoon in late July, Bill and I sat by the street at a tiny, battered metal table at a tiny, battered restaurant. Though it was stiflingly hot, we sipped a popular local-style coffee: flavored with natural cinnamon and loaded with sugar and cream. I was tired from a long morning of wandering the streets and soaking up whatever culture I could glean from the fish markets. Bill was tired from a long night of drinking.

We didn't speak, having little enough in common, and quietly watched the passersby. It was a rare moment of peace, which I preferred over our usual haunt: a pool hall where we could escape the heat amid dark spaces and cold beer. But I knew this moment of quiet reflection was doomed to a short existence.

"Let's get a drink," Bill piped up suddenly. Yep, I could always count on Bill!

"I don't want a drink," I replied. "I'm gonna chill here awhile longer."

"I'll buy."

"I'll accept."

And so we went to Papas & Beer. This was a typical resort town drinking establishment along the lines of Señor Frog's, which featured a drunken frog, or Carlos & Charlie's, which featured drunken monkeys. Papas & Beer featured drunken papas, I guess. We heard it long before we saw it: a multi-story wooden monstrosity bristling with filthy decks wherever they could fit one, safely or otherwise. While I understood the huge inflatable beer bottle on the roof, I was perplexed by the many fat inflatable tubes zig-zagging across the facade. Pennants and banners fluttered madly in the hot wind, topped only by the chaos inside. I was reminded of the movie *Gladiator* and Maximus's first arena in north Africa.

And chaos it was. It was packed with cruisers from *Ecstasy* and day-trippers from San Diego, all who had mere hours to expunge their stress in one wild, frenetic orgy. The beat thumped so loudly that bottles shivered sideways on the bar, and the screams, oh the screams! The revelry apparently required shrieks to carry above the music, which was punctuated by shrill whistles that signaled everyone to down shots.

Bill waded into the crowd, while I placidly smoked a cigar and observed a strange ritual common to port parties such as this. An ugly, round Mexican man who looked distressingly like Sancho Panza wandered until he found a suitable victim for his fun. He blew piercingly on his whistle to signal the action was to begin, and pulled a middle-aged, portly American woman from her friends.

Standing behind her, Sancho pulled her head way back until she was bent nearly double, then poured a long, long shot of tequila directly into her mouth. Finally she spluttered to indicate that she could receive no more, so he clapped a sweaty hand over her mouth to shake her head. Without any warning, he flipped her into the air upside down and pushed her head between his legs. As she kicked frantically in the air, he gave her a few smacks on the ass before pretending to rub his face into her crotch.

Dazed and confused, the woman was set down to stagger back to her friends. Sancho Panza would then nod to her in thanks and work his way through the crowd for another victim. I watched him do this several times to women of all shapes and sizes, most of whom were much larger and heavier than he. I was impressed by his strength, but even more impressed that he didn't get his ass whooped.

I was bored by it all. This was all trite port party action, even if particularly well done. A change in the music signaled a water balloon fight that was surprisingly enjoyable, but for the fact that it doused my cigar. Annoyed but accepting, I worked my way up the rickety wooden steps to an upper deck where Bill was working over an attractive young woman.

"Ah, Brian!" he called loudly from afar. "This is Tina! Dance captain on *Ecstasy*!"

Tina was very pretty with high cheekbones sprinkled with the fairest hint of freckles. Her hair was bleached platinum blonde, parted down the middle and just long enough to curve under her dimpled chin. She had a beautiful smile and the smoothly muscled physique one would expect from the dance captain. Indeed, her thighs were powerful enough to crush a man, but I'm sure Bill had only reacted her impressive breasts.

As I approached, the music changed again to signal it was body shot time. Numerous bartenders had been discretely clearing the bars, and now I saw why: employees everywhere were shoving women up onto the counters. Sancho Panza's twin waddled over and, without ceremony, pushed Tina flat onto all sorts of unknown pools of sticky liquid. She squeaked, but acquiesced, as he yanked her shirt up to reveal her tight belly. Before our very eyes, Sancho Dos poured tequila so that it pooled in her navel. He paused a moment to regard his work dripping down Tina's defined abs, then gestured to all that she was ready to receive.

Bill pounced like a lion on a gazelle, crushing his lips onto her and grossly slobbering up the alcohol. Tina was a good sport, that is until Bill's hand slid up her body towards her breasts. She reared up and smacked him forcefully across the face. I could hear it from my distance. Sancho Dos guffawed and disappeared back into the crowd, his task accomplished. I finally neared as Tina sprung off the table and vaulted down the stairs.

"Well done, Bill!" I said, stepping up to him as he rubbed his jaw.

"That one packs a Hell of a punch!" he replied. "She could kick my ass any day!"

"No doubt she will!"

Later that day found me in the Society Bar at the back of the Promenade deck. *Ecstasy* was in port until morning, so my only task for the day was merely to schlepp tickets with Bill at the occasional guest still on board. I was exhausted from a long run on the track in the heat, having foolishly thought I was used to it by now. Every day I was hitting the weights and running several miles. It was wonderful to get back into my workout routine, but sapped my strength of some evenings.

I stood wavering before the cigar selection, too tired to read. While I nodded, nearly napping, suddenly there came a tapping, a gentle rapping upon my rear door. Petra was to meet me for a drink, but I hadn't expected to be greeted with a spank! I turned to accost her, but was even more surprised to see not Petra, but a small, mystery brunette. This man-handler grabbed my hand and drug me over to a love seat. Curious, I obligingly plopped down onto the leather beside her. Her brown eyes bored into mine as I waited to hear what she had to say.

"You should have a facial," she said in sharp English with a thick Bulgarian accent.

Ah, a Steiner! I should have known. I grinned and said, "Now that was one hell of a sales pitch!"

Her face was dominated by an exceptionally, almost alarmingly, long and sloping nose that was only just barely tamed by her fine features. Her dark hair was swept up in some sort of well-rolled sideways bun. I realized this was the Steiner boss whom Bill had mentioned earlier, who had endured the 'walk of shame' from the previous auctioneer's cabin.

"You are very handsome," she said, squeezing my hand. "I think you are an ideal candidate to model some of the treatments. I sell a lot more when I have a male model. You're perfect because you're still a macho guy: tall and strong, tanned and tattooed, always smoking a cigar."

The mere thought of Bill's verbal attacks should I partake of a facial at the spa already had me jumpy. An electric jolt of nerves flashed through me, and I suddenly sensed I was being watched. I glanced up to see Petra standing over us, eyes locked onto my hand held tightly by the other woman.

"Oh, uh, hi Petra!" I stammered. "I was just talking with... uh...?"

"Leonora," the Steiner replied. I became very self conscious about how she wouldn't release my hand.

"Talking," Petra repeated blandly. "Yes, I see that."

Had I been a lesser man, or a smarter one, I would have just blushed and gone with it. Instead I defended myself with perhaps the most moronic statement I could make. "Leonora wants to give me a work over."

"It certainly appears that way."

"A *makeover*," I quickly amended.

"Freudian slip?" Petra inquired with a fine brow raised.

Leonora released my hand and rose. She casually smoothed her skirt and gave Petra a long look. As she sashayed out, she called over her shoulder, "Think about my offer."

Petra immediately sat beside me and leveled a heavy gaze at me. An awkward moment commenced, but then she said, "You've been getting lots of offers, I see."

"What do you mean?"

Petra grabbed my hand and observed, "Your palms are sweating. First you're seeing Vladka, now you're seeing Leonora, and you asked to have a drink with me. Yet you claim you have a girlfriend."

"I do!" I protested. "I just thought a harmless drink would be nice and, wait, what did you say about Vladka?"

"You really do get around. If Bill were capable of seduction, I would expect that from him... but not you."

"I am *not* sleeping with Vladka!" I protested. "I hired her to pass out flyers for me. She's part of Camp Carnival and walks all the guest hallways anyway. It was a no-brainer."

"Whatever you say," Petra replied sweetly, patting our held hands.

"Really, Petra," I defended. "It's all about my Bianca."

"Bill says differently."

"Bill would. He's just jealous because I'm so vastly superior to him."

Suddenly that sense that we were being watched flared up again. Sure enough, I looked up to see Bill towering over us. A wave of deja vu washed over me as Petra released my hand and rose, precisely as had Leonora, and smoothed her skirt. With an uncanny repetition, Petra gave Bill a long look, and sashayed out with a devilish comment called over her shoulder, "Think about my offer."

Bill's flat stare at me changed at hearing her parting words, and he chortled, "Oh, you dog, I knew you were bangin' her!"

"That was weird," I said to him, referring to the deja vu. "You're not going to try to hold my hand, too, are you?"

"Ticket time, bitch," Bill ordered, obviously preferring to ignore my comment. "Let's go. On the way you can tell me how it is to screw two European chicks in one day."

With a sigh, I rose and followed him to the Rolls Royce. Time passed slowly, as there were few enough guests around. The sun began to set, and the hot yellow glare slanted into warmer, orange streams that ran the length of the deck. Bill and I enjoyed the tranquility of the scene in silence for while, but then occurred a rare moment of disclosure when Bill commented about the days of old.

"No more lone wolf days," he began simply. "They're about gone, so enjoy them while you can."

I waited for him to continue, sensing that this would be an all too infrequent opportunity to learn something from him.

"When I started, I was a DJ, you know. Gene was one of the very first auctioneers working for Frederick. There weren't two hundred of us, but only a few. We met in the club. Gene was selling art using all the old used-car tricks, wearing his Uncle Sam suit and even honking a horn to get attention, if you can believe that shit. We got to talking and when he learned that was my second contract he offered me the job on the spot. I was American, see, and had actually returned to ships. That was the greatest hurdle in those days, because non-entertainer Americans don't last more than a few weeks at sea.

"We were lone wolves in those days, leaving the pack for a new forest every week. We had to learn on our own, learn to adapt or die. We had no background, no knowledge, no staff, no structure: just hunger and instinct and the will to survive.

"Now we have all those things, *and* training, *and* assistants. Each new addition, each step closer to organization, takes another bite out of our commissions. In those days, Sundance was so desperate for bodies to work the ships that we made double what we make now, but sold half as much. But things are changing. As they develop the infrastructure, they retain a greater chunk of the money. This is the last hurrah, my friend: enjoy it. Soon this business will be clogged with associates jockeying for advancement like every other goddamn cubicle office job.

"Is this why you refuse to train me, then?" I asked. "Because you never had any help yourself. During auctions I'm too busy with my own duties so there's only so much I can observe and replicate. How about a word or two of help, something that you wish you had had?"

"I taught you all you need to know already," Bill said gruffly.

"All you said was to not lie!" I protested. "That's a no-brainer."

Bill harrumphed and muttered, "Only to a goddamn Boy Scout."

To signal that the moment of clarity was over, Bill barked at a group of three sexy young women walking by, "Free raffle tickets for the art auction!"

One of the women, a tall and slender blonde, broke from her girlfriends and slid right up to me. As she approached her lips curved into mischief and her eyes glinted. She came within inches of me, so close her peppermint breath wafted over me as she asked slyly, "Do I want tickets?"

"You want it alright," I teased. "There will be art, champagne, and me. What more could you ask for?"

"What more could I ask for?" she repeated. Lashes lustrous with black mascara flitted as she glanced down to my mouth. "You're right!"

Suddenly she grabbed the lapels of my suit and pulled herself in for a big, wet kiss right on my lips. Her girlfriends howled in approval for the long kiss. She released me, smoothed my lapels affectionately and replaced my shirt outside the suit's collar with red-tipped fingernails. Then she plucked a handful of tickets from my nerveless grasp and spun about.

"Nice suit," she commented as she wiggled all curvy and sexy back to her girlfriends, who welcomed her back with giggles and knowing smiles.

I turned to say something victorious to Bill, but he was busy folding his shirt collar atop his suit.

Being a rockstar isn't as easy as one would think. My so-called frustration revolved around not having the freedom to completely embrace my 'celebrity'. As ludicrous as it sounds, the babes became a burden. Remaining celibate for my Bianca had always been a privilege and a pleasure, and almost easy. We had such a chemical connection that it could never, ever be topped by a quick bang from a stranger, regardless of who she was. Well, true, I was never tested by Angelina Jolie, but as a waiter on Carnival ships, gorgeous foreign women sought me out in hopes of a Green Card. I was offered anything and everything a man could want, but always said no. Somehow on *Ecstasy* things proved a bit more complex.

It all revolved around the dance captain.

A week after first observing Tina at Papas & Beer, I met her in the crew mess. She was sitting alone before a dry salad, and looked positively bored. Having come for coffee, I brought my steaming brew beside her for a little small talk.

"Good morning," I said, picking some mysterious bits from my supposedly clean plastic cup. It was actually noon, but I had no doubt it was morning to her. Her sunken eyes and pale, tight lips said as much.

"Oh, you're Bill's gay boy."

I suffered a flashback to the Widow Maker and Shawn's assistants, Denny and Jesse.

"A dry salad?" I asked. "That's not very American."

"Huh?"

"Most Americans drown their salad in fat and sugar," I explained.

"Not if they are dancers," Tina replied grimly, pushing some painfully browned lettuce around her plate. "But ships have nothing else healthy for the crew, and we are supposed to stay skinny. You going out?"

"I am," I replied. "Today I opted to eschew the titty bar in favor of Ensenada's indigenous flora and fauna."

She stared blankly at me a moment, then nodded in understanding. "Oh, so *you're* the faithful one I keep hearing about."

"Wow," I muttered, blinking. "How on Earth did you get that from what I just said?"

"Rumor has it there is a smart, faithful one on board. I have no idea what you just said means, so..."

I resisted the urge to say 'post hoc ergo proptor hoc.'

"Well, maybe I'll run into you later," she said. "I'll be at Papas. See ya."

"OK," I said as I rose. "Ciao."

"Ciao?" she teased. "That's not very American."

"Touché!"

"Huh?"

I left her there, but didn't run into her until that night at the crew bar while looking for Bill. Bill, bless him, doesn't want connection, only penetration, so the crew bar was his nightly haunt. I arrived at about eleven, knowing there would be few enough people present, for at this hour the restaurant staff was all still working. Barring a few Italian officers huddling together in a corner, the only occupied table was filled with dancers and musicians. A quick glance through the dark room verified Bill's absence, but Tina caught my eye and called out loudly to me, "I'm bored. I want to do something exciting!"

"Steal a car," I suggested, approaching.

"Just because I'm in Mexico doesn't mean I want to steal a car," she replied, giggling.

"Well, when in Rome..." I joked, but trailed off when I saw the very large, very Mexican musician sitting next to her. A hugely intimidating man, easily two hundred and fifty pounds of tattooed muscle, he glared at me openly until I was uncomfortable. Then the long and rather creepy goatee clinging to his chin began to waggle as he laughed.

"Join us!" Tina cried, holding up a beer from the surplus on the table. Considering the group consisted predominantly of dancers, how could I not? I sat at the corner next to Tina, Carrie the singer, and Josh the bass player.

Though from Vancouver, Carrie oozed her Irish heritage with pale skin and long, flowing copper locks bound up tightly. Her figure was lithe, revealing her energetic personality translated into athletics. I had not initially recognized her, for on stage she wore a bobbed platinum wig. Though Carrie's job required a glamourous look, her interests lay elsewhere and our heads were close together as we conferred about wilderness hikes. Amusingly, I noted more than one jealous glance from Tina. Most likely she just liked being the center of attention. Certainly the huge musician gave her enough.

The bass player lived in San Diego and, despite being Mexican, insisted his name was Josh. I quickly dubbed him Joshua Tree because of his immense size and hairy arms. He wore a button-down shirt with the sleeves torn off to reveal trunk-like arms sleeved entirely with wild and unruly ink. Upon his knuckles were letters, but I could never make out what they were in the dark, smoky atmosphere. Joshua Tree's focus was entirely devoted to Tina, who regally deigned to give him just enough attention to keep him obedient.

I had planned on a late-night cigar on the open deck, and happened to have a stick with me. Tina, seeing her chance for my undivided attention, snatched up my cigar and began playing with it with a great lack of subtlety. With great relish she fondled it and caressed it with her lips. When that failed to get me hot and bothered, she threw it at me. Joshua Tree, however, had been utterly absorbed in her flirtatious behavior. Upon the end of the symbolically explicit performance, he actually shook his head to clear it, like a dog casting off water.

"You know how to tell if a cigar is a real Cuban?" he asked me, loudly clearing of his throat. "It smells like elephant shit."

"A brilliant insight," I replied gravely. "I feel ashamed to admit that regretfully, to date, I have not yet smelled elephant shit."

"Oh, that's right, you're American," he said, as if Mexico obviously had herds of wild elephants. "Your loss."

"No doubt."

Josh shifted beneath the table and reacted sharply. He bit back a bellow of pain, then propped up his leg with a wince.

"Oh!" Tina cried, "Did you hit your hurt ankle?"

She leaned into him, and no doubt his pain vanished. But he obviously didn't want to let such desirable sympathy disappear too quickly.

"I was running today in Ensenada," he explained casually. "No more of that!"

I frowned with understanding and concern. "Why, what happened?"

"The sidewalks are so damned uneven, I tripped. Stupid Mexican streets. I fell hard, man, and smashed up my ankle pretty bad. I stayed on the ground, catchin' my breath, and took off my shoe to rub my ankle. Can you believe that some goddamn Mexicans stole my shoes!"

"What? Come on."

"Can you believe that shit? Three of them. One grabbed the shoe from the ground, and another hit me on the back of the head. Not very hard, because he was so goddamn small, but he flashed a knife and his buddy told me they only wanted my other shoe. They didn't even ask for my money, not that I had any. Goddamn, dirty Mexicans."

"Aren't you Mexican?" I asked.

"Yeah, but I ain't a goddamned *dirty* Mexican," he clarified with profound insight. "Whose ever heard of a Mexican wearing size 13 running shoes?"

"Well pluck my chicken," I agreed in wonder. "That is officially bizarre."

"Yeah, and I was just getting back into running," Josh lamented. "I gained a lot of weight when I had to stop running from a knee injury. I was in a bicycle accident and just about ripped off my kneecap."

Both Carrie and Tina gave desired squeaks of concern, so Josh continued. "My knee swelled up like a balloon and grew into this huge hematoma. It was horrible, filled with all sorts of nasty blood and shit. This was in San Diego, so the doctor was great. When he cut into the hematoma, the blood had already turned dead and black. It smelled awful, man, stank up the whole damn room."

Tina began giggling.

It began softly, but soon grew into snorting efforts at control. Josh paused his horror story and all three of us stared at her as she snickered louder and louder. Finally Tina could contain herself no longer, and burst forth with laughter like a river gleefully jumping its banks.

With all the social grace of a child, she blurted, "Your knee *farted!*"

I glanced at Josh. I glanced at Carrie. Had I really just heard that? It seemed all too apparent that I had, yet both my companions ignored the outburst. Josh continued with his story as if nothing had been said at all, while Carrie hung upon his every word. It was a marvel how they they maintained composure in the face of such a moronic statement. I had to excuse myself before I lost my control. I stepped outside of the crew bar, into the fresh air, and bellowed out a laugh. It was so forceful I frightened a couple of room stewards who happened by. Oh, how I dreaded to be judged by the company I kept!

⚓

Yet nightly, inexorably, I began to join this trio at the crew bar. I was far from a crew bar ghost in the manner of oh so many lost souls at sea, but being openly courted by a couple of sexy entertainers is a slippery slope. While many dancers rotated in and out like Steiners, the core of our little corner became Tina, Carrie, Josh and I.

From the outside, our group likely appeared as two men and two women sharing a table, wherein focus tends to shift into two would-be couples. The dynamic was not that simple, however. I was present primarily because of Carrie and our shared interest in nature. Tina, as quickly became apparent, was jealous of the attention Carrie received and tried to get more of mine. Josh worshipped Tina and was jealous of the attention I received from her.

Tina was used to being the object of universal desire among men on *Ecstasy*. This was understandable, as she was the dance captain and had the gymnast's body that comes with it. But she was thrown off that my interest in her, as with all of *Ecstasy's* women, was entirely platonic. Tina wanted the only man aboard who didn't want her and, as she said to her confidants, she decided to 'bag the brain'.

This manifested itself quite obviously, and the entire crew quickly assumed that we were bunking up. My protestations mattered not at all, and certainly Bill was quick to compliment me in front of others for my apparent sexual conquest, followed by a quick expectation of assistance in doing the same. True, Tina was gorgeous, but she was just so incredibly childish I could not think of her as a woman.

Indeed, the social circles of a cruise ship are remarkably like high school: everybody wanted what they couldn't have. Joshua Tree was jealous of me and Tina. Indeed, so was Bill and every other male on-board. Tina was jealous of me and Carrie, or me and Petra, or even the tenacious rumor of me and Vladka. The more it became clear I didn't want Tina, the harder she tried to get me. Finally, after years of wondering what it would be like, I learned what it felt like to be considered a mere piece of meat.

One evening, before the entertainers' late-night stage performance, I was in the crew bar chatting with Bill about work. Tina swept through the room with Josh in tow, and came right up to our table. The song changed and, with great showmanship, Tina insisted on dancing. She stood before us and worked herself over to great effect. Bill openly stared, as I would expect, while Josh just stood back and observed in silence. Suddenly Tina pulled me from my seat and began using me as a stripper pole. I stood stiff, pardon the pun, and somewhat resistant, as she rubbed her amazingly pert bottom all over me.

The song ended, and Tina boldly announced, "We are going to bed now."

"Oh no we're not!" I replied with an unlikely mixture of flirtation and aversion.

"Then at least give me a kiss," she pleaded, face close to mine.

"I will not."

Her lips puckered into a pout, but then she pushed away, stating, "I *will* win, Mr. Brain."

Josh just looked me straight in the eye and said with flat sincerity, "I want to be you for just one minute."

But the entertainers had time for just one drink. As they rose to leave, I commented to Bill that I was going to the sports deck for a late night jog in the cooler air. Tina would have none of it, however, and demanded that I watch her show.

"But I've seen all your shows," I defended.

"Not this one," she replied with a grin. "You won't want to miss this one. Bill, you're coming, right?"

He nodded over his double Jack Daniels, and that was that.

Half an hour later I sat beside Bill in the main lounge, on the first floor near the wings. The show was the usual mixture of music and dancing; some routines were Vegas-style acts with Tina leading a line of dancers kicking like feathered showgirls, while others depicted Carrie singing in a series of sequined gowns. I had never been interested in dance, to be honest, perhaps in part because I was so horrible at it. Not only had I no rhythm myself, I was incapable of even getting it when watching professionals flaunting it. It was fun to identify the various performers as friends of mine, to be sure, but I must admit I listened to the music more than anything else.

But the announcer changed all of that.

"LADIES AND GENTLEMEN," a thunderous voice called over the hushed, darkened theatre. "ECSTASY'S ENTERTAINERS SHALL NOW PRESENT YOU WITH A REMARKABLE DILEMMA."

Startlingly, the lights burst over the crowd to illumine nearly one thousand curious souls. But this did not signal that the show was not over; it was just beginning a new, oh-so awful segment. Carrie and her singing partner Carlo stepped onto the brightly lit stage in tuxedos with swallow-tails and black top hats. With large gestures, they pantomimed a deep visual search of the audience by raising a hand to shield their eyes. I thought little enough of it, until Bill suddenly stood up beside me and began waving his hands over his head.

"What the Hell are you doing?" I cried.

"Volunteering," he answered smugly. My stomach sank as I knew damn good and well he wasn't volunteering himself for anything. Sure enough, Carrie leapt down into the audience and grabbed my hand. She pulled me from my chair and led me reluctantly up the steps, only to have Carlo assist in dragging me center stage.

"THIS GENTLEMAN STANDS FORTH," the announcer continued melodramatically, "TO SEEK THE PRIZE."

The lights over the audience dimmed, while the singers released my arms and melted into the shadows. Now the limelight bore down on me with the power of a thousand suns. Under that searing, soul-revealing spotlight, I felt ridiculous. I was used to being on stage before large crowds, delivering introductions at the beginning of a cruise. But that involved a line of reluctant vendors, each with only a moment to step forward and talk at a largely uncaring crowd. But this was me, and me alone, and I could feel everyone's focus on me. Thank goodness I still had my suit on, because I had almost changed into my shorts and to reveal my chicken legs would be to die a thousand deaths. Within a minute I would want to die, anyway.

"BUT IS HE WORTHY OF THE PRIZE?" the voice continued. "WILL HIS OFFERING PLEASE THE LADY OF LIGHT?"

Though blinded by the main spotlight, I sensed other beams roving across the stage as two lines of female dancers rushed from the wings to cross before me. As the dancers converged around me and spun away in neat lines of pirouettes, a single blue beam of light glowed upon a new figure. Tina, body caressed by a seductively tight body-suit of glittering stars, teasingly entered the periphery of the stage. Her dance was cut with a strobe light, making her nimble movements twinkle like the night sky. The music oozed a mysterious, night-sky vibe.

Alarm bells went off in my head when the music began to morph into a decidedly pop music beat. The bass grew louder and louder, and my heart inched lower and lower, dropping all the way into my bowels when I began to recognize the world-famous bass line.

"BEFORE HE ENJOYS THE PRIZE," the voice boomed, "HE MUST PAY THE PRICE OF DANCE!!!"

The Bee Gee's *Stayin' Alive* burst forth from the bass line, and the crowd roared with approval. All spotlights converged on me, and I was obviously expected to dance. Oh, the horror! At first I just stood there, frozen in fear, but the dancers converged over and around me, prodding me to move. The audience began chanting the words of the song, and my face became so red that surely it was visible through the white-hot spotlight!

Hapless and helpless, I had to embrace my fate. Reluctantly I began to imitate John Travolta's *Saturday Night Fever* to the best of my feeble ability. What else could I do, but ham it up? My dignity had already been shredded by a thousand knives.

I don't know how long I was out there, shaking my hips and jabbing the sky to the rhythm of the Bee Gees, but surely it was less than the 13.7 billion years it felt like. Sometime around the ten billion year-mark, when the Earth slowly coalesced from the devastating loneliness of space, so, too, did my ordeal end. The dancers streamed off stage and the bass line faded, to be replaced once again by the starry night music. Tina waited in the far corner of the stage, glittering and magical and gorgeous in her blue glow.

"THE LADY OF LIGHT PONDERS HIS OFFERING," the narrator explained over the swooshing, cosmic mood music. I stood there, panting and humiliated, yet also terrified of what might come next.

"HAS HE EARNED THE PRIZE... OR WILL HE BE REBUFFED?"

Suddenly Tina spun in a long series of cartwheels. The blue strobe and her glittering bodysuit gave her graceful movements an entrancing, shimmering quality as she whirled across the stage like a shooting star. She whirled to a stop directly before me and, with barely a pause, grabbed me bodily. With an amazing display of her supple yet powerful physique, Tina forcefully dipped me and planted a deep, long kiss right on the lips. The music swelled in celebration as I lay back, completely at her mercy. My vision swam and the crowd applauded, but I swear I heard an annoyed plunk from a bass guitar.

I was then wrenched back up to my feet, stunned and dizzy. Tina twirled about me, trailing a finger across my chest, and whispered in my ear before she spun off into the dark once more. I blinked and stood there like a deer in headlights, when the stage lights rose and the singers, Carrie and Carlo, escorted me back to my seat with shaky legs.

"What did she say to you?" Bill asked when I got back.

Numbed from the entire experience, I answered, "She said 'I won.'"

After the show, Bill and I went to the crew bar to meet Tina, Carrie, and any other pretties who wanted to share a laugh at my expense. I was a good sport, if annoyed that my pathetic dancing promised to live in infamy long after this cruise. As a conciliatory gesture, Tina bought me a drink. Then another, and another, and before we knew it the lights came on, signaling the close of the crew bar. At a quarter to three in the morning, we decided to raid the crew mess.

I followed the stream of sweaty, slender dancers through the corridors, wondering if I would be able to find anything to eat other than bread and ketchup. Tina tapped me on the shoulder and said, "I need to get something from my cabin. Come with me real quick?"

"Sure," I replied, following her down a narrow side corridor and into her cabin. Being the dance captain provided Tina with her own cabin, small as it was. I sat at a makeup table bristling with bottles and containers and tubes and brushes and lipsticks and glitter and all-around secret babe-stuff.

"Good God," I commented, picking up a new tube filled with an arcane recipe for controlling men. "Did you have to go to school to learn how to use all these?"

She snatched the tube out of my hand with mock severity, but I was already exploring the other mysterious potions and alchemical concoctions on the table.

"Body Butter?" I asked. "What's Body Butter? If anything here involves bacon, I'm yours forever."

Tina gave me a sour look and using a red-tipped fingernail, pointed for me to return the item. I complied with a shrug, which was a mistake. As I set it down, I knocked over a huge box of Q-tips. The little swabs shot out of the box to rain down everywhere, scattering over her bunk, floor, and into every fold of every article in her laundry basket.

"Brian!" she criticized sharply.

I mumbled an apology and dropped down to pick up my mess from her laundry basket. Laughing, we dug through her clothing, gathering up Q-tips by the dozen. I was about to comment on a particularly seductive pair of panties, when it happened. We kissed. Tina grabbed me, actually, but I must admit that I was about to. The moment was too perfect to pass up.

We rolled across the floor, kissing and panting and grabbing. It was not passion, but aggression. Our kisses were lip-crushing violent, and our bodies pressed into each other and smashed into furniture. Tina was a powerful woman and she fought savagely for dominance. It was hot and primal, and I battled with a head dizzy from the scent of her sweat and the taste of her salt. I don't even remember what I was doing, but could only focus on her fingernails tearing my flesh and ripping my clothing.

Yet suddenly I was overcome by a moment of calm, serene clarity. The ferocity and immediacy of our sexuality faded, and I realized that I didn't want this. I pulled back from her, dodging clutching hands but unable to unlock myself from between her powerful dancer's thighs.

"What's wrong?" Tina panted.

"I can't do this," I answered, pulling away. "It was a mistake."

"Are you kidding me?" she snarled.

"I have a girlfriend," I explained. "I should never have gotten going. I'm sorry."

Tina regarded me skeptically for a long moment. Our hearts thumped in our chests, but slowly eased back to sanity. Finally she said, "I see."

We rose shakily to our feet and silently re-buttoned buttons and re-zipped zippers. Numerous parts of my anatomy burned from her scratching, particularly below my navel and the nape of my neck. Blood actually trickled from lacerations criss-crossing my shoulders and neck.

"Let's get to the crew mess, then," Tina said simply.

Our friends had long since retired, leaving Tina and I to scrounge through the crew mess ourselves. We cobbled together some peanut butter and jelly sandwiches, and sat tiredly across from each other. Our actions had been so fierce that we could not have been more exhausted even had we fully consummated the act. More than just moving like zombies, our skin had a death-like pallor from the light bouncing off the empty white tables. Our love-wounds glowed red.

My mind raged. Why had I begun? Why had I stopped? Would this keep Tina from stalking me? Would I carry guilt from this?

Strangely, what began to dominate my mind was a shoe commercial. I kept seeing a solitary man running an empty stretch of road, oblivious to the storm that raged around him. Go Nike, Brian: just do it. How on Earth was it even *possible* to stop so close to having sex with Tina? But I had merely been going through the motions. If I had been younger, or less experienced, I surely would have gone all the way. But after the passion and chemicals of Bianca, simply nothing else was worth the effort. I categorically did not want Tina. I wanted Bianca.

I don't know if Tina won, but I knew I lost. We chewed in silence.

16. FIRE WALK WITH ME

The next night I reluctantly sat at our table in the crew bar. I had to deal with the Tina situation sooner or later, and had chosen the former. Carrie was the first to arrive, and was quietly sipping a beer. She gave me a huge grin when I arrived, but quickly discarded it in favor of the gossip I knew was coming.

"Tina's very angry with you," she said.

"You think?"

"Did you really *not* go all the way last night?"

"It was a mistake," I replied. "I have a girlfriend, you know."

"Several, it seems."

I was getting used to my protestations being dismissed out of hand. Yet, barring last night's near miss, all I had done was flirt with a few women. People could bitch and moan all they wanted, but I simply refused to believe that public flirtation equals penetration.

Tina arrived with Joshua Tree in tow. Wary of the dance captain, I tried to focus on Carrie as if this were just another night and we were all hanging out, but Tina would have none of it. Suddenly I understood how a woman feels when a guy won't leave her alone. She babbled unceasingly about all sorts of inane things, gossip, and fart jokes. She was trying to lure me into conversation, but was about as intelligent as an ice cube. No wonder she liked me!

But I was here to bury the hatchet, so we shared some beers and kept things light. Actually, Tina was in a grand mood, beaming and bouncing as if she had won the lottery. She kept the pedal to the metal on the fun, and her stories bubbled with enthusiasm. And tricks. I caught her secretly switching my half-empty beers with full bottles. Obviously she was trying to get me drunk. The time flew so pleasantly that I let her. When the ladies left together for the powder room, Josh gave me a satisfied smile.

"Tina is happier than I have ever seen her," he said approvingly. No doubt he knew nothing of my final, ignominious retreat.

"Josh..." I began, but he cut me off.

"Take care of her and treat her right," he warned with tremendous gravity. He cracked his massive, scarred, and tattooed knuckles for emphasis.

The ladies returned, with Tina toting a square blue box marked with a circle cut into multi-colored wedges. I groaned, recognizing it immediately. A world of hurt awaited me.

Tina slammed the box on the table and cried, "Let's play Trivial Pursuit! They have the Genius Edition!"

I cringed, thinking of the years in my youth spent playing the original *Genus* Edition.

"What's the point?" I squeaked faintly.

"To prove you aren't as smart as you think you are," she replied brightly.

"Well then," I boomed with intentional smugness. "Good luck with that!"

"Here," she said. "Have another beer."

Carrie and Josh were game, however, so of course I joined them. This was my favorite game in the world, after all. We opened the box and cleared the table of bottles to make room for the board. While Josh set up the pieces, Tina snatched up the box of question cards and randomly selected one.

"A sample question to get our brain juices flowing," she said, scanning the questions. "Ha! How 'bout this: *What was the name of Sir Isaac Newton's dog?*"

Carrie snorted, and Josh hesitantly warned Tina, "I don't think this is going to be much fun."

"How about you, *Mr. Brain*?" Tina challenged, dripping mockery. "Think you're so smart now?"

"Diamond," I answered. This time I tried desperately *not* to sound smug. All three of them stared at me, open-mouthed.

"Now I *know* this isn't going to be much fun," Josh quietly whined.

"How the Hell did you know that?" Carrie marveled.

"I used to play this game with my brother," I explained. "That was the very first question we read, and we got scared that everything would be that hard. They're not, so don't worry. But I will always remember that one."

Tina frowned and muttered, "Maybe I should have given you shots all night instead of beer."

The game ready, we began. Tina went first, and Carrie read aloud her question.

"*What is in popcorn that makes it pop?*"

Tina giggled and blurted, "Sperm!"

Chuckling, Carrie asked, "Anybody else know the answer?"

I waited, but with no other takers, I said, "The answer is water."

Glares ensued, and Tina stuck her tongue out at me. We moved on to Josh's turn. Tina read out, "*Who was Minihaha's husband?*"

Josh cleverly asked, "Mini-hoho?"

I laughed, and Josh beamed at his successful joke. Tina, however, was bent on proving her point. "Mr. Brain?"

I sighed and said, "Hiawatha."

"Oh, come on!" Tina cried, throwing up her hands. "How could you know that?"

"I grew up in a town called Hiawatha," I explained. "It's a suburb of Cedar Rapids, Iowa."

"See Tina?" Carrie chided. "There'll be no living with him now."

Yet the game proved to be a lot of fun for us all, once the three of them teamed up against me. After drinks and laughs, the night drew to a close. Apparently having heard about my encounter with Tina last night, Josh had abandoned his usual, lustful focus on the dancer and focused on the singer. As we left, Josh and Carrie skipped arm-in-arm, playing and joking closely as they had all night. As the two continued ahead, Tina pulled me to a stop before the side hall to her cabin. She trailed a fingertip teasingly across my chest.

"Will you come with me tonight?"

I paused, searching for an appropriate answer to her loaded question. She just grabbed my hand and led me to her cabin. While she fished through her purse for the key, I struggled to dash any shoe commercials from my mind. I resolved through my alcoholic haze to just have a good time and go with the flow. I'd just have to deal with the fallout later.

Tina finally unlocked the door, just as her neighbor happened by. He was a painfully skinny, big-eared British chap from the gift shop. Tina latched onto him with both hands and said, "I need to talk to you."

Two seconds later she had hauled him bodily into her cabin and slammed the door shut in my face. I blinked at it for a blurry moment, then roared with laughter.

A few days later, after a long auction, I was relaxing in the blessedly Bill-free lounge on the Promenade deck when Carrie happened by. It was formal night, so she wore a beautiful, flowing green dress that looked smashing with her flowing, coppery tresses. She invited me to join her in an hour for the late comedy show, being performed by a guest comedian. I freshened up and put on my khaki suit over a black silk shirt. I was looking and feeling good. Why, just a month ago I was sweating and stressing over my career and money, but now life was in every way rich and leisurely. Despite the booty calls, I really was living the good life.

Now *that's* a phrase I never expected to say!

I was surprised Carrie met me for the show alone, figuring a host of entertainers would join us. We had a grand time, laughing until our sides hurt, and afterwards decided to keep the fun going at the crew bar. Our usual table was overflowing with the dance troupe, and we 'paced ourselves' with the drinking. For entertainers, that meant drinking at a *fast* pace, of course.

Suddenly Carrie's male singing partner, Carlo, rose to his feet and ripped off his wig with enthusiasm. Though wearing a handsome men's suit, his face was made up as a woman's: lipstick, eyeliner and all. His dark skin contrasted strikingly with his favorite Marilyn Monroe wig.

"It is time for the disco!" he cried, to much applause.

I had never been in a cruise ship disco with guests before, and was excited to experience it. I followed the flashy line of glittering dresses and sharp suits towards the Promenade deck, but suddenly everyone piled up like traffic around an accident. There was enough commotion at the front of the line that I could not see what caused it, but I had a good guess.

"You're going to the disco?" I heard Tina holler over the drunken buzz of our group. "Why didn't you tell me?"

"Yeah, come on," Carrie replied cheerily. "Let's go!"

"But I didn't dress up!" Tina cried. "I haven't done my makeup, nothing! Why do you always do this to me? Why don't you want me there?"

"You said you needed a nap," Carrie answered. "So I went to the comedy show. What, you wanted me to leave in the middle to call you?"

"Who'd you go with?"

The line rippled, indicating that Tina was bringing the drama to the back. I was not particularly thrilled about that. Neither was anybody else, for dancers melted away to find their own path to the Promenade. As soon as Tina saw me, she marched right up and waggled a finger under my nose.

"You went with Carrie to the show, didn't you?"

I leaned back, surprised at the ferocity of her onslaught. I shouldn't have been surprised, however. The lacerations all over my body from before still ached.

"Why wouldn't I?," I replied innocently. "I assumed you'd be there, too."

"Well I would assume so, too!" she snapped. "Thanks for checking, *dear*."

Tina's words dripped with tremendous venom. I received the full brunt of Tina's displeasure, and kept waiting for Carrie to step in front of me protectively, in the manner so pleasantly demonstrated by Rebecca de Mornay in Pittsburgh. But it was not meant to be, and there was nothing really more to say. Tina stormed off in a huff, and Carrie and I went to the disco.

The disco was a great time, a whirlwind of pumping music and erotic dancing. I had nothing to do with that last part, of course, but was thoroughly entranced by the dancers cutting loose beneath the disco ball. Male, female, heterosexual, homosexual, transvestite, or otherwise, they were a pulsing mob of gorgeous limbs and torsos working each other over. The guests in the club were in as much awe as I.

Because the disco was smoke free, there were many cigarette breaks at the aft bar of the Promenade. A smoky corner of the Society Bar was taken over and whenever the dancers needed to catch their breath they would ironically come here for a smoke. Entertainers rotated in and out constantly, though usually the musicians lingered because of the many Steiners present.

Since I was not a dancer by any stretch of the imagination, I lingered as well. I smoked a long, leisurely cigar and joined many a conversation before they turned private and a newly-formed couple would wander off for a dirty dance in the disco or, more likely, in the cabin. Carrie spent a lot of time drinking and chatting with me. At first I thought she simply felt obligated to be a good host, or remorse for the drama I was sure to get from Tina. But as time flowed, and the shots, too, we found ourselves specifically enjoying each other's company.

Eventually the disco closed for the night, and our smoking corner swelled with bodies. To my great amusement Leonora, the spa manager, wedged herself between Carrie and I. Without ceremony she downed my drink and leaned drunkenly into me.

"Hi Brian!" she blurted drunkenly. Then she fell face-first into my lap.

I leaned back and held my arms up, surprised.

But it was Carrie who spoke first. "A little premature for that, don't you think, Leonora?"

Leonora pulled herself up awkwardly, pawing me roughly in the process, then blearily glanced at Carrie. These women were a study in opposites. Carrie sat regally and composed in her emerald gown, despite having downed more shots of tequila than even Joshua. Leonora, on the other hand, had long-since unlaced her disheveled blouse from sweaty dances with who-knows-who. A long tear in her fishnet stockings traced her thigh.

Leonora guffawed at her own behavior, and stated the obvious. "I'm so drunk!"

"Why of course you are, dear," I said to her sweetly.

"Not as drunk as last night, though," she boasted. "Last night I was so drunk that I started kissing Carlo!"

Carrie laughed. "Carlo? Was he in his Marilyn wig?"

"He was in a suit," Leonora defended with a sway in her seat that nearly dropped her to the floor. "I think."

"That's the second gay guy you've been macking on this week," Carrie chided. "But I don't think you'll find any luck with Brian, either."

"Whose Brian?" she asked, blinking heavily as she looked around.

"Finally my reputation does not precede me," I deadpanned. But Leonora was a handful and I had to endure several minutes of come-ons and groping before I could excuse myself. By that time, Carrie had disappeared.

Though Carrie held her alcohol well, I knew she was tanked. Before I retired, I wanted to make sure she got back to her cabin all right. Upon reaching her cabin, I found the door wide open and she was not inside. Her laughter tinkled from across the hall. The door behind me was also wide open, and I recognized it as the guest comedian's cabin. The old man sat upon the chair heavily, like a grandfather spinning yarns to a cluster of children before a fireplace. Carrie and two other ladies lay strewn across his bed, listening with rapt attention.

They waved me in, and the wrinkled, white-haired comedian offered me a cup of coffee.

"I always bring the real deal," he said, rising to pour me a cup. "Ship coffee is like paint thinner."

"I quite agree," I said, taking the steaming brew. It smelled delicious and tasted even better.

"But not fresh thinner, mind you," the man clarified gravely. "Had the captain himself painted a masterpiece called 'Black ship at night', and put all his brushes into an old mason jar filled with thinner; even that fails to describe it. But the crud that settles on the bottom of the jar? That, my friend, is ship coffee."

"Profound," I congratulated. "I see you've given this a lot of thought."

"Part of my contract with Carnival is that I have a coffee machine in my cabin," he explained. "I don't drink and I'm too old for sex. So, on ships, that leaves only good conversation and good coffee."

"Both rare commodities among crew," I agreed.

Carrie patted the bed beside her. I climbed onto the bed to lay next to her. Time flew as the comedian made us laugh and laugh, and laugh some more. Like many comedians on ships, his shows for guests were necessarily family-oriented and, thusly, clean. But in his own cabin with his own private audience, the comedian let loose with all sorts of jokes about sex, politics, and religion. His grateful audience was already primed with alcohol, so it was a grand exhibit. We were shocked when he announced it was nearly 4 a.m. and time for him to retire.

Carrie's drink had finally caught up with her, and I helped her across the hall to her room. Though her cabin was smaller than mine, I was instantly jealous of Carrie's because of the huge, full-sized bed. There was hardly any room to walk at all, not that Carrie needed any. She flung herself onto a thick, lustrously-soft alpaca blanket. It was rare for anyone to bring such a comforter on a ship, but evidently Carrie felt the special bed required a special blanket. It was dangerously inviting, even if Carrie hadn't motioned for me to join her while unzipping her dress. I sat at the edge of her bed, pondering what to say.

But I needn't have bothered. She passed out.

I sat there, indulging in one of those moments where you debate through an alcohol-thick mind what to do. I pulled off her shoes and she rolled over to snuggle with a pillow. I tenderly adjusted the alluring blanket over her, then stumbled back to my cabin like a good boy.

And what did I get for behaving? In bed by 3:45, and at 4:00 the awful screeching of the halls being waxed woke me up. I should have stayed with Carrie!

"So," Bill said to me the next day in the art locker. "You joining me in Ensenada later this afternoon?"

"No," I replied. "I'm meeting with Tina. She said she had something she needed to talk to me about."

"I'll bet," he chortled. "Maybe she's mad you screwed Carrie last night."

"What?" I squawked. "Where did you hear that?"

"I had breakfast with the comedian," he explained. "I'm starting to get jealous of you, which is bullshit. You're sleeping with the goddamn dance captain—"

"I am *not* sleeping with Tina," I protested, but he pressed onward.

"You're banging hot-ass Tina, hot-ass Carrie, hot-ass Petra, and even ugly Vladka."

"I have slept with no one," I defended heartily. "And Vladka's not ugly. You're such a jerk, man. What's wrong with you?"

"Bah, Vladka's skinny with no tits, a flat ass, and bad teeth," he continued. "But what I don't get is why you still pretend to be faithful to your Russian."

"Romanian!" I snapped. "And I *am* faithful. I made a promise. Why is that so hard for people to understand?"

"Whatever," he scoffed, then changed the subject. "I requested my vacation, you know. We have the repositioning cruise coming up, but I want to get off before then. I told the fleet manager that you would be good to take over *Ecstasy* while I'm gone."

"That's awesome!" I cried, "But very early. I don't know if they'd let me already."

"Well, they have a plan for that. The fleet manager said you wanted to go to October's training class or something. You can whet your whistle on *Ecstasy* for one cruise to show your stuff, then go to advanced training with your chick from the Urals."

"The Carpathians," I corrected.

"Goddamn it," Bill complained. "I was actually trying that time."

"Close," I said. "The Carpathians are in Transylvania. You've never read or seen *Dracula*?"

But I was too excited and heady to bicker with Bill. "Where you going on vacation?"

"Thailand."

"That sounds awesome," I said. "Why Thailand?"

"You'll see why. But I need to clear the photos from the memory stick in my camera. You know how to burn those to a CD?"

"Sure," I replied. "But I may have to look at them in the process. Is that OK?"

"You can make copies for yourself for all I care," Bill answered gruffly. "Then you'll forget about Romania and want to join me in Thailand."

Bill's reason behind Thailand became vividly clear when I transferred his photos. Intrigued by his choice of words, my curiosity got the better of me and I had to peek. He had mentioned some great photos from earlier that week when he had gone out to Venice Beach. The photos revealed that he had gone with his Thai room stewardess, but he had not bothered with any photos of the beach. Rather, he had a dozen pictures of them together in a hotel room taking a bath together and, well, other things. Picasso's *Woman with bracelet receives gentleman with a cat* ain't got nuthin' on Bill!

Tina had made it abundantly clear that she had something important to discuss with me, so we arranged to meet at a restaurant called Mango Mango. Her machinations were evident immediately, because when I arrived she was already with another man.

"Ah, Brian!" she called. "Meet Auggie. He works in the gift shop."

I shook his hand, an act he had difficulty performing with Tina dripping off his broad shoulders. Auggie was a powerful man easily six foot four inches tall, and was clearly the largest man on-board beside Joshua Tree. But while Josh was merely bulky, Auggie's physique was well-defined and obviously well-used. His features were blunt, almost brutish, with a nose obviously broken at least once in the past and several scars across his shaved head. As rough as this countenance was to behold, his big smile was warm and genuine.

Tina could not keep her hands from caressing Auggie's massive shoulders, yet her attention was obviously directed at me. With great delight she commented, "Carrie is mad at you, you know."

"Carrie is? Why?"

With a smug air, Tina explained simply, "Last night, of course."

"Nothing happened last night," I said. "I was a perfect gentleman."

"Oh, I know," she articulated. "I know."

I rolled my eyes and debated walking out right then. What kind of creep did Tina expect me to be? Carrie had passed out! While I could be accused of playing with fire, I maintained that I was just dancing around the bonfire's circle of light. I was still in the dark and cold, but being accused of hogging up the heat. While I couldn't win, that did not mean I had to flee. Instead I ordered a mango margarita, for which this place was famous.

"Auggie here played football in college," Tina bubbled. "Where was it again, dear?"

"Quebec," he answered. "I was a defensive tackle."

"I didn't know they played American football in Canada," I said, marveling that I had not recognized any French Canadian accent.

"With all due respect, dude," he rebutted with a grin, "Most Americans know nothing about Canada. We have a large football program. In fact-"

"Oh, let's not talk about football!" Tina interrupted. "There's so much more interesting things happening. Did you know on our repositioning cruise we are visiting Acapulco? I can't wait to see the clubs!"

Tina had obviously planned this meeting so Auggie and I would vie for her attention. She was not prepared to deal with boy things like football. Her chagrin deepened when we began discussing engineering history.

"The repo cruise, yes," I agreed. "I can't wait to see the Panama Canal. One of the architectural wonders of the world."

"Begun by the French, you know," Auggie added. "By de Lesseps, the builder of the Suez Canal."

"Ferdinand de Lesseps," I said with a complimentary nod. "But de Lesseps drastically underestimated the jungle and didn't account for the continual flooding of the Chagres River."

Auggie beamed. "You're right! I can't believe you knew that!"

"Actually, I'm reading a huge book on the Panama Canal by Pulitzer Prize winning author David McCullough. It's called *The Path Between the Seas.*"

Tina groaned, but Auggie leaned in. "Did you know the Americans had to literally remove *all* the mosquitos from the Canal Zone? Image removing each and every mosquito from a jungle!"

"Why would they do that?" Tina asked, despite herself.

"Malaria," I answered. "The connection between malaria and mosquitos was discovered after the French left, by Dr. Gorgas, I believe."

"I can't believe this!" Tina lamented. "I'm surrounded by librarians! Auggie, I thought you were a football player."

"I was," he said simply.

"Let's go to Papas & Beer," Tina offered, realizing the situation was not going the way she had envisioned. She opted for a place too loud to converse. "It's just across the street. We can do body shots!"

"I was born in France," Auggie continued, ignoring her. "I lived there until I was ten and listened to stories as a child about Panama. My great grandfather died working on the canal."

"You're *French*?" Tina wailed.

"Auggie is short for Augustus," he explained. "The Roman emperor? I grew up on the Mediterranean coast."

Tina, finally beginning to realize the situation she created was now completely beyond her control, commented, "My mother would die if she knew I was talking to a Frenchman."

Augustus looked at her in surprise. "Why?"

"Freedom fries!" Tina shouted. "Freedom fries!"

Auggie and I both rolled our eyes. The look of betrayal on Tina's face was precious.

"You see?" Auggie said to me, indicating Tina's behavior. "We are very different than Americans, but have one big thing in common: ambition. That's why both of us wanted to build the Panama Canal. We are like brothers, and brothers squabble over petty things."

"Petty?" Tina barked. "You're saying 9/11 was petty?"

"Not at all," Auggie replied calmly. "We weren't talking about 9/11. Americans always do that, by the way. Look, in the first Gulf War France was your biggest ally. Way, way more than England. But it ruined our economy. And this current mess America got itself into violates the

United Nations. Why would we ruin our own economy again for your mistake?"

"Because we asked you to!" Tina retorted. "You'd be speaking German if not for us."

"And you'd still be an English colony if not for us," Auggie replied sweetly. "George Washington never won a single battle in the entire war, you know."

"That's true," I said, cutting off Tina before she strained herself with misplaced indignation. I tried to change the subject back to engineering.

"What I want to know is how the French were the world's foremost engineers for so long. I was on *Majesty of the Seas*, built by the French, and it was the worst design ever. And it had all these stupid, soldered lips across the halls that served no purpose."

"America has the best military in the world," Tina muttered to the bar, sulking.

"Yes," Auggie agreed.

"And France has, what, the best wine and cheese?" I said, playfully repaying the compliment.

Auggie grinned back at me, making his broken nose twist ungainly. It made his reply even funnier when he said, "Style before substance."

All good things must come to an end, and Bill's and my time in *Ecstasy* was about to change forever. On the last port of call on our last cruise before repositioning to the Gulf of Mexico, Ensenada gave us one helluva farewell.

The day started with quiet reflection and sizzling carnitas: two of my favorite things in the world. I was not entirely alone, however, as my margarita was company enough, and I was sitting among crowded curbside tables. Eventually Auggie happened by and joined me. Because he worked in the gift shop and was therefor free until midnight, he had a few margaritas as well. From there we wandered the streets in a nice buzz, until we heard our names falling from the sky above. A dizzying glance up revealed Bill waving at us from a balcony. Our trek upstairs was rewarded with some big ass green drink oddly called a 'purple hooter'. Then came some beers. Then came the drinking games.

I refrained from too much liquor, still hoping to have a bit of sobriety for later in the day, but Bill and Auggie were going full-on. Bill insisted on a strip club, and things went downhill from there.

There's little enough dividing line between strip club and brothel in the U.S., and none whatsoever in Mexico. The most popular establishment of this kind in Ensenada was clearly Club Paris, only a few blocks away from Papas & Beer. The exterior of the building was nondescript, but the interior promised something special, all right.

Within five seconds of walking in, we were escorted to a table and brought icy, sweating Coronas. Five seconds after that the small, sweating waiter loudly demanded we pay for the drinks and give him a sizable tip. This was not the customer service we had expected, by any stretch of the imagination. On that subject, we were surprised to see only a solitary, fat woman lounging about the stage. I suffered nasty visions of Salsa in Cozumel, and the nightmarish cramps that resulted from my forced afternoon there. I decided to bolt.

As I finished off my beer and prepared to leave these two juveniles to their fun, Bill barked at the waiter to bring the hot chicks before he brought any more overpriced beer. Instantly from behind a curtain bounced three exceptionally gorgeous Mexican girls with fake tits. While the label 'girls' was probably a misnomer, it was a close call.

Instantly one was on my lap and my shirt was on the floor. I hadn't even blinked in the time it took her to start caressing my chest and curling her fingers in the hair. She purred and pouted into my ear that she was thirsty. I knew that would cost me and, sure enough, the corona was ten dollars... in Mexico! But in essence we all received a free lap dance while the girls tried to convince us to sleep with them.

I wanted to leave. Bill wanted to stay. And Auggie?

Auggie was going absolutely insane. He was so filled with lust that he made Bill look prudish and me look dead.

"My God!" he cried, leaning back to look at us as his stripper wiggled nicely on his lap. "I must have her! I've got to screw this chick or I will die!"

"Calm down, Auggie," I started to say, but Bill interrupted me.

"Take her in the back, man," Bill said. "Where do you think we are? You ain't in Canada, amigo."

Auggie began shaking in his seat, convulsing as if suffering a seizure. His stripper was so freaked out that she leapt off him and padded away to safety.

"Jesus, Auggie," Bill chided. "Calm down, man."

"I can't help it," he admitted.

"Come on," I scoffed. "You work on a ship."

"Tina's got me flopping on the end of her line like a fish," Auggie admitted.

The music changed away from Spanish hip hop to begin a flamenco beat. Speakers hidden in the dark all around us resonated with the sounds of clapping hands and Spanish guitar until we felt the beat in our chests. All stage lights converged on the red curtain at the back of the stage, shivering just enough to tease us and the smoke that swirled about. The music began to build, and suddenly the curtain parted to reveal a woman of devastating beauty.

Somehow, a Spanish Catherine Zeta-Jones stepped out from the movie Zorro and onto our stage in Mexico. She had lustrous black hair bound by a red flower, and golden hoops from her ears glinted brilliantly. Upon the shoulder of her flamenco dress were red bundles of lace that accented the chocolate skin of her bare arms to perfection. The top of the dress was a tightly laced black bodice, below which flowed multiple tiers of red laced skirts.

As one, we all gasped and gaped at her like fish. I honestly could not recall having ever, ever seen such a beautiful woman before. She grabbed her skirts and spun with the music, kicking and thrusting her hips to the hot Flamenco beat. It was a mesmerizing performance, so entrancing as to be sublime. Just when we thought it couldn't get any better, she began unlacing her bodice and the back of her dress. She spun about, creating a pattern as the light shimmered off the tips of the loose laces of her dress, and her voluminous breasts risked breaking free.

Auggie began shaking in his chair again.

With a dramatic whirl, she dropped her skirts to the stage, revealing long, dark legs and a superb bottom snugly trussed in fishnet stockings and nothing else.

"Oh... my... God..." Auggie breathed.

I concurred. For the first official time in my life, I was struck speechless. But Bill could be counted on, as always.

"She take your mind off Tina?"

"I must have her!" Auggie roared. His words were loud enough to carry over the music, and the Flamenco Goddess floated off the stage and light into the dark towards us. She leaned into Auggie seductively, her heaving bosom barely hidden behind the loosely-laced bodice, and whispered in his ear. His face drained of color with each word. I couldn't hear what she said, but could detect her sexy Spanish accent. That was hot enough.

"I can't!" he cried to her.

"You can!" Bill said.

So drunk that he could barely enunciate, Auggie screamed at the Heavens with all the rage and self-loathing of Hamlet decrying the cruelty and betrayal of the world.

"Oh God!" he cried, "I don't have any money!!"

He began desperately pawing at his watch. "I have a Rolex, think she'll take a Rolex? I'll give her my Rolex!"

"Calm down, Auggie," Bill said, becoming all business. He leaned away from the stripper on his lap and motioned to the Flamenco Goddess. They conversed briefly, then she stepped back to wait.

"What is she waiting for?" Auggie said with a painfully defeated voice.

"She's waiting for you," Bill said. He handed Auggie a thick wad of cash and said, "You can pay me back later."

Auggie gaped at Bill in much the same fish-manner as he had the Flamenco Goddess, then abruptly leapt up. He took the dancer's hand and she led him across the floor to disappear behind a blue velvet curtain.

"She's so hot I'd be done before we even started," Bill commented, "That's OK, though, 'cause I'd still have an hour just staring at her."

"I'm inclined to agree."

"Jesus, Brian," he chided. "Even here with a stripper on your lap you sound like a goddamn librarian."

Then Bill's lady led *him* behind the blue curtain. That, of course, left me there with a stripper on my lap.

"Yes?" she said.

"No," I replied. "Thanks, honey, but I'll just wait for my friends."

Reluctantly she slipped off my lap. I suffered a moment of self-loathing as well, but comforted myself by pressing my ice-cold Corona to my forehead. And in my lap. I settled back while the stage was repopulated by various Hispanic angels of the night. To my surprise, however, Auggie came lumbering back to the table in just a few minutes. Now it was my turn to again gape like a fish.

"What the Hell are you doing back already?"

"I screwed a hot stripper!" he boomed with a slur.

"In five minutes?"

"That was only five minutes?" he asked blearily, falling into his seat. He was so drunk that he couldn't even stand.

"You have a fifteen hundred dollar watch and didn't bother to check it? You paid for an hour with her!"

He swayed dangerously in his seat and repeated moronically, "But I screwed a hot stripper."

"At my age," I commented, "If I was that fast I'd have a heart attack."

"Well..." he admitted, "She took care of me, anyway."

"Wow," I marveled. "That was *a lot* of money for a couple of minutes and only having to wash your hands."

Auggie just grinned stupidly at me and asked, "You know what? I screwed a hot stripper!"

"You sure did," I congratulated. He was too drunk to hear my snicker.

All night Auggie staggered around Ensenada proudly shrieking his accomplishment to everyone. No less than twenty unsuspecting victims were accosted in the street by his drunk self-congratulations. Every time I turned my back, I ended up hauling him off a bewildered innocent. Once he came back without a shirt, for some reason.

His raving included children. A group of local kids loitered around a vendor's cart sitting beneath a street light. Auggie barged right up to them, though he knew no Spanish. He tried to compensate with volume.

"Ay!" he cried. "You know what? I... yo... screwed a hot stripper! Comperndy, kids? Comperndy bonita? Ha, *bone*-ita! I'm funny!"

The children understood nothing, of course, but were greatly entertained by his failing efforts at equilibrium. But the fruit vendor was not at all impressed by this screaming, staggering, powerful sailor. The vendor shooed him away with cross words and threats of *policía*. Yet Auggie was undeterred. Finally realizing that his words did not have the proper effect on his audience, he began illustrating with motions.

"That's enough," I said, grabbing his hands to stop the carnal miming.

"Uno, dos!" he cried as I drug him down the dark street away from his intended audience. "Yo bone hot carne mama!"

Auggie was a huge guy, so my struggle to get him back to the ship was difficult. I pushed and prodded, but he tugged forcefully back. He tripped on the sidewalk and dropped like a stone. That seemed to have broken his will, so with his arm around my shoulder, I hauled him off. He wouldn't shut up the entire agonizing trip.

But the problems were just beginning. Crew are not allowed to come aboard drunk, and it would be hard indeed to hide Auggie's inebriation. We stopped just out of sight from the gangway, and I propped him up against the wall.

"OK, Auggie," I said clearly and forcefully. "We need to get you on the ship."

"No!" he cried, "There is no hot mamacita carne grande on the ship!"

"That's OK," I said, "Because you already did her. Remember?"

"That's right!" he declared brightly. "I did! I screwed a hot stripper!"

"The first thing we need is a shirt. I guess I can buy one at a shop around here. Do you have your ID?"

Auggie's attempt to pick through his pockets was pathetic. As I scanned the area for a shop selling T-shirts, a petite Bulgarian crew member approached. Before I could stop him, big, brawny Auggie leapt out of the shadows and bellowed at her, "I boned a hot stripper today!"

With a shriek, the poor woman leapt back in terror. She crouched protectively, but was reassured when I wrestled her assailant back. Only then did she recognize Auggie as her coworker in the gift shop.

"Auggie!" she snapped at him, waggling a finger. "They've fired two people this last month for drunkenness! What's wrong with you?"

"We need to get him in bed," I said to her. "Can you help us distract security?"

She marched over to Auggie and promptly kicked him in the shin. Hard. Auggie howled in pain and grabbed his shin. It was a mess trying to hold him up as he hopped around on one leg.

"What was that for?" I asked.

"For scaring me!" she snapped at Auggie. "And the price of my help. Now you have an excuse for his staggering. See? He's bleeding. Just say he tripped and hurt himself."

The Bulgarian pulled from her bag a souvenir T-shirt that barely fit across Auggie's broad shoulders. We tag-teamed security., with me distracting with questions like, 'I have an MP3 player here, do you need to scan that? Here's my bag, I don't think I have any metal in it, let me see...'. Meanwhile the Bulgarian helped Auggie get his ID into the card reader because he was unable to hold it without dropping it.

Amazingly, we made it through security. Getting Auggie to his cabin was a nightmare, because he was too drunk to tell me which way to go. Just when I thought he would end up sleeping in my cabin, he slurred that we were there. Auggie flopped onto bed and, just before passing out, murmured, "I have to be at work at midnight."

"What?"

"Get out!" he roared, suddenly flaring to life. "I have to be at work in an hour!"

"OK, OK," I said, stalling as I set his alarm for him.

At midnight I called Auggie's cabin, but there was no answer. That could either mean he was asleep or he was already at work. I decided to stroll by the gift shop and check. When I arrived he was standing ramrod straight behind the counter, as if over-compensating for his obvious inebriation. A middle-aged, somewhat portly guest was chatting with him about football.

"My son played football, too," she was saying. "But never attended college. He says he likes vodka, so I want to get him the best vodka in the world. Any suggestions?"

"That's easy," Auggie answered. "Grey Goose."

He handed her a bottle, and she beamed up at him with gratification.

"Sure looks pretty," she said. "You say it is the best?"

Auggie showed her literature on all of its international awards and credentials, and she seemed satisfied. Until she began spluttering with indignation, that is.

"Why, this is from France! Oh, I'll never... ugh! I'll never buy anything from those horrible little people who don't support our holy war in the Gulf."

Auggie remained silent, but glared down at her.

"You do agree, don't you? You look like a good, solid American boy."

Auggie rumbled like a volcano about to blast apart and spew fiery destruction. Amazingly, the lady was unaware of her imminent danger. She just looked up at him, waiting. Finally she asked, "Where are you from, anyway?"

"France!" he thundered, towering over her.

In terror, the woman dropped the bottle with a crash and fled. Auggie stared at the deck bristling with dangerous shards of glass. He ignored it and marched over to the snack aisle. He popped opened a can of Pringles and began cramming them into his mouth. When another lady wandered into the shop, he marched menacingly right at her and shouted with a mouthful of chips, "I don't want anyone in my store right now!"

She fled, screaming, and Auggie blithely chomped away.

And so came an end to my glory days on *Ecstasy* with Bill. We had made a killing here, but the ship was repositioning to a different home port and Bill wanted nothing to do with it. We stood together for a moment before the gangway, waiting for clearance.

"This is your chance to get into the big boy club," Bill said tiredly. He was obviously hung over, but had already bragged about how drunk he was going to get on his flight over the Pacific.

"I must admit that I'm nervous," I said as the security chief finally waved us through. "I'm not going to have an associate for my cruise, right?"

"You won't need one," Bill said. "It's a two week cruise, man. Lots of time. When you dock in Miami, there'll be another auctioneer to take over from there and you go on vacation. To your communist shit-hole or wherever."

"Just me and the *Ecstasy*," I said, possibilities swirling through my head.

"Not exactly," Bill said, hefting his suitcase on the gangway. "Sundance is sending someone here for the first four days to make sure you know what you're doing."

My excitement melted. I asked, "Who?"

Bill's answer was a smug smile. I watched him depart down the gangway and disappear across the pier. Slowly I turned about to glance up at *Ecstasy*. My ship. My first step to getting my Bianca for good. But who would they send to supervise my performance?

"Well, my little tadpole!" an arrogant voice called behind me. "You claim to be frog worthy. We shall see."

Part IV: The End of the Beginning

"Eating words has never given me indigestion."
—Winston Churchill

17. FEAR AND APATHY IN ACAPULCO

My nemesis from auctioneer screening, Lucifer, boarded the ship in all his hyena-like glory. His traveling had obviously been wearying, as he slouched visibly and his hair was in wild disarray. It made his pronounced ears look even more dog-like, complimenting a snaggletoothed grin large and fierce.

Lucifer wore his usual blue pin-striped shirt with white French cuffs, though this time it was so unkempt as to appear pulled from a garbage can. The horrendously wrinkled article was half-pulled out from his pants, and a ring of perspiration darkened his slovenly belly. This want of an iron was perhaps less due to travel than to his manner of packing: his only luggage was a gargantuan sack which he drug across the floor. It appeared designed to hold a set of golf clubs, but its disproportionate lumps bore evidence of clumped clothing.

Disheveled and sweaty as he was, Lucifer still strut as if he owned *Ecstasy*.

"Why, if it isn't the Father of Lies himself," I greeted with a forced smile.

I extended my hand, which Lucifer absently shook. His sweating palms were unpleasant. Without ceremony he hauled his bag to the elevator and kicked it before the doors. Spinning around, he contemptuously looked me up and down.

"Asking for your own ship this soon is pure arrogance," he barked without ceremony.

Before I could retort, Lucifer jabbed the elevator button and added, "I like that."

That's a first, I thought.

"From on high I was pleased to learn that you have begun to talk the talk," he continued. "But I wonder if you can walk the walk?"

As the elevator doors opened, he kicked his luggage so as to block access for anyone else.

"On Lido I'll explain why you have been so blessed with my presence."

"Shall I kiss your ring?" I mocked.

"You shall kiss my ass," he retorted as the elevator doors closed.

Fifteen minutes later I sat in the Lido restaurant watching Lucifer eat. It was disgusting. He ordered a triple burger, without cheese or any pretext of nutritional merit. I watched him scrape from the white bun any bits of toasted onion, as well as discard the lettuce, onion, and tomato as having no place in his culinary regimen. He squeezed ketchup over the top so liberally that it flowed down the flanks like lava from a volcano.

I was rapidly becoming uncomfortable with my comparing of him to a hyena, because he provided such ample evidence in support of the analogy. He ripped apart his meal without even a ruse of civility, tearing off huge mouthfuls of food as if trying to secure it from a squabbling rival. It was revolting. Ketchup splattered everywhere from his violent, rending bites.

"I am not playing the same role as in Pittsburgh," Lucifer mumbled with a mouth stuffed with half-chewed beef and fat. Ketchup streamed from the corner of his mouth in suitably predatory fashion. "On land I am there to break, but at sea I am here to help."

"I see."

"Ah, but you won't see!" Lucifer rejoined sharply, losing onto his belly a flap of grease-soaked bun. "I will be in the shadows."

"Lucifer lurking in the shadows to 'help me'," I replied drily. "Finally I have proof for my mother that there *is* a worse alternative to my atheism."

"I know where you *should* be," he mouthed crassly. "And that's where I *will* be. If you're not there, then Bill loses his vacation."

Lucifer ate without speaking for a while, obviously preferring his burger to anything I might have to say. Yet he was far from silent: I cringed at his noisome chewing and the wheezing breath between gulps. I pondered the import of his presence, my stomach churning at more than just his poor table manners. What if I didn't anticipate everything he thought was important? What if there was some event that was common to auctioneers that Bill, in all his arrogance, eschewed? Further, I was terrified of Lucifer's hyper-critical eye reviewing my first fully autonomous auction. And I was rusty, because Bill didn't even give me five minutes of podium time.

"Well," I began slowly. "It's a fourteen-day cruise, but we are low on inventory. I'm planning four auctions."

"I am here four days," Lucifer said. "You'll do the first auction before I get off in Acapulco."

So much for stalling until he left!

"I'll get you a copy of my scheduled events," I offered. "Tomorrow we are in port all day, so I'll only hand out raffle tickets and such on the Promenade. The next day I'll have the first auction. I want art-excited people to attend an auction first, rather than my lecture on-"

"A lecture, of course!" Lucifer interrupted, showering me with bits of burger. "I expect nothing less from a goddamn art-loving pussy such as yourself."

"The lecture will be the day *after* the auction," I explained. "Because I don't want people to attend a lecture and feel they have satisfied their art cravings for a few days, you know?"

"Oh, I know," Lucifer boomed. "I'm shocked that you do, my little sea slug. Care to lecture on color as well?"

"What's that supposed to mean?"

"You had plenty of shite to say about pink shirts in Pittsburgh. Perhaps you would prefer to lecture on color coordination and fashion as well? I think you'd make a better interior decorator than art auctioneer. You seem gay enough."

"And I think you'd make a better janitor than a trainer," I snapped. "You swept up more dust dragging your luggage than half the cabin stewards on board."

Lucifer chortled appreciatively as he masticated yet another grossly-overdone bite. Sensing that my temper was getting the better of me, I opted to change the subject.

"Have you heard any news about Charles and Tatli on the *Majesty of the Seas*? When I left, they weren't doing so well."

"They weren't," Lucifer agreed. "They had lots of problems, but I went to their ship. Charles followed my orders and now they are doing fine."

Of course, I thought cynically. I bit my tongue.

"And what about my class of trainees? Anybody else asking to be an auctioneer yet?"

Lucifer's eyes flashed as he boorishly chomped with his mouth open, teeth stained red with ketchup. He did not answer.

The next morning I sighed as Petra handed me a cappuccino. I stared deep into the cinnamon-dusted foam, seeking comfort. Instead I found a sneeze.

"What's wrong?" she asked.

"He's going to eat me. I just know it."

Though the Rolls Royce Café was empty but for the two of us, I still leaned in conspiratorially before explaining further. "Lucifer is going to eat me. You should see the way he tears flesh, with bloody teeth like in that Dalí work, *Men Devouring Themselves*. When you hear me screaming, don't try to help. Just run, 'cause it'll be gross."

I glanced at the café's walls, filled with neat rows of artwork hanging floor to ceiling. I had taken great care in their arrangement, but was already second-guessing all my labor. Was this not art I was to feature as mystery works on tomorrow's auction? The flyers I had printed featured the same artists, didn't they? And what about those easels marching up to the bumper of the vintage Rolls Royce? Was it enough?

"I need to get a bracelet that says WWLD."

"What's that mean?" she asked, frowning in confusion.

"What Would Lucifer Do?"

"Brian," Petra soothed. "You'll be fine."

"What if he walks by and doesn't see me working? Maybe I should be, oh I don't know, scrubbing the artwork or something."

"I've never seen you like this before," Petra chided gently. "If Bill didn't intimidate you, which is amazing in itself, why would you let this guy?"

"Bill did intimidate me," I admitted. "At least a bit. But this guy is horrible. He gets off on destroying the hopes and dreams of man."

"You act like he really *is* Lucifer."

"Close enough," I agreed. "Tonight I need to be on the ball advertising tomorrow morning's auction. The flyers are ready and scheduled for delivery into the staterooms and I bribed the cruise director for a larger advertisement in the ship's paper for tomorrow. I am advertising free champagne mimosas in all the relevant places. I am about to put signs on some of the artwork scattered around the ship, as well."

"Sounds like a lot."

"It *is* a lot," I replied. "But help me go through it again. What do you think the guests will be doing tonight?"

"The show," Petra answered. She paused a moment before asking, "You aren't doing any promotions with any... entertainers... are you?"

"Oh hell, no," I said, almost recoiling. "The last thing I need right now is another Tina drama. Or Carrie. Or Joshua... are they all dysfunctional, or is it just me?"

Petra nodded slightly in satisfaction. "There is karaoke tonight. Hundreds go to that."

"That's right," I said, perking up. "I can do a promotion there. You know, give away a prize for the best and the worst performance. That sort of thing. Good idea."

"I meant that you should sing really badly," Petra replied. "Then the whole ship will know who you are."

I sat down and loosed another sigh. Petra took advantage of the empty café and lightly rubbed my shoulders.

"I just have a lot of bad habits to unlearn, you know? When Bill was here, we hardly worked at all and rolled in the money. We got drunk every day and every night, in port or in the crew bar, everywhere! But that was because he knows how to talk to his people. I'm not from L.A. and I just don't get them."

"But this is a repositioning cruise," Petra offered, squeezing my neck.

"Yeah, but we left from Long Beach. A repositioning cruise is a mixed blessing. I have lots more time to reach goal, but G2 is accordingly much, much higher. The ports are all new and exciting and I want so badly to go out and play. I've never been to Acapulco, or through the Panama Canal. That's exciting stuff, but I need to focus on the job."

"Your habits weren't as bad as you thought," Petra commented, fingers teasing the nape of my neck. "Or as bad as some of us hoped. Tina and Carrie come to mind. Or Vladka, or..."

"Oh, you damned women!" I cried, throwing up my hands. "I need to just keep my head down and focus on my Bianca."

Petra released my shoulders and stalked off, leaving me to bury my head in my hands. A moment later I heard her footsteps returning and her slap something on the table before me.

"I just remembered this," she said crisply. "You wanted to see proof I was a model."

I lifted my head to see two magazines, including an issue of Cosmopolitan presumably written in Czech. Petra had folded it open to an ad focusing squarely upon the trim waist of a woman in panties.

"What's this?"

"This ad is for Veet hair removal creme," she answered. "I have no say where my pictures go."

I frowned and studied the nearly pornographic photo closely. It was easy to do.

"And you're trying to convince me that this is you?"

Petra's thin lips quivered into a smile. "Look at the other one."

I paged through the second magazine, apparently in German, and stopped when I encountered the same photograph. Yet this ad was not zoomed in on her crotch, more's the pity, but revealed her entire figure and the lower half of her face. Though her eyes were absent, there was no mistaking the curvature of her thin lips and trim, muscular figure.

"Well I'll be damned!" I exclaimed.

"See?" she said. "I knew I could take your mind off this Lucifer fellow. Some of us 'damned women' have ways of relieving your stress, not just adding to it. Perhaps you should try one sometime."

My phone rang at a quarter past midnight, waking me. I had gone to bed early because of the importance of my morning auction. I really hoped this wasn't another booty-call drama from Tina, or perhaps Petra offering to 'relieve my stress'. Strange how I labeled those things 'bad.' Mom would be proud. Stranger still, though, was my actual relief that my late-night caller was the very gay assistant cruise director, Timothy.

"Brian!" Timothy screamed hysterically, "Where are you?"

"In my cabin, obviously," I grunted, barely stifling a yawn.

"You are supposed to be hosting bingo. What are you doing in your cabin?" My yawn finally overcame me, and the phone squawked with indignation. "You're not sleeping are you? What the Hell, man?"

"Why on Earth would I host bingo?" I asked. "That would not exactly be an art auctioneer's job."

"Not for the guests, dumb ass. The crew bingo."

"You woke me for the crew bingo?" I snorted. "Screw 'em. I'm going back to bed."

"You never do *anything* for the crew," Timothy protested with painfully non-masculine sentimentality. "As a department head, you are required to do things like this. But you never *ever* do."

"I've only been a department head for two days, Tim."

"Well, you put up the posters last week for Bill. Don't you remember?"

My fatigued brain recalled vaguely that Petra and I had, indeed, posted some flyers on the I-95 some time ago.

Sensing an opening, Timothy rallied. "If you don't do this, I'll tell the cruise director. That's right! And he'll stop promoting your auctions."

Just what I need on this, of all cruises! I grunted an answer into the phone, "All right, all right. When and where?"

"Ten minutes ago in the crew bar."

"You realize, of course, that I have absolutely no idea how to host bingo."

"I already sold all the bingo cards and took in the money. I'm giving it to your assistant because I have to get out of here."

"What, do you have a hot date or something? Why don't you do it and I'll make it up to you. You're already there and half-way done."

"Just host the thing, please," he begged. "Everyone's getting very angry, so hurry!"

Swearing liberally, I threw on some wrinkled clothing and trudged to the crew bar. Crew activities usually began at midnight because everyone labored every other hour of the day. When you rely on a mere handful of hours of sleep every night for months on end, losing an extra hour or two ironically becomes less traumatic. I, on the other hand, had the most important auction of my life in the morning. This sucked beyond belief.

Outside the entrance to the crew bar, I was nearly bowled over by Timothy in his haste to escape the noise and commotion inside. Relief flooded over his features as soon as he saw me, and he spritely flung himself down the metal steps to the I-95.

"What's the rush?" I called after him irritably. "It's not like you have a Steiner waiting!"

Already a level down, he shouted back, "Oh yes I do! Have you seen the new spa manager? He's gorgeous!"

The crew bar was surprisingly fully lit. The air was hot and moist, and the unruly mob that filled it was entirely of brown and black skin covered in tropical T-shirts. Upon becoming one with the crowd and smoke, I was lashed by boos and curses. I suffered a flashback of being kicked into the lifeboat by Roosevelt Reddick. Certainly this group was as irate at my entrance as that other had been.

Petra obviously had not forgotten tonight's duty, because she came dressed to kill. She wore a mini skirt and an emerald spandex top that hugged her body lovingly. Despite my fatigue and the hostility being thrown at me, I forgot everything in favor of staring at her small, perfect breasts. Her perky nipples pushed through spandex like exclamation points. Before I said a word, she grabbed my arm and led me through the hisses to the ping pong table. Upon it rested the bingo cage and a microphone.

"Timothy already did all the prep work," Petra explained. "The prize money is in this envelope. There is $600US. Oh, and he gave me this. He said it may help you win over the crowd."

She handed me a thick, dog-eared book called *The Almighty Book of Bingo.*

"I am Maximus," I said. "I will win the crowd."

I took up the microphone and motioned for the jeering to stop.

"OK, OK," I called out, voice cutting through the haze of smoke. "Quiet down, I'm here now. Sorry to keep everyone waiting, and—hey! You spit on me again and I'm leaving with the money right now, you bastard!"

A muffled apology rose, and the angry shouts simmered down to a tense buzzing.

"So, before I start... do you know how much the prize is?"

The room finally fell into complete obedience. Sensing I now had control, I decided to show them who was boss.

"The prize is a lot of money," I teased. "Way more than I ever thought it would be. But before I tell you, shall we read from the good book?"

Confusion rippled through the mob, until I held up *The Almighty Book of Bingo*.

"First, a joke!"

Shouts and curses and groans rose into the air to swirl with the cigarette smoke. Some were good natured. Most were not.

I flipped through the book until I found a random joke.

"A man walked into a bingo hall and chooses his bingo cards," I boomed to the horde of drunk internationals. I paused, and the rabble actually became civilized. I continued onward with smug satisfaction. "Seeing a fly land on a particular number on one bingo card, and thinking this was a lucky sign, he bought that card. Later on that night, he lost."

My narration slowed to a halt as I sensed the punchline should be next, but simply couldn't find it.

"And so he said, 'It must have been a house fly.'"

That was it. Some joke. Silence descended upon the sea. This was, perhaps, the first time a crew bar had ever been silent at midnight in the entire history of Carnival Cruise Lines. I swear I heard a cricket chirping somewhere. Bedlam ensued.

"What the Hell does that mean?"

"Shut up and start!"

"Screw your jokes, turkey lips!"

Blinking beneath the hailstorm of epithets and hatred, I still managed to lean into Petra and ask with surprise, "Did someone just call me turkey lips? I didn't know they had lips. I know they have that dangle-thing, but I'm pretty sure they don't have lips."

Petra's own thin lips wriggled in amusement. "And you think you're so smart."

"OK, OK!" I called out again for calm. "The prize money totals $600US!"

Instantly the thunderstorm of discontent eased into a gentle rain of disdain. While they were compliant, Petra and I quickly began the bingo. She spun the little metal sphere to mix up the balls, and pulled them out in suitably game show-assistant fashion. Time progressed and things seemed to be going well.

That is, until *Ecstasy* was hammered by a rogue wave.

The entire bow of *Ecstasy* shuddered, and the crew bar's location front and center amplified the jolt. A roar of surprise rose from the crowd, quickly followed by the shattering of dozens of bottles and glasses as they slid off tables. The very floor itself pitched to the side, dumping everyone into a raucous pile with mixed furniture and shattered glass.

Powerful as it was, the blow to *Ecstasy* was more surprising than damaging, and crew members were used to such things. Within a moment everything was as it had ever been: crowded, hot, smoky, and impatient. Half the players' bingo cards had been tossed to the ground, but our master list was amazingly intact. Unfortunately, the bingo cage was a casualty, and had spilled its insides all over the pitching deck. Petra scrambled after the wildly scattering balls, assisted by crew members who jumped and sidestepped to avoid crushing them.

Sensing some commanding action was required, I did the only thing I could think of: I sought the solace of *The Almighty Book of Bingo*.

"Another bingo joke!" I called into the microphone, even as people jostled to fix bingo cards and scuffled after loose bingo balls.

"Knock knock," I said authoritatively.

"Who the Hell is there?" someone screamed back.

"Bee eye."

"Bee eye who?"

"B-I-N-G-O!" I shouted enthusiastically, then much more lamely followed up with, "And Bingo is my name... oh?"

"Put that book away before I shove it up your ass!"

Just as I lost control of the crowd completely, I observed a slovenly figure working his way towards the exit. It was Lucifer, shaking his head in disgust.

The next morning saw plenty of people enjoying free mimosas during the auction preview in the Stripes Lounge. Though I had not delivered an auction in many months, I was not nervous about how I would perform in front of the guests, plural, so much as in front of *the* guest, singular and odious. As it turned out, I needn't have been worried about Lucifer watching the auction at all.

He screwed me before I even got that far.

The preview was going splendidly, with all my employees making me proud. Amazingly, Petra and Tina worked surprisingly well together on a delightfully long check-in line, and my art movers swept through the lounge to snatch up tagged artwork with great efficiency. I dripped over the microphone tasty bits about the artists I was to feature shortly, and answered questions about how things work. Foolishly I began to anticipate an unmitigated success.

Then came Lucifer's ruckus. I heard his voice calling loudly and provocatively from the center of a large cluster of guests.

"I say," he exclaimed. "I saw this very same artwork on my last cruise. I bought it for way more than it was worth!"

Lucifer pretended to speak directly to a tall man with a halo of pale blonde hair around his balding head, but he didn't fool me. His volume was designed to attract a crowd, and several guests paused to oblige him.

"The same work, you say?" Mr. Halo asked. "How is that possible?"

"How indeed?" Lucifer goaded the crowd. "When they said it was a painting! How can I see the very same painting two cruises in a row, I ask you?"

My jaw nearly dropped to the floor. The son of a bitch was sabotaging my auction!

Rarely have I hated another man more than right then. Lucifer and I locked eyes for one long, awful moment, and his flesh-rending mouth twisted into that obnoxious, snaggletoothed grin. Somehow I resisted the urge to march right up to him and punch him in the throat.

"To what work are you referring, sir?" I asked as calmly as possible. "Surely you don't mean this lithograph here from Marcel Mouly?"

"Yes," he answered for all. "I bought that painting last cruise for $1500. I found out later that I could have bought it for only $1200! And even at that lower price it would have been bullshit, too, because here it is again! What, you got a bunch of Chinese sweatshop workers cranking them out, or what?"

"This work exactly, you say?" I repeated for clarity.

"Yes," he snapped. "Are you guys deaf as well as crooks?"

"But this is not a painting at all," I replied. "See the numbers there in the corner? This is a limited edition. Of course you will see another like it from Sundance. We are among the largest and most successful international fine art purveyors in the world, after all, and Marcel Mouly is a renowned French artist."

"I don't know nothing about all that," Lucifer scoffed. "Looks like a painting to me."

"He's right about that," Mr. Halo said, agreeing with me. "Those numbers make it a lithograph or something."

"Marcel Mouly is a master lithographer," I touted. "He's received the Premier Prix de Lithographie, the highest award from France, not to mention that he's a Knight of the Order of Arts and Letters. I assure you, an original, unique painting from Marcel Mouly of this size is worth tens of thousands of dollars."

"Yeah, well I still paid hundreds more than it was worth!" Lucifer repeated. "I saw that online."

Mr. Halo did not seem inclined to side with me on this one, nor any of the others crowding around to overhear. I sensed a riot brewing.

"Online from whom, may I ask?"

"All sorts of sites," Lucifer obfuscated. "One guy sold a similar painting on eBay for just $600, in fact!"

"Anyone can sell anything on eBay," I scoffed. "On eBay I found my auctioneer's gavel by a retired woodcutter in northern Minnesota. It looks exactly like the ones used by Christie's in London, but are they the same? I think not. On eBay there is no way of ever knowing if two works are truly comparable. Not all Picasso paintings are worth one hundred million dollars, after all. But none of that is really the point that matters."

"And what is that?" Lucifer asked.

"You didn't buy the Mouly at the opening bid, did you?"

"I don't think so," Lucifer replied, frowning in recollection.

"May I kindly remind you that the entire point of an auction is that bids go... *up?*"

Lucifer's frown deepened, and Mr. Halo actually chuckled to himself. The crowd dispersed and resumed their viewing. My answer apparently pleased the majority, for most remained for the auction. As the first work was brought onto the auction block, I was surprised to see Lucifer actually leaving. As much as I wanted him gone, his not even observing my auction left me perplexed. Was it good or bad?

Good, it would seem, because by the end of the auction G1 already hovered nearby. Not bad for only the second day out of fourteen! Even better, I had some rather hefty prospects on the horizon, including a family who purchased two paint-overs by Peter Max and were considering another. I was in, baby, and couldn't wait to meet up with Lucifer to gloat about my results. Right after I beat him senseless for his performance during the preview, of course.

Yet Lucifer was nowhere to be found. The remainder of the day passed tensely, as I waited for him to arrange a meeting. None came. I did not see him until the next afternoon at my 'Art Through the Ages' lecture.

Lectures are entirely my cup of tea. Because I knew Lucifer hated them, I took extra pains to properly balance sales strategy with impartial history. I respected history too much to spin it into a sales pitch, as he would have preferred, but did fill Stripes with artwork from masters we had for sale to illustrate my points, rather than show slides of famous paintings. My lecture began in 17th century Holland with the portrait and etching genius of Rembrandt, then moved to 19th century France for the color colossus of Matisse and the iconic marketing of Toulouse-Lautrec. Next came early 20th century Spain, with the globe-altering images of Picasso and cultural collision of Dalí. I finished with the present era comparing the radically different but undeniable economic powerhouse artists, Peter Max and Thomas Kinkade.

It was an hour of all things art, both philosophically and economically. While not about closing sales, it was nonetheless about placing our best artwork in front of a roomful of art enthusiasts. I was very proud of it. The audience enjoyed it. And then there was Lucifer.

He had arrived about ten minutes after I had begun, loping in with his toothy grin. His tardiness was a good thing, because had he come early I would surely have yelled at him and been too agitated to complete the lecture. He took a seat in the back and observed in merciful silence for the entire forty minute presentation and twenty-odd minutes of questions. Lucifer then remained quietly in the back while everyone left and the stragglers remained to ask more in-depth questions. Finally, inevitably, it was just us. I took a long sip of my now-cold latte and tried to hold back my growing apprehension of speaking to the hyena.

"Aha!" he chortled, arms behind his head. "I see you once again hide behind your coffee when you don't know what to say."

"What does that mean?"

"Whenever someone asked you a question you didn't know, you hid behind your coffee."

"A pause to think of an appropriate answer," I defended.

"To hide, you lousy tadpole!"

I regarded him carefully before I said, "I thought you said you were here to help."

"And so I am, my little tube worm."

"You call that stunt at the preview helpful? I call it sabotage. And so would Gene, I might add."

Lucifer rose to his feet and sauntered towards me. "Oh, you think to invoke the name of Gene, do you? You might be surprised to learn that he bet you would fail."

I tried to hide how much that hurt to hear.

"I don't believe you."

"Oh, yes," Lucifer gloated. "It's true. And would you believe that I, of all people, bet you would succeed?"

Sensing my disadvantage, Lucifer strut around as he explained further. "Gene thought you had potential, but would buckle under the pressure because you are too nice. I, on the other hand, sensed that the momentum of Bill's huge sales would carry you through this test cruise, but you will fail when given a ship of your own."

"I'm going to reach G2 and you can all be damned," I snapped. "And I'm going to do it my way, lectures and all."

"You're right that reaching goal will prove them wrong," Lucifer agreed. "But you are wrong about your lectures. The money is in the auction. Nothing else."

"There was a lot of interest in Picasso," I defended.

He laughed a loud, derisive laugh. "Yeah, right! What a colossal waste of time. What, you think that old guy, Mr. Payne, asking all the questions at the end is going to buy a Picasso? He looks like a bloody school teacher. He's just retired and has a pension of twenty bucks a month."

"He claims he already has a Picasso linocut," I defended. "And he summers in different countries around the world. He was asking me all sorts of very intelligent questions about our Japanese woodblocks the other day, and telling me stories of his travels there. They smacked of the truth. And did you see how hot his Russian wife was? You think a hot piece of ass like that would marry a high school teacher?"

"Bah!" Lucifer scoffed. "Mail-order bride."

"You never know who has money on a cruise ship," I continued. "People act different while on vacation, and I've met millionaires in jeans and a T-shirt."

"That's true," Lucifer reluctantly agreed. "But anyone with a brain can still tell them apart. Did you see the guy's watch? It was a twenty year-old Casio. Still had the little calculator built in, for Christ's sake."

"Penny pinching doesn't mean they don't buy art," I rebutted. "It means they don't waste a hundred dollars on a pink tie because GQ says it's hip today, you damned sheep."

Lucifer stalked towards the exit, once again shaking his head in disgust over my performance. Just before stepping onto the Promenade, he paused.

"You *do* know a lot about art history," he conceded over his shoulder. "But I wonder if fourteen days is enough time for you to learn about art *selling*."

"I wonder if four days is enough time for you to kiss my ass."

Lucifer turned to regard me with his goofy grin.

"I don't need to watch you auction or any of that other crap," he explained. "If you reach goal, you prove Gene wrong. But if you want to prove *me* wrong, you'll have to sell a Picasso. If you do that, I'll personally proclaim you the Frog Prince before Frederick himself."

Like everyone else, I had heard of Acapulco as one of Mexico's oldest hotspots. It was a port of hot nights and midnight seafood dinners, of dancing until dawn or until passion overcame you and your lover. It was a place to sleep off the hangover on gorgeous beaches covered with even more gorgeous bikini-ladies. It was, in short, all things Hot Cocoa. OK, so she was not Mexican but Brazilian. Potato, *potahto*. But instead of Hot Cocoa, what did I get? A slovenly, dyspeptic Brit.

Ecstasy docked so very early that it was nearly yesterday. Lucifer arranged for early clearance and an early flight, necessitating a wake-up call at 3 a.m.. Since 3 a.m. was the Witching Hour, when the devil chose to mock the Holy Trinity by inverting the hour of Christ's Crucifixion, this seemed appropriate. Being an atheist, I presumed that such things things could not inconvenience me. But I was wrong, because Lucifer woke me up to personally see him off. Why, I have no idea, for we hardly spoke. Asshole. At least I didn't have to wait for him to lug around his gargantuan, lumpy bag. Security did it for him, because once scanned they didn't want him near it until off the ship and through the port facility.

We sat together in *Ecstasy's* main lounge and sipped our coffee in silence. Not surprisingly, we were the only ones waiting. A cabin steward wandered by to polish the brass railings, and I was shocked to recognize her as the one Bill had ogled while vacuuming his cabin so long ago. I had forgotten that regular crew work any shift, any time, and every day. It was an uncomfortable reminder that being an auctioneer was really my only way to remain at sea with any semblance of comfort.

Time crawled by slowly and the atmosphere grew heavier with each minute of additional silence. We had nothing to say to each other. Neither of us liked or respected the other. Since he was no longer in a position to belittle me and he was in no way inclined to advise me, he ignored me. I was thrilled.

"So," Lucifer said finally. "You gonna shag that barista?"

I chuckled. "I see that your observations extend to beyond all things Sundance."

"It's obvious she wants your johnson or a Green Card," Lucifer continued. "No doubt it's the latter. Regardless, I suggest you shag her and get it out of your system. You are too new and too shitty an auctioneer to be sidetracked by quim."

"Inspiring words," I said. "I'll be lost without you."

The chief of security emerged from the passenger's gangway and motioned that Lucifer was cleared.

"Yes," Lucifer agreed as he rose to his feet.

Without further ado, Lucifer strode away. He did not shake my hand or even nod. In fact, he didn't even say goodbye. I was tempted to let him leave on that note, but my curiosity had been burning too long and hot to let the moment slip away.

"You never answered if any other trainee has their own ship yet," I called out.

Lucifer paused before the angled hallway descending to the Acapulco terminal. He cocked his head to the side, but did not turn around when he answered.

"You're the first."

The sun sluggishly rose, and day awoke with a hang over. Because the sun rose over the steaming land of Mexico, it cast a sultry purple and red haze over the sea. Hands in my pockets, I strode along the gorgeous, vast northern curve of Acapulco Bay. This section of town was older and almost exclusively Mexican. It was interesting to see how the tourist-centric areas catering to Mexicans differed from those catering to Americans. There wasn't a single McDonald's with requisite concrete parking lot and bored, teenage employees, but instead dozens of cafés right on the beach worked lovingly by grandparents, aunts, and uncles.

I squished through damp sands teased by greenish tidewater, then across rusted and ruined night club concrete lapped by floating rubbish, then onward into a forest of towering, swaying palms. I passed a stretch of sand containing thousands of tiny, beached jellyfish. So quickly had they dissolved in the humid air, I needed time to realize what I was looking at. From the beach I watched the fishermen rowing back towards land with the night's catch.

I opted for breakfast in a café that caught my fancy. It had the thatched roof, open walls, and on-the-sand thing I would have expected from paradise. I was the only guest present and preferred it that way. I was tired of people and the games they played. I was done worrying if Lucifer thought I should or should not be present here or there or wherever. I just wanted an untrammeled port, though this one already felt tainted by Lucifer.

Yet I was, for the moment, Lucifer-free. The morning was rich and soft, much like the air that blew in from the sea. Ah, the morning smell of real life! The air was so thick with humidity that breathing it in was almost difficult, yet certainly more wholesome than the artificially scrubbed air of my cabin. It was so hot, in fact, that I marveled what the atmosphere would be like in summer. Right now was late September, for the love of Chicken!

I ordered some chilaquiles, which came with a thick steak in truly American-sized portions. It was matched with minutes-old bread baked by Tía Guadalupe and a huge tankard of papaya juice squeezed by Tío Jose. I was intrigued by the bushel of papayas resting beside the bar, and Jose's lavish use of them. This gargantuan feast set me back a mere $7.50. Acapulco, I love you!

After breakfast I wandered among the recently arrived fishermen now selling their night's catch upon the beach. Wooden planks were placed atop coolers and rocks, or balanced upon the gunwales of rowboats. Each board boasted the freshest bonitos, jacks, or Spanish mackerel one could find. Row after row of fat fish glimmered silver in the morning sun, or flashed purple and red being cleaned behind a boat. The youngest boys were invariably assigned to gutting the fish, whereas the shirtless men marched up and down the sand with their wares, also working over the women who came for the day's freshest and best.

I moved beyond the market in order to pass the strong smell of fish, and scrunched through a sandy parking lot of boats. Dozens of working fishing boats had been pulled up onto the beach away from the morning tide. They wore names that surprised me, such as Patricia, Bella, and Xanadu. Beyond the resting boats the bay curved ever onward, and behind another copse of palms stretched the modern high-rise section of the south bay. They were vast, these modern luxury apartments and resorts, and muscled back the trees along fully half of the huge bay. The flanks of each of the massive buildings was nuzzled by fawning, lush trees.

I expected Acapulco to be cool simply because I had heard of it. I had the same fantasies of Mexico as anyone else. But the beauty of this place was far more stunning than I anticipated, and far different. When *Ecstasy* passed by famous Cabo San Lucas yesterday, so close that I actually feared we would go aground, I had noted the archipelago was exceptionally arid. But Acapulco is lush, green, and gorgeous.

Too bad I couldn't enjoy it.

Alas, Lucifer had given me time-sensitive parting instructions. A whole slew of paperwork was due to be emailed him by this afternoon, including a revised auctioneering schedule for the cruise and a detailed list of advertising strategies that was to include flyers, posters, rotating artwork on easels by the vintage Rolls, themed presentations in the Rolls Royce Café, and, for some bizarre reason, auctioning off a wooden horse for the cruise director. By the time I compiled the list of duties and emailed them off to Lucifer, the afternoon had grown long.

But eventually I finished my chores and opted for a late lunch out with a former fashion model from Slovakia. Bitch as I might, it was hard to spin it that life was rough for me nowadays. For all her help, I had promised Petra I would take her out in Acapulco. Regardless of my johnson —a statement rarely made by man—or Green Card as motivation, Petra's help had been a Catsend.

Though I usually eschew such touristic places, I planned on taking Petra to Señor Frog's. I had been assured all day that it had the best view in the entire city, from breakfast through fish markets, from the excursion manager to the ship's translator. So for perhaps the first time, all the little voices in my head were right! In the back of a tiny Volkswagen Beetle we chugged along through congested traffic, taking nearly thirty minutes to pass beyond the high rise section of the bay and into the southern cliffs. The road wound ever upward, and I stared in awe as we ascended up and away from the beaches. I was fascinated by a huge cargo ship that rested at an angle in the shallows. Its dark, rusting bulk sat empty and forlorn and completely out of place. As the road wriggled higher and higher, the hulk became a long, black smudge against the otherwise impeccable half-moon of Acapulco Bay.

Finally we arrived at Señor Frog's, which rested right on a cliff overlooking dozens and dozens of world-class resorts. They extended around the southern curve of the bay like tiny blocks. Individual buildings and houses behind them were nothing more than scattered glitter over the rolling green hills behind.

We were thankful for the breeze that blew by the heights. We found a table on the deck overlooking the awesomeness of Acapulco, and ordered ice-cold margaritas as further remedy to the heat. My Tommy Bahama shirt was shamefully soaked through with sweat and my hair tightened into tight, damp curls. I presume it was the heat that made me sweat but, to be honest, Petra's outfit was a contender. Her skin-tight black dress was designed to show off her trim, muscular figure. The lucky dress clung to her body closer than her own sweat and blushed darker from the moisture.

Petra pulled from her tiny purse a cigarette case with great aplomb. She extracted a stick and lit it with the European's inherent love of ceremony. Cigarette smoking behavior where I was from, whether male or female, differed from the smoking habits of European women. Though they smoked so regularly as to even light up during a meal—a rarity in the States—European ladies still solicited each and every cigarette as a coy lover. I never once saw a European rush outside in the cold for a 'quick smoke', as I saw in the States. As a cigar smoker, I appreciated the courting of the right moment for a smoke and the rituals associated with it.

So we smoked and watched the humidity pulse over Acapulco Bay. Eventually, inevitably, the sun began its slow descent. We watched the orb, swelling orange as it dipped ever closer to the water, eventually drop down right across the bay, right behind the *Ecstasy*. It was a perfect afternoon of tranquility and accomplishment. And a bikini model. Yes, I had passed the first hurdle and gotten rid of Lucifer. I was on top of G1 and had almost the entire cruise to finish off G2, which wasn't too far away. Everything was so perfect that I thought something surely had to go wrong.

Something surely did.

A tiny sound caught our ears, teasingly familiar but too far away to accurately identify. It sounded a second time, and I leisurely asked Petra, "What is that, do you think?"

Petra suddenly gripped the table as if in danger of falling. She clawed at my watch and demanded, "What time is it?"

"Chill. It's only 4:25."

"But the sun is going down."

Realization flooded over me. "Pluck my Chicken, that was the ship's horn!"

"Oh my God!" she cried. "It's 5:25! We have to be on-board at 5:30. It took half an hour to get here!"

The panic of watching your home leaving without you is one I hope most people never experience. It is a gut-wrenching feeling, far more intense than merely the inconvenience of missing a flight. On the surface you feel just fear and anger over having made a bad, bad mistake. But more than having to scramble to fly to the next port, missing the sailing is a firing offense. Too, there is another emotion when your ship leaves you, a deeper, more loathsome feeling. You feel small and insignificant. How could home abandon you?

"Run out front," I ordered, "And grab one of those taxis. I'll pay."

With a frenzy we flew out of there, throwing pesos and dollars both at everyone we encountered to help things move faster. Two taxis waited outside the front entrance, and we rushed across the steaming concrete towards them. But they weren't waiting for us—they were waiting for their drivers! Petra pounded on the car door in frustration, while I raced back into Señor Frog's and demanded the driver. Several painfully long minutes later a portly, late middle-aged woman trudged across the parking lot towards her taxi, where Petra hopped up and down as if she were waiting outside a restroom.

"How long to get to the terminal?" I demanded of the woman as we rushed into the back seat. She took her sweet-ass time looking at me blankly.

"Carnival Ecstasy!" I cried, adding in bad Spanish, *"El barco muy muy grande. Sí?"*

"Sí, sí," she answered. *"¿Quiere ir a la terminal del transatlántico?"*

"Yes!" Petra fairly screamed. "Yes, that!"

"Uh, mucho speedo!" I stammered. I flashed two twenty-dollar bills at her and added everything I could recall from Speedy Gonzales, *"¡Andale! ¡Andale! ¡Arriba! ¡Arriba!"*

Our lady of the taxi certainly proved herself worthy of the extra fare. We must have broken every land-speed record for that trip around the bay. Certainly we broke every traffic law, Mexican or otherwise. To this day, I don't know how we actually made it back in time. We had to literally run the last few hundred yards through a shopping mall to the gangway, Petra barefoot and clutching her high heel shoes.

We were applauded on our return by security.

18. ROMANCING THE STONE

Greg Gregg is a very big, very bearded man. His wife calls him Cube, as in Greg times three. That's because he's so big, he counts as two. I suggested that perhaps Cube would be a better nickname for their son, Greg Gregg, Jr., but they told me that he's called Square. Shows what I know.

Greg and his wife Shirley were guests on the repositioning cruise, and I was exceedingly grateful for their presence. They loved to have a drink or three at the Society Lounge I frequented with a cigar, and we immediately hit it off. My appreciation ran far deeper than merely libations and small talk, however: they had already purchased $15,000 worth of artwork. Greg liked to bitch and moan that I was fleecing him, but he was a genuine and generous supporter of Shirley's interests. Actually, he accused her of being more interested in *me* than the art. He even offered me escalating sums of money to sleep with her and just get it over with. He figured he would save a fortune by the end of the cruise if it meant she wouldn't buy any art. Theirs was a complex relationship.

When *Ecstasy* docked in Puntarenas, Costa Rica, I happened to stumble upon them and their entire family near the pier. It's hard to miss Greg, because he towers above crowds like a mountain over rubble. The Greggs were debating whether they wanted a tour of the jungle or not. Greg was in favor of anything smelling even remotely of danger or adventure, as were the two twenty-year-old twins, Chris and Cliff. Both boys were slender and athletic motor cross enthusiasts who had already broken forty-seven bones between them since high school. Even Chris's fiance Amber was game for the jungle. Scrawny little Square, however, was dubious of the wild and more inclined to shop for local trinkets with his mother.

Foolishly, Shirley asked my advice.

"Once a man swings on a real vine in a real jungle," I began orating, "He is forever changed. That tapping into something primal, no matter how fleeting, alters outlook and skews expectation. My awakening happened here in Costa Rica, though on the Caribbean side, at Parque Nacional Cahuita. From that moment on, I knew I would never again sit in traffic on my way to the office, contently or otherwise."

"Shit, Shirley," Greg complained. "Maybe you should just stick to art."

"Oh yes," I continued dramatically. "I am now a man who can read *Heart of Darkness* with deep clarity and understanding. True; working on ships is good for that, but I assure you that Mowgli of the *Jungle Book* ain't got nuthin' on me."

"Please make him stop," Greg pleaded.

"I am Michael Douglas in *Romancing the Stone*," I boomed. "And I declare that nothing short of Kathleen Turner herself will pull be back to civilization!"

Here I stopped, panting and sweating from my fiery oration. A small crowd had paused and were watching, apparently waiting for the authorities to throw me into the drunk tank.

"Oh," I added sheepishly to Shirley. "And it's safer than motor cross."

"Sold!," Shirley cried, elbowing Greg in the ribs. "You could use some manliness like that. Before we married, you assured me that you're a Tarzan in bed. I'm still waiting."

"Oh, being a firefighter isn't manly enough for you, now?" Greg mocked. He scratched his thick beard in contemplation. "Hmm... perhaps this is my chance to finally escape. Is a wife's unhappiness with a husband's career a legal grounds for divorce?"

"Father!" Square chided with painfully real shock.

"I need a primate in the *bedroom*," Shirley emphasized. "Not in the bathroom."

"Mother!" Square uttered in despair.

"Don't panic, son," Greg smoothed in smarmy fashion. "Your mother's just being coy."

Suddenly I understood why they called this poor young man 'Square'.

So I tagged along with the Gregg family, numbering six, and about half a dozen miscellaneous others. The bus promised adventure from the start, seeing as it was far older than myself and had obviously needed repairs more often than the twins. While the bus boasted an air conditioner, it was in no way capable of competing with the Central American summer. The heat was so humid and oppressive that it would send an Eskimo into cardiac arrest. I was more than a little concerned that those present not of the Gregg family were all well into their retirements and overweight. Yet it seemed only Square wasn't game, so in we squeezed and sweated.

We rumbled painfully away from the coastline and into the steamy, dense interior of Costa Rica beneath rain-swollen skies. One of my favorite aspects to this nation was their overwhelming appreciation and prioritizing of their natural environment, so within just minutes we were deep into pristine jungle. We chugged along fully adequate, if poorly maintained, roads for nearly an hour before things went wrong. That was better than I expected. We hit a pothole so hard that everyone was flung into the air like popcorn in a hot-air popper. Immediately the bus groaned and shouldered itself off to the side of the road. We were thrown again to the side when the right wheels dropped into the muddy shoulder.

About half of us filed out of the bus and into a huge pool of muddy water. The pool was surrounded by thick, knee-high grasses agitated by the humid wind. Not one hundred feet before us was a bridge that spanned a wide, muddy channel. While it had concrete protective walls, I was dubious about their ability to stop us had the bus decided to leave the road on the bridge rather than here. From far down the river valley the clouds bullied each other in their haste to be first to rain on us. The valley was exactly the kind of meandering brown stripe wiggling into the hilly, dense green that one would expect from Central America.

"Look at that!" I called to Greg. "Isn't it amazing?"

"What?" he said curtly. "Breaking down in the middle of nowhere? Yeah, great."

I gestured broadly to the immense panorama. "It's so gorgeous, powerful, and primal!"

"So's my penis," Greg quipped. "Anybody got any beer?"

"*Cervezas aquí,*" called a guide, gesturing to the other side of the bus. Greg and I walked around the vehicle and shared a chuckle when we saw a restaurant nestled in the trees. Chris and Cliff were already on their way. Shirley, Square, and the older folks opted to remain on the bus. Amber stood in the doorway, as yet uncertain if she wanted to leap into the mud to join Chris.

"How much you wanna bet the owners put the pothole there themselves?" Greg asked as he scratched his beard. "You should buy me a beer, you know. It's the least you could do after getting fifteen thousand dollars of my money."

"Can't bully your wife, so you're trying me?" I asked. "Good luck with that. I'm going to check out the bridge. I'm not here for beer, but adventure."

"*Cuidado,*" the guide warned, waving his hands in a very international 'watch out' manner. "*Muchos cocodrilos en el río.*"

Greg and I wandered across the long bridge and stared down into the wide, messy river of ugly brown water and mud. The river itself was perhaps fifty feet across, but easily one hundred feet of thick, slippery mud lined both its banks. This was indeed a hangout for dozens of crocodiles, all chillin' in the mud at the water's edge.

"Look at that," Greg said, pointing into the trees that nuzzled up to the mud flat. "I see a cow. In fact, there's a bunch of them. Are they really that stupid that they would hang out with crocodiles?"

Sure enough, half a dozen large but skinny Brahman-style cattle were blithely munching on the grass not one hundred feet from the nest of crocodiles. Ah, this is exactly what I wanted! Large wildlife plain to see, and stunning jungle views. Both sides of the rich, brown river were packed with lush trees spattered with the brilliant, clean white dots of birds.

After a while the guide returned. He looked up at the huge man and paused, suddenly unsure of himself.

"Well? What is it?" Greg demanded with an irritated tug of his beard.

"*El borde es doblado,*" the man said slowly, enunciating each word carefully.

Greg looked at me and asked, "Didn't we hire this tour from a guide who spoke English?"

"We did."

"And it wasn't this guy?"

"It wasn't. I was watching for a switch like this but I got distracted by macking on your wife. Surely this will be our only inconvenience today."

"Very reassuring, Brian."

Seeing Greg's complete lack of understanding, the guide glanced at me for assistance, but I knew very little Spanish. Finally the guide pointed to the river.

"*Allí!,*" he said. "*Llanta.*"

We looked at him, perplexed, as he pointed again and opened his mouth wide. He gestured emphatically to his open mouth and bared his teeth. Then he pointed to the river again.

"What the Hell kind of tour did you lure me onto?" Greg demanded of me. "They got cannibals in Costa Rica, or what? Don't you know any Spanish?"

"Not really. I learned *dónde está la zapatería* from *Pulp Fiction.* That means 'where is the shoe store.' That's about it."

"What good are you, then?"

"Ask your wife," I teased. "Hey, it's a start. If we were in the Philippines, I'd know how to say 'the boy threw the ball at the wall', so give me a break. But I think he's pointing to that crocodile."

"*Sí! Sí! Cocodrilo.*" He opened his mouth wide again and pointed to his teeth. Glancing down into the valley below, understanding dawned on me. One cute croc, a mere six feet long, rested with his mouth wide open. I checked for a bird picking his teeth clean, but didn't see one. So much for fable. What I did see, however, is that it was resting beside an abandoned truck tire.

"Aha! He's saying the tire's rim is bent. I think that's what *borde* means. Like border, you know?"

"*Sí,*" the guide said, relief flooding over him. "*No problema. Veinte minutos.*"

"What's that?" Greg asked.

"Twenty minutes," I translated. "See? Four years of Spanish weren't totally wasted, after all."

"Maybe you should have studied the lessons more than you studied the teacher, eh?"

"No," I replied. "The French teacher was the hot one. Mrs. Marcel wore tight leather mini skirts. We all wanted to be *her* student."

"I'll bet," Greg agreed with a smile. "Well all right then: all's well that ends well. Plenty of time for you to buy me that beer."

We walked back towards the restaurant, and I said, "Seeing as how you haven't yet decided to buy Shirley that Peter Max, I'll be happy to oblige. Will that be enough, or shall I work her over on this trip, too?"

"She wishes," Greg laughed. "Hey, if you kept her entertained so I didn't have to for the rest of the cruise, one more Peter Max would be a small price to pay."

We returned to the restaurant and saw the twins and Amber marveling over a partially-restored 1970's Dodge Charger resting on blocks beneath a corrugated-metal roof. Though the garage had no walls, the side closest to the jungle was defined by a row of nasty oil drums filled with all manner of alien refuse, garbage, and food waste. Wrinkling his nose at the smell, Greg offered to bring his family a fresh round of beers, but they declined.

So Greg and I entered the restaurant ourselves and were pleasantly surprised by just how nice it was. A long wooden deck lined the compound and extended deeper into the jungle, paralleling the river. The posts were shellacked trunks of trees that supported a roof of thatch. Tables lined the railing and Greg and I sat down to enjoy a Costa Rican beer called Imperial.

The late morning was quiet, and we reveled in the lack of a crowd. Cruise ships are fun, but can be very congested. The only other person present was a wrinkled and nearly black-skinned ancient local in a broad straw hat. His heavily lined face was relaxed in a well-deserved nap.

"Wow," I commented idly to Greg. "Have you noticed this guy's wrinkles? They seem to cover every single Nazca line in Peru."

"Uh huh," Greg said, sipping his beer and staring at the chaotic greenery as it dropped into the river valley. The breeze was enjoyable, but everything was still muggy and hot. The beer perspired nicely in our hands. Suddenly the tranquility was pierced by a noisy ruckus from the trees opposite us. Two huge, brilliantly colored macaws chased each other in the trees. After watching them a while, they disappeared into the steaming rainforest.

"Really," I said to Greg as I resumed my perusal of Old Man Nazca. "I see all sorts of familiar patterns there. You know what I'm talking about, right? The mysterious lines in the Peruvian coastal desert that are miles and miles long and serve no obvious purpose? They are best seen by airplane, yet were made about fifteen hundred years before flight. Absolutely fascinating."

"So's my penis," Greg answered again, blowing the foam off the top of his beer.

"Look, I even see the hummingbird on his right cheek! There, below the crow's feet."

"You really need to get your head out of your books, man."

"That's funny," I chuckled. "My ex-wife always said my head was in my ass."

Suddenly Greg leaned towards the railing and stared, wide-eyed, into the jungle. He pointed to where the thick undergrowth shivered.

"What the Hell is that?" he cried. "It looked like a goddamn jungle cat!"

"What, you mean like a jaguar? Bullshit."

"Look, man!"

I scanned the pitching shrubbery, then nearly fell over when I saw a sleek, black body pass behind some fronds. "Holy Cat!"

"You think it's a jaguar?" Greg asked in wonder.

"No, it's all black. That's got to be a panther. It was huge! What, over five feet long?"

"At least. I never saw it's head, though."

"Me neither," I agreed. "But I understand that panthers are very reclusive and hunt only at night. What would it be doing here in the morning, close to humans?"

"Coati," our napping neighbor suddenly said. We turned to look at Old Man Nazca, but his eyes remained closed. Greg and I spared a quick glance at each other, perplexed.

"That's no coati," I replied. "It was way too big. Coati are like weasels and stuff."

Old Man Nazca did not reply. He did not even open his eyes. The only sign that he had heard me at all was a twitch of his right eye. The hummingbird's wing flapped.

"Do you know about nature," Greg asked. "Or just art? I'm from Chicago, so I don't know anything about this stuff."

"I know enough to say with authority that *that* is no coati. Look!"

We watched the large creature slink through the underbrush. It was a mere twenty feet from us and was separated by only a simple, rustic railing. Needless to say, that was not much protection. While a big cat was certainly capable of taking down animals as big as Greg and I, it was highly doubtful it would do so here.

Right?

"You think it's attracted to the garbage cans, like wild bears are?" I asked. "Even I could smell the garbage in those oil drums from a mile away. I can't think of any other reason it would be so close to people, and during the day, no less."

The panther moved towards the front of the restaurant, and finally exited the brush to pass the entrance of the deck. It seemed in no hurry, yet moved with a quick, fluid grace that was mesmerizing in an animal so large. There was no mistaking that it was a black panther.

"Holy Cat," I repeated breathlessly, in awe of its beauty and poise. "After this, I swear that I shall never again invoke the Chicken."

"It's heading towards the front garage!" Greg said, leaping suddenly to his feet. He pounded towards the front with great energy, and I quickly followed when I realized that the big cat was heading directly towards the old Dodge Charger that Chris, Cliff, and Amber were reviewing.

Greg and I thundered around the corner and paused, breathless, looking for the animal. We caught just a glimpse of the beast passing behind an old, rusted Volkswagen Beetle parked at the edge of the forest. Then it was gone, presumable back into the jungle whence it came.

"False alarm," Greg panted. He glanced around the oil drums and the Charger, but the twins and Amber had moved on. Though pleased, Greg was also a little disappointed that his kids hadn't at least caught a glimpse of the animal.

We returned to our beers on the deck, and sat down heavily. The excitement was over. Brief as it was, it was exhilarating. Just as we were putting beer to our lips, a gravelly voice called to us from the neighboring table.

"Coati," Old Man Nazca repeated. His eyes were still closed.

"My ass," Greg snorted, swigging his beer. "I'll bet it's trained to come whenever it hears a car running over that goddamn pothole. Like Pavlov's dog running when it hears the dinner bell."

"Why Greg," I said, impressed. "How very erudite of you. The wonders of the day never cease."

"Thank you," he said smugly, stroking his thick beard. "And you still haven't even seen my penis."

"Surely that will be our only wildlife incident today," I mused.

"Surely," Greg repeatedly mockingly.

Thirty minutes passed quietly, while I debated relaying this panther visitation to my long-suffering mother. No doubt she already had a list of all the dangerous animals of Costa Rica on hand, as well as the statistics of how many Iowans have been killed by them. A mother's worry is a wonder.

The bus finally fixed, we drove another hour deeper into the heart of Costa Rica's world-famous bird-sanctuary jungles. We went up and down several hills so steep that we worried about our bus making it out. At least the roads were concrete. If they had been unpaved and as muddy as the ditches we passed, we would have been doomed. Finally we ended up at an amazing resort nestled in the jungle. Each building was in a style pleasantly mixing Spanish architecture with the openness one would expect from a dwelling in the deep jungle. Everything was gorgeous beyond belief: the grounds were surrounded on all sides with attacking vegetation, yet sculpted minimally and artistically within to provide a place of calm, Eden-like peace and reflection. Flowering plants exploded with color. Everything was dense, rich, and lively. Costa Rica's saying is *'Pura Vida'*, and now I knew why. 'Pure Life' indeed.

Here the older folks of the tour split off for a jungle canopy tour. I had assumed we would join them on the series of bridges set high up in the foliage of the trees, enabling a bird's-eye view of, well, birds. I was excited for such a trip, being a great fan of the wild outdoors. Few things are more exciting for me than simply being surrounded by nature's glories. But then we became intrigued by a couple of locals in a pickup truck resting leisurely. One was short and stocky, the other tall and lanky, and both rested their feet atop a placard that caught our eye.

Zip lines!

Imagine sliding across high wires through a jungle canopy, eye to eye with the monkeys and the birds, far, far above the earth. Platforms are hundreds of feet apart, and you fly through the air from tree to tree. While it wasn't exactly swinging from vine to vine a la Tarzan, it was far more practical. All the Greggs were eager except Shirley and, of course, Square. When Shirley acquiesced into going, Square was shamed into the same.

The seven of us piled into the back of the pickup truck and raced off even deeper into the jungle. We were half a dozen extremists: the largest firefighter I had ever seen, two motor cross freaks, a timorous paramedic, and companion adventuresses. Oh, and a book-loving art dealer. After about twenty more minutes of driving, Greg knocked on the window separating the cabin from the back of the truck, and shouted to the stocky driver named Lucio.

"You *do* speak English, right?"

"*Qué?*" the driver asked. After receiving the expected sour look, Lucio smiled broadly and said, "Just kidding. I speak very good English."

Finally we arrived at our ultimate destination. The foothills of this area were very steep indeed, and any misstep could drop you into a ravine one hundred feet deep. A cluster of low, long buildings nuzzled up next to a towering, moss-draped hill like children hiding in a mother's skirts. They were all clean and new and nice. Each had a uniform base of navy blue paint, topped by cream-colored stucco. Connecting the buildings were well-laid tile walks, which wound through flowering jungle plants of all manners.

Step one was to gear up. We were assisted in this by our two Costa Rican guides, of the Hispanic variety common on the nation's Pacific coast. Francisco and Lucio were as youthful and apparently reckless as Chris and Cliff, as revealed in their joking and taunting of what we were to expect. Amber, in particular, was unnerved by what we were about to do, though she tried to hide it. Visibly paling, she gingerly stepped into her harness to allow tall, gangly Francisco to tug it up and around her body. She was far too distracted to see how much pleasure this Goofy look-alike had in strapping up her beautiful body. His laugh was goofy, too, but wholesome. Amber's trepidation, however, was nothing compared to Square's.

"Get it snug, now," he ordered Lucio. From his mannerisms it was clear that Square felt superior to Lucio because of his greater height. No doubt living in big Greg's shadow had given him issues. "Is that tight enough, little man? Ouch, too tight! Too tight!"

Lucio flashed a smile to Francisco as he loosened the strap that ran between Greg Jr.'s legs.

Everything went particularly smooth because the Gregg family was very familiar with safety equipment of this variety. Body harnesses, hard hats, rock-climbing clamps, and the like were all in a day's work to these men of daring-do. Ironically, the man most familiar with a vastly larger array of safety equipment, Greg the firefighter, posed the greatest challenge. He was just too big. Not only was Greg about six inches taller than me, making him nearly six foot eight inches tall, but his hands were literally double the size of mine. Lucio found a solution in the machine shop for *el jefe* with a pair of gargantuan welding gloves.

Step two was getting to the site. Lucio led us ever deeper into the steaming jungle via a thin, barely-visible path through the growth. Even leaf-cutter ants would have trouble finding *that* trail. Single-file we progressed up and down ruts and ravines that obviously had just arrived with the last rains. The jungle was amazingly thick, as much as one's wildest imaginations; a stupefying and dizzying 3D maze of green. We brushed aside countless branches and smacked aside countless leaves and shook our limbs free of countless snagging vines. Despite my years of hiking in the woods, not to mention being the son of Boy Scout Masters several generations deep, I honestly could not follow the trail. Acknowledging humility was a rare and distasteful moment for me.

And it was hot. Really hot. Jungle hot. I love heat, but I was sweating far more than in any sauna I had ever encountered. The air was filled with so much water it almost hurt to breath.

After about twenty minutes of this extreme hiking, we found ourselves surrounded by massive chicken-foot trees. The base of each tree was a bizarre series of above-ground roots that really did look like chicken feet, only three meters wide. These trees were hundreds upon hundreds of feet high and created the world-famous jungle canopies of Central and South America.

Then I saw it, something I have always wanted to see in real-life: a slender, swaying bridge in the jungle stretching precariously over a chasm bottomed by a crocodile-infested river below. Eureka!

The bridge was about two hundred feet across, and looked all the narrower because it was less than a yard wide. It flapped in the breeze as if in sore need of support, though in fact there were plenty of rusted wires holding it in place. While disappointingly not floored of rotting wooden planks that would threaten to drop us into the chasm, the bridge did boast transparent grillwork. Yes, each step across that chasm offered a perfect view straight down to the crocodiles splashing around. OK, so the drop wasn't one hundred feet or anything dramatic like that, but closer to thirty. That merely meant we would survive the fall that brought us into contact with the crocodiles. Cool.

Being in the lead, Lucio led Shirley, Square, and Amber across. Chris was about to follow his girlfriend, but Francisco ordered him to stop.

"Why?" Amber asked, halting on the slippery metal grid of the bridge bottom.

"Too much weight," Francisco answered.

"What?" Square squawked. "This isn't safe?"

"It's safe," Lucio called reassuringly from the front.

Though obviously nervous about the bridge, Square hurried towards his mother rather than the safety of the earthen ridge.

Francisco casually motioned for Amber to continue. "I cross with brothers. Then *el jefe y chico grande. No problemo.*"

"So I'm Chico and you're the Man, eh?" I asked Greg as we enjoyed the sight of the twins carefully tip-toeing across the bridge. They grabbed both rails tightly and kept their feet away from the center of the flooring. A few times Chris or Cliff would pause and lean over the side, but the entire bridge would wobble and a squawk from the far side would bring them back to center.

Finally our turn came. Greg stepped onto the bridge and I brought up the rear. Each step we took rocked the bridge precariously, even more so than when the wind gusted up the canyon. Our destination, the opposite ridge, was nothing but thrashing trees. It was the coolest moment of my life. I was experiencing my greatest jungle fantasy! Well, barring the one about being captured by a tribe of horny Amazonian babes looking for a mate. But that one was a bit unrealistic.

The bridge was so narrow that the helmet buckled to my side drug along the railing, even as my waist pressed against the other. Once I set my feet into the middle of the flooring and the metal grate dipped severely, twisting like a snake caught in an eagle's beak. The handrails dipped with each footfall, and the whole bridge constantly threatened to dump us over the side. It was far, far less stable with Greg and I than it was for the others.

When Greg reached the middle of the chasm, the swaying became uncontrollable and he stopped. Together we held onto the wriggling metal rails and glanced around with mild alarm.

"Hey!" Greg yelled to the far side. "How much weight can this thing handle?"

"*No problemo!*" Lucio called back over the blowing wind. "Two hundred kilos!"

Greg twisted to look at me, but the wiggling of the bridge stopped him. Instead he called over his shoulder.

"Is that a lot?"

"Well," I stalled as I waited for the swaying to steady. "I weigh two hundred pounds, which is ninety kilos, as I recall."

"That's just great," he called in amusement. "I weigh three hundred and sixty pounds."

I blinked in alarm.

"You do? That's a problem."

"That's a problem," Greg repeated, laughing into the wind. "I don't think our little local friends have any idea how big Americans are."

"Surely this will be our only misunderstanding today," I added drily, warily glancing over the side.

"Surely," Greg replied with a snort as he ever so gingerly crossed the remainder of the bridge while I remained in the center. It shifted and jerked and wriggled beneath me with each of his footfalls. I spent the time staring over the edge at the crocodiles below. They didn't seem particularly expectant for me to fall, but that may have just been me rationalizing. Finally I crossed the chasm without any trouble. Our destination lay much further, however, and we had another such bridge to cross as well. The second bridge was shorter but far, far up in the canopy. It was exhilarating. That is, until a wind gust nearly made me drop my camera.

I enjoyed the trek and lost track of time. I was therefore startled when the group suddenly halted and I stumbled into Greg. Thankfully, he was as immovable as a megalith, because before us the ground dropped away into a precipice. I gasped as I reviewed a vast panorama of dense jungle hills spreading into the far distance. The valley below us was gargantuan and untrammeled by mankind, home to only nature and a thin layer of mist draping over the deeper valleys. We had ascended the flanks of the mountains and it was all downhill from here.

The first platform was built into the earth at the edge of the precipice, and Francisco was already preparing for the first trip across the zip line. With my eyes I followed the delicate cable that extended easily one hundred feet above and through the dizzying green expanse of the tree tops. It passed right beside two brilliantly-colored toucans that hopped from branch to branch to get a better view of us.

And then Francisco was gone. Without a word he slid into the depths of greenery and I lost track of him. A second later he burst from a thicket of branches, already so distant that he looked one foot tall. So far and so fast did he go that I never saw where he stopped. The toucans flashed away in a mad scramble of black, red, and yellow.

The group zipped in the same order as we had hiked, which made me last. Lucio hopped about the platform like a monkey, readying the lines and our safety gear. With a playful whoop the female Greggs flashed through the air. With a painful wail Square followed. Soon it was just big Greg and me. I was ever so anxious to get going, but Lucio slowed down to give Greg a second check. After the bridge fiasco, we both certainly appreciated it. But Greg's calm was very reassuring. He was a fireman, after all, and recognized all the gear as safe and its usage as correct. Considering he was 360 pounds and not worried, why should I be? Still, Lucio and I both caught our breath when Greg leapt into the green with a bellow and the cable dipped alarmingly.

Finally Lucio stepped over to me and strapped my helmet on. I was wearing my jungle hat, but he pressed the helmet over it which smashed the flaps around my ears. I could hardly hear his instructions, but heard only something about 'fat lady' and 'squeeze.' That was hardly reassuring.

And then I was flashing through the air. With amazing speed I slid through the sky above the canopy, filled with the wonder of flight. The trees were mesmerizing, and there was no seeing through their tiers of branches to the earth below. The second I grew comfortable soaring over the treetops like an eagle, I plunged into the green. Thick, flat leaves slapped me harmlessly, and I was completely disoriented by flashing foliage on all sides. It was like I had plunged into the sea and didn't know which direction lay the surface.

All told, I slid about one hundred meters on this first zip line, alone and zipping through the jungle canopy. Then suddenly a massive tree loomed up. A tiny platform clung to the titan's flanks, crowded with Greggs hugging the massive tree that anchored the cable. Francisco gestured wildly to me as I fell towards them ever faster, and

I realized he was motioning for me to slow down. Grateful for the thickness of my gloves, I squeezed the cable until my descent became more controlled. Still moving faster than I had anticipated, I flew into Francisco's arms, forcing the others back in a wave.

"Jeez, slow down!" Greg teased with a grin. "You trying to push my family into the great green yonder?"

Francisco expertly unclamped me from the zip line and instantly hooked me up to the safety rail of the narrow platform that circled the massive trunk, which must have been six feet thick. If it was that big here, I could only imagine its foundation! I glanced over the side, but could not see the earth. Both above and below was a mass of living, breathing greenery shot through with brown branches and trunks. Even those were predominantly covered in vibrant moss.

"You worried me," Francisco said with a laugh. His laugh sounded like a donkey yet was strangely pleasant to listen to because it sounded absolutely genuine. "Last month, a fat old lady from America hit tree."

"Yes," I replied sourly, "My athletic abilities are frequently compared to those of a fat old lady."

Francisco guffawed further, but continued. "She no try to slow down at all, though we taught her. She no even grab the cable."

"Oh, that's what Lucio meant," I said in understanding. "I couldn't hear him clearly. He must have said to squeeze the cable to slow down."

"Yes. She no do, and two of us grab her, but she hit tree."

"Was she hurt?" Square asked, pushing through the crowded platform. His face was terribly pale and he was visibly impatient for Francisco to finish assisting Lucio onto the platform. After clamps were transferred and everyone was safe, Francisco worked his way back towards the front of the group.

"Only bruises," Francisco answered as he swung out over the edge to get around big Greg. His movement was as casual as if he were born one hundred feet up. "She try to sue us in American court. When that no work, she try to get cruise line to sue us. They say no, but we lose contract with them. Very bad for us."

"But good for you," Lucio added. "Without worrying about cruise line rules, you can swing upside-down and backwards."

And that is precisely what we did. The next several zip lines, in fact, we spun around and whirled upside-down. What a rush *that* was, careening through time, space, and jungle with no idea where you are going, but just exhilarating in the moment. The whole experience was part pure adrenaline and part tranquil observation from the unparalleled view of the platforms.

On the next platform an additional guide waited, and we switched our zipping order. Now I got to go first. Unbeknownst to me, this was also the line where they decided to play a prank on us. When I went out, the guides grabbed the cable and yanked it up and down. The result was a heart-stopping lurch up and down over the green expanse. I had to laugh as both guides hung uselessly on the cable when trying to shake big Greg around. It wasn't as funny when we heard Square's pitiful wailing from the distant green above us.

On the last platform I met a surprise visitor. Here the platform was only about thirty feet above the ground. The air was denser here, wetter, and hot. This last platform was anchored in the claw-like crotch of the tree, where the main trunk split into three that towered up into the sky. Each was nearly a meter thick alone. Piled into the bottom of the crotch was a mass of earth covered in wet, rotting leaves. Right beside the platform was curled a sleeping snake.

Being the first in line this time, I nearly stumbled into the sleeping serpent, who looked so cute and content in his nap. I resisted the urge to lean in for a closer look, but noted that the diamond pattern on his back reminded me of a Western rattlesnake. He must have been about two meters in length and about two inches thick at his middle.

"What kind of snake is that?" I inquired of Lucio, who was busy preparing from Greg's imminent arrival. When he saw the snake, though, he nearly jumped out of his skin.

"*Díos mío!*" he cried. "Very dangerous, do not touch!"

"OK, OK," I laughed. "Don't shout then, or you'll wake him up. What is it?"

"Is called Fer-de-Lance. Very dangerous. It kills more people than any other snake in Central America."

"Fer-de-Lance doesn't sound very Spanish," I gently chided the snake. "Don't you know you're in Costa Rica?"

I had long ago learned how to remain calm around poisonous snakes. After having accidentally kicked several rattlesnakes while trail running in Nevada, one finds the stimulus to learn about them. Older, larger snakes have no reason to waste their venom on you, unless they think you're dinner. This guy was far too big to be a young and restless type, who bites first and asks questions later. Thusly I figured that if I don't kick this guy, he probably won't bother with me.

"Enjoy your nap," I told the serpent quietly. "It's a very, very hot afternoon and your cold blood probably doesn't want to be agitated. Don't you worry."

"Be very careful," Lucio repeated, worriedly eyeing the snake's proximity to the platform. "His average bite has 100 milligrams of venom. That's no laughing matter."

"So how much venom does it take to kill a man?"

"Fifty."

The Gregg troupe managed to gather on the platform without any difficulties or stirrings of the snake. I was prepped for the last zip line, and I reluctantly stood at the edge of the drop off and stared into the distance.

"This one is not very high up," Lucio instructed. "But is very long. It will look like you are going to slide into the river, but you won't. Well, maybe *el jefe*. Have fun!"

And then I was gone in a flash, screaming across the river. I immediately flipped upside-down and began spinning a 360. Below me, or rather, above me, the river slithered over rocks. The water was not deep, perhaps only a meter, and slid smoothly over round stones and mud. As exciting as it was to soar across the skies up high, cruising just above the water like a duck preparing to land was even more thrilling. The proximity to the ground made every second feel like a prelude to a crash into the wet stones. Somehow, amazingly, it was my favorite of the day's dozen or so zip lines.

Alas, the zip lining came to an end. The final platform sat above the muddy banks of the river and offered a paved walk directly into a fantastic resort. We were given a few hours to wander the grounds and relax before returning to Puntarenas. The Greggs and I parted so they could spend time together as a family without a seventh wheel. They dined in the restaurant, which was truly amazing. A complex series of wooden decks ran along the sluggish river. Each deck was lined with gargantuan and aggressive jungle flowers of all types and meandered past the trunks of huge trees that shot up through holes in the thatched roof. Each place setting boasted ornately folded linen that stuck up from a glass like another flower. It was hard to tell where the restaurant ended and the jungle began.

All public buildings were open-air to allow the breezes to caress away the sticky jungle heat. Some structures had massive roofs to cover large congregations, while others were intimate bungalows. I wandered the stone walks that wriggled past rental bungalows boasting thatched roofs and private hammocks. Many a grassy clearing was adorned with tropical flowers luxuriating in the humid air. I paused briefly upon a stone bench by a spring-fed swimming pool of crystal waters. Everything had the appearance of a world-class resort without having any feel at all of a hotel. Just more and more cool places carved out of the jungle, yet still a part of it. Each flower obviously thought itself still at home in the wild, even when flanking a moss-covered fountain. Even the big ash trees kindly held up lanterns for after hours. Very neighborly of them.

I wandered the grounds alone, contentedly puffing upon a cigar that had nearly met its end while zip lining. I paused to enjoy a pool filled with a variety of lilies complete with tiny multi-colored frogs. Everything was rich, healthy green. The air was moist and natural, and it began to lightly rain.

I hopped into the shelter of a Spanish mission-style chapel. The small one-room structure had two rows of heavy-wooden pews facing an altar made of a stone slab atop two boulders. The back wall behind the altar was all uneven stones covered in thick vines designed to trickle water liberally down their sides. Above this was a huge open-air triangle because the wall did not rise to meet the peaked roof. I watched the rain crashing gently onto the forest outside and puffed away. This did not feel like a desecration of any sort, because a sign in English revealed that at night the altar was used as a bar. This was my kind of chapel!

If ever there was a single resort I would want to return to with my far-off Bianca, it was this. I have been to world-class resorts in all corners of America and several corners of the world, covering the entire Caribbean Sea, the Mediterranean Sea and companion Seas Alboran, Balearic, Ligurian, Tyrrhenian, Ionian, Adriatic, and Aegean. I've covered the breadth of the Baltic Sea, the Red Sea, and the Black Sea. I even lived in Las Vegas, on the edge of the ancient, long-dead Salton Sea. *This* was my favorite resort. Strange, then, that I never got its name. Another of Brian's strategic moves.

When it was time to go, we had the van to ourselves as our previous, older companions had found alternate transportation. Not surprisingly, our van broke down on the return trip. Where? Where else? Right in front of *Restaurante Cocodrilo*. These guys must make a fortune. This time the van overheated and came to a stuttering halt on the bridge itself. No longer fearing a stomp through the mud, the entire Gregg family and I trekked to the restaurant to have another beer.

We sat about a couple tables on the deck as the sun lowered into the west. Amazingly, Old Man Nazca remained right where we left him hours ago, still with eyes closed beneath the brim of his straw hat. The jungle was dark, but the twilight still lit much of the greenery with a warm, golden sheen. Rain drops glistened and fell as drops of pure gold. It was the perfect evening setting to regale ourselves with talk of the adventurous day we enjoyed. Well, that most of us enjoyed: poor Square still looked pale and pathetic.

"Right here is where we saw the black panther," Greg was saying to Shirley. "It was magnificent!"

"You weren't scared?" Square asked, lips all but quivering at the thought of a big cat encounter.

"Well, Brian was," Greg roared with satisfaction. "He almost pissed his pants. But I was here to protect him."

I rolled my eyes, and Shirley reached over the table to pat my arm.

"Don't worry," she reassured. "I am on your side."

"What a surprise," Greg muttered into his beard, hiding his grin.

"You saw coati," the waiter corrected as he delivered another round of Imperials. "No panthers here."

"Oh, please," Greg muttered after the waiter departed. "Are these guys trained to say that? Worried we'll go home and scare off potential tourists, or what?"

Suddenly Amber leaped up with a shrill squeak.

"Ouch!" she cried, rubbing her thigh. "Something bit me!"

"Oh my God!" Square cried, as if he had been waiting for this all along. "A Fer-de-Lance? Oh my God!"

"No, no," she muttered, eyeing a large wasp that squirmed on the deck below her. "I must have sat on a wasp. Damn it, I'm allergic to stings!"

Chris immediately leaned over to get a better look, and Greg and Shirley rushed around the table. Greg ordered Amber to stand for a clear view. In the fading light, we could already see a huge welt spreading across the back of her thigh.

"Don't worry, dear," Chris reassured as Amber began to pace. "You know I've always got your prescription of Epi-Pen."

Chris felt in his pocket for the self-injecting device, then paused with alarm. A bit more frantically he fished in all of his pockets before his eyes bulged in realization.

"It must have fallen from my pocket zip lining!"

"Oh my God!" Amber repeated, now genuinely scared. "How far are we to the ship? Is that piece of shit van even going to work? If I don't get my epinephrine, I am in big, big trouble. Last time I almost died from this, and that was just some dumb bumble bee. Who knows what the Hell is in this goddamn jungle!"

"And I can't believe my own son would litter in the jungle!" Greg teased, earning a big ol' wallop from Shirley.

"Cube!" she chided roughly.

Greg held up his arms in surrender, saying, "I was just trying to prevent the panic that's already brewing. Junior, you're the paramedic. Take a look."

But Square was even more panicked than Amber. "Yeah I'm a paramedic, but I don't have any of my equipment. What am I supposed to do? I need equipment, medicines, things! I have no things!"

"I'll go see if they have any antihistamine in the restaurant," Cliff volunteered as he rushed off into the main restaurant.

The red welt on Amber's leg continued to spread angrily, even as she tried to remain calm, unsuccessfully. The moment she complained of being dizzy she nearly fell down on the bench. Square felt her pulse and noted that it was quickening dangerously. Her throat and face already visibly swelled.

I had never seen an anaphylactic reaction to a bee sting before, and was shocked at how quickly the symptoms were wracking her body. After merely two minutes, Amber was literally having trouble breathing!

Yet lo and behold! Old Man Nazca leapt forward with all the energy of a man who had rested for twenty hours. He boldly threw aside his bulky hat and snatched up the table's salt shaker. Unscrewing the top, he upended all the salt into his palm. Without a word to Amber, he roughly pushed her over to expose her swollen thigh. His coarse hands smashed the salt into the welt and aggressively rubbed it in. Amber squealed.

"*Mas!*" Old Man Nazca ordered, reaching out for more salt. Greg poured another shaker's worth into his palm and the old man returned to his work. For five solid, long minutes he rubbed and pressed and scoured Amber's thigh with the salt. Amazingly, Amber's rasping pants began to ease.

"I'm, I'm feeling better," she eventually stammered.

We all watched anxiously as Square counted her pulse for a tense sixty seconds, but it was obvious that the danger had passed. Amber looked OK. Square looked like he was about to faint.

"Well," I remarked gently, "Surely this will be our only medical emergency today."

"'*I have no things*'," Chris mockingly whined to his brother before being swatted by their mother.

"Thank you," Amber said to the old man. He replied with a big, toothless grin, then casually collected his straw hat. He paused to look up at the towering figure of Greg. Though the brim of his straw hat barely reached Greg's beard, the old man puffed up with great authority.

"Coati!" he said, then marched back to his bench. As if nothing had happened at all, he closed his eyes and went back to his nap.

19. PICASSO AND A CAT

My three checkout girls and I shared a martini at the Society Bar. Dressed in sweaty auction attire, we looked like survivors from a wild night on the Las Vegas Strip. Petra's ultra-mini-skirt tube dress somehow managed to pull up even further to reveal more than a little thigh, but her sleepy gaze never passed her appletini. Not to be undone on the 'I'm so sexy without even noticing' department, Tina's pink lingerie-style halter-top was completely unlaced so her impressive cleavage could explode out.

Ironically, my low-key third assistant from Australia, Sarah, was the most presentable. She eschewed makeup in deference to her tom-boyish personality, yet wore a classy pantsuit outfit. Sarah slouched deeply into her chair directly opposite me with legs spread wide open. Sadly, the pantsuit made this posture decent.

I leaned back on the couch between Petra and Tina, casually blowing cigar smoke at the ceiling. Though hot, I was too tired to take off my jacket, so instead just loosened my tie. We had just finished the last ball-busting, crazy-busy auction, and I was infused with a deep sense of relief and accomplishment. I had not only met Goal 2, but blew it away.

What's more, I had accomplished this feat on a ship heavily depleted of high end art, and without the assistance of an associate auctioneer. That is not to say I did it alone. I would have been lost without the borderline adoring assistance of Petra, or the undeniably dubious assistance of Tina. Sarah had provided a much-needed peacekeeping force between the two women, who even now shot glares at each other from my right and left.

The post-G2 celebration was a ritual that I had not enjoyed for quite a while. With Bill as auctioneer success was a foregone conclusion. We drank like fish anyway, Bill and I, and partied hard, but it was never accompanied by a sense of achievement. I found myself strangely longing for my time with Charles and Tatli. While life was stressful on the Widow Maker, a sly drink with them had always felt right. Being in such hot water together, the three of us made a pretty solid connection in a comparatively short time. Unlike many of the international folks I worked with at sea, I could envision myself inviting Charles and Tatli into my home on land. My thoughts drifted to poor, ulcerated, impotent Rookie of the Year Shawn. Maybe. And Bill, invited to my home? Forget about it. I had no illusions about Bill: he was never coming back from Thailand.

As the four of us sipped martinis and chatted languidly, another dancer joined us. Angela was yet another beauty, with short-cropped black hair, a statuesque figure and *huge...* tracts of land. Then a rather pretty shop girl came to join us. Before I knew it, I was the sole male in a rotating group of women, like some sort of mini Hugh Hefner. What really made me sit up and reflect on the moment, however, was when Jurita joined us.

Jurita of Lithuania was undeniably the hottest babe on *Ecstasy*. She was staggeringly beautiful, truly world-class, with naturally red hair and emerald eyes and a smoking hot body. Jurita was so sexy, in fact, that once, when she sunbathed on the open deck below the bridge in her booty shorts, the navigator almost rammed another ship. Literally. Klaxons went off and everything. Despite being off the coast of Mexico, people panicked thinking we hit an iceberg.

And now she was talking to me. But why? She was the chief officer's squeeze, so was obviously not interested in trying to move up the social ladder. For the last few months Jurita would not look at me without turning her nose up. She never even gave Bill a sideways glance. I was in such shock, yet still so fatigued, that to me her voice sounded like the adults in a Charlie Brown cartoon.

"Wah wah WAH?" she asked with a Baltic accent.

She was so damn gorgeous that she made even *that* sound sexy! Yet for some inexplicable reason I ignored her query and said something really, really dumb.

"I'm a tadpole," I said.

Jurita's almond-shaped eyes glittered as she pondered my arcane response for a moment, then she turned back to her other friends. Before I could feel too much the loser, however, Petra gave my arm a reassuring squeeze. Sarah cocked her head to the side, reminding me for a moment of Shawn. Only a pretty blonde version, of course.

"What does that mean?"

"It means," I replied quietly, "That I have earned the right to be with my Bianca."

"You're so sweet," Sarah commented, accompanied by a few romantic sighs from the ladies.

That's when it occurred to me why I was surrounded by all the babes, including the super-sexy Jurita. They didn't want a Green Card: they all thought I was harmless. But really; despite my position of apparent authority and apparent wealth, these ladies knew I would not hit on them. I recalled having listened in on Sarah's conversation and feeling a pang of jealousy when she laughed about a recent tryst with another guy. I was attracted to Sarah on several levels, sure, and Petra, too. But I was not looking for romance: I was only days away from finally getting my Bianca! But the reality was that being lonely for affection on a ship is trying, especially when surrounded by mostly charming but predominantly fantastic women. Ship life.

When working the Carnival restaurants, I had turned down countless offers for anything I could desire—the allure of a Green Card is beyond comprehension to those out of the know. I was faithful to my Bianca, and further reinforced that with the excuse that I didn't even have my own cabin. Getting less than four hours of sleep month after month lowers libido, after all. But here on *Ecstasy* I had my own cabin and the good life, with good clothes, free time, money, and an alluring nationality. I was hip deep in hotness, and their comfort level and advances grew daily. Was fidelity after almost a year of separation truly that powerful? Or was it something else?

Alas, one real reason for my past denials of sinful pleasure suddenly became clear. Despite being an uncontrollable flirt, or rather because of it, I was really just trying to mask my lack of self confidence to act. But was I really just all talk? Should I really think so poorly of myself? After all, actions speak louder than words, and I never once cheated on Bianca. The irony was that these hordes of hotties were reassured by my track record of self-control, and maybe attracted to the happiness I exuded at the thought of Bianca.

I gave Jurita another glance, then shook my head. Who was I kidding? They all thought I was gay. They all thought I made up the whole Bianca thing to hide it. Sigh.

"Well," I finally said with a last puff of smoke. "There's one more sea day this cruise, and there is one thing I have left to do."

Lucifer had issued the challenge of selling a Picasso, and I accepted. Well, in my heart I had, so this was my 'sell a Picasso or go home' cruise. That was what I thought on day four when he threw the gauntlet, anyway. After a few days it became 'sell a Picasso or go home' week. Now, the next-to-last day of the cruise with a full port day tomorrow, was officially 'sell a Picasso or go home' day. I really really really hoped it wouldn't get to 'sell a Picasso or go home' port, or, worse, 'sell a Picasso or go home' night.

I awoke with high expectations. Mr. Payne and his delectable Russian wife had been all but drooling over Picasso's *Minotaur Seduces the Sleeping Girl* etching all cruise. They already owned a fine international collection, mementos from his many summers abroad. After a summer in Spain he brought home a Picasso linocut. A later summer in Russia brought home an insanely sexy wife. Most recently they stayed in Japan, where he brought home several historical Japanese woodblocks. His questions about the few we had to offer were extremely astute. He utterly exhausted all my knowledge gleaned from a semester on Japanese Art at the University of Iowa oh so long ago. In the end he was not as interested in the woodblocks as he was the Picasso, but the entire process served to reinforce my credibility.

Aside from woodblock talk, three separate times Mr. Payne and I had delved into the market for Picassos. Today I was going to sell one. He was already hot and bothered by the Picasso etching, but with my mini lecture this morning, I was going to give him a Picasso orgasm. The cruise was all but finished, so it was time to put out or get out. Whenever Mrs. Payne was around, my metaphors turned naughty. I couldn't help it.

Every couple of mornings this cruise I had arranged for an informal art lecture in the Rolls Royce Café, called Coffee With the Masters. *Ecstasy's* regular weekend cruises were too short for such things, but a two-week repositioning provided plenty of relaxed mornings. So the night before I would fill the café walls with as many good works as I could from my chosen artist, say Marcel Mouly or Salvador Dalí, then in the morning give a relaxed, fifteen-minute lecture. Today's featured artist was, of course, Picasso.

True, we had only two works of his on board, but there was more to talk about with him than anyone else. I had placed teasers all over the ship asking 'why is Picasso so famous?'. I expected a dozen or so folks to show up, but this lecture was really directed at the Paynes. For this lecture I waited until morning to set up the two Picassos on some easels. I wasn't particularly worried about their theft, but certainly I was about controlling exposure of the pornography. I covered it with a cloth.

I had a few minutes before the lecture, so I ran to check my email. I wish I hadn't. Some asshole auctioneer on another ship had sold my *Minotaur Seduces the Sleeping Girl* for $120,000.

I shuffled back to the Rolls Royce in a haze of demoralization. Mr. Payne had, of course, scrutinized both Picasso etchings we had on board. Not surprisingly, he preferred Picasso's iconic minotaur over his admittedly also-iconic pornography. While any red-blooded heterosexual male would instantly think pornographically after one look at Mrs. Payne, that didn't necessarily translate into Mr. Payne saying 'hey, honey, let's buy this and hang it above the couch'.

When I returned to the café, there were about twenty people waiting patiently as they sipped their coffee. I waved to Greg and Shirley Gregg in the back row, then my eyes locked on Mrs. Payne. I mean, the Paynes. Man, I truly *was* obsessed with the babes lately! I really, really needed to see my Bianca again.

"Good morning everyone," I greeted. "Welcome to Coffee With the Masters. Today we are featuring Pablo Picasso."

People shuffled themselves into attention. I reached for the cloth covering *Woman With Bracelet Receives Dandy and a Cat*, but paused before presenting it. I scanned the crowd for children, but there were none. When I revealed the artwork, a middle-aged lady at the nearby table gasped.

"Oh, my word!" she exclaimed. She rose to her feet and looked down upon her husband, who was trying to hide his fascination of the image.

"Come, Ralph," she ordered. "I will not sit here and be subjected to this filth! Why does art always have to be lewd, rude, and inappropriate? Wouldn't it be so much better if they just painted something wholesome and inspiring, like angels? Don't you agree, Ralph?"

She glared down at her husband, who was completely ignoring her in favor of the intricately intimate cross-hatchings of the Picasso.

"Ralph!" she snapped. He jumped as if yanked from a trance.

"Yes, yes, dear, of course we're leaving," he muttered as he meekly followed her. She marched out with her head held high, and he trailed along behind with a few quick, regretful glances back.

This was going to be a rough lecture, I realized. I sipped from my latte, but Lucifer's mocking laughter echoed in my head. I set the coffee aside and began.

"Why is Picasso so famous, you ask? He is undeniably the most famous artist ever. People use his name mindlessly because it has become part of our language, a noun synonymous with over-the-top excellence. But why?

"If pressed, most people would say that Picasso is famous for creating Cubism. We've all seen the funky angle-twisting portraits he made. Technically, he was a Modernist, which is a larger, umbrella-term that covers all those *isms* of art, such as Cubism, Surrealism, Abstract Expressionism, etc. He did them all, actually, not just Cubism. He mastered one art form and moved onto others continuously, even into his nineties. But he did more than merely drop one movement to master another, he was a *pioneer* who blazed a trail into the wilds of unknown art. Picasso was the greatest *artistic inventor* who ever lived."

I paused for a moment to let my audience shake their heads in doubt.

"Most people revolt at that statement," I acknowledged. "Wasn't Da Vinci the greatest artist/inventor? After all, he made the most famous painting in the world, the *Mona Lisa*, and invented scissors and tanks and stuff. All true, but did he change the world for all time? Did any of the greats that come to mind?

"I'll start with Da Vinci. His big contribution was bringing new perspectives to classic themes, such as *The Last Supper*. For the first time, someone painted Jesus at the center of the table with the room's architectural vanishing-point right on his halo. All objects and even the people's postures reference this vanishing point. Genius? Yes. World-changing? Not even close.

"Who else? Michelangelo comes to mind, of course. His Sistine Ceiling is a masterwork of grand vision and revered by two billion Christians around the world today. All that and he wasn't even a painter, but already the world's greatest sculptor! His statue of David is truly awe-inspiring. Yet he was also an engineer, who had to design the scaffolding that allowed him to paint that big ol' ceiling while church services continued below. Genius: absolutely. World-inspiring? Yes. But world changing? Nope.

"If those giants didn't change the world as we know it, who else could have? Monet? Ah, now we're getting somewhere. He was the start of something new. He pioneered Impressionism, which was a whole new way of looking at and presenting a scene. But remember that in his day photography was fast replacing the need for portrait and landscape painters. Art had to adapt to survive, and it began to show us that simply being *more accurate* was not enough. Monet was on to some change, but his genius petered out and he retired to painting billions and billions of lily pads, as Carl Sagan might say. The door of change was ajar, though, and Matisse tried to toe it open further by using colors in non-realistic ways. He would paint a room with red walls, red ceiling, red floor, and red furniture just to shock you. But that was it. So he mastered color. Big whoop.

"All of these guys, from Da Vinci to Michelangelo to Rembrandt to Monet, have in common one simple thing that keeps them below Picasso on the genius scale. I'll get back to that thing in a moment. This is where we introduce Picasso and *his* origin.

"Picasso, born in Spain in 1873, was a child prodigy. By age 8 he was already painting bull fights, man. I was watching Smurfs, and he was composing the chaos of bullfights! By his teen years he already mastered all aspects of late 19th century Realism and had qualified for the most prestigious art school in all of Spain. The entry exam was a solid month of grueling testing. Picasso passed it in *one day*.

"But none of that matters. What matters is what he did in 1907, when he painted *The Ladies of Avignon*. This is a huge painting of five crazy-ass, nude women and a bowl of fruit. Some women are painted kinda-sorta normally, but others appear with wildly distorted faces. It begins on the left with his earlier Rose Period style, but as the eye moves across the scene, the styles morph and, suddenly, so do the perspectives. There was actually progression *within* a single painting. In short, this was the first Cubist painting. The door of change had not only been kicked open, but blasted off its hinges.

"Cubism, you might say. So what? Remember, until this moment, the only type of painting ever done were either obvious images, such as landscapes and portraits, or an allegory. He did many allegorical paintings of his sexual fears, be it scary whores, performance anxiety, venereal disease, or pregnancy. Typical young man fears, more or less. But with this painting he *embodied* his fears, and the fear of sexuality was transformed into fear of the painting itself. It's huge, raw, filled with sharp angles where there should be feminine curves, horrid masks where there should be smiling faces. Even the surface of the painting is spiky and dangerous. This canvas was not a neutral space for presenting an image. It was downright dangerous to behold. This painting wants to eat you alive!

"This one painting, *the Ladies of Avignon*, is why Picasso is the greatest artistic inventor who ever lived. It's not because Cubism is so awesome, but something else. These are not nudes with African tribal masks on their heads: the masks *are* their heads. Within a single image these five women transform from simple nudes, past the beauty, past the sexual, to the primal. Yet in the end they are just women. A person is far more than just the body you see before you. You see, he painted the *abstract* of a woman. The abstract.

"*The Ladies of Avignon* broke away from all art of the past, ever. For all time henceforth, everywhere on Earth, there will always be at least *two* types of art: Realism and Abstract. And that, my friends, is what Picasso did that was beyond the wildest aspirations of Da Vinci or Michelangelo. Those other guys mastered better ways of depicting images, but they were grounded in the image. Picasso made art about the idea, not merely the means of presenting it. Forever."

I paused to let it all sink in.

I gave a mischievous smile and added, "By the way, Avignon is not a reference to the city in France, as most people assume. It was the name of a brothel in Barcelona. See? I just *knew* that being a lustful young man in a brothel could bring about good things. Unfortunately I just didn't know I was supposed to first master 500 years of artistic method. Damn it."

The artist brief was over, and as guests filed out I tried to hide how anxious I was to talk to Mr. Payne. After most people filtered out of the café, I wandered over to him and his luscious wife. We made small talk for a few minutes, but soon enough I cut to the chase.

"So what do you think?" I asked him. "I understand if the graphic *Woman with Bracelet* is not suited to your tastes, but if we find the right Picasso on our electronic gallery, would you be interested in having it in your home?"

"What, me? Oh, no, I could never afford a Picasso," Mr. Payne admitted. "I'm just a High School art teacher. How else do you think I would get every summer off from work? School is out."

As smoothly as possible, I scrambled to salvage my dashed hopes and dreams of ascending beyond tadpole status. "You do already have a Picasso, do you not?"

"Well, true," he admitted. "But I had just inherited some money. That was a long, long time ago. I was just hoping to get an idea from you of what it would be worth nowadays. I can't afford to have it appraised. Aren't those several hundred dollars?"

I answered mechanically, trying to hide my disappointment. "Yes, they can be. But you really should get one to have it properly insured. There could be some sort of tragic accident when a blimp crashed into your house or something. You never know. Thank you, Mr. Payne, for your time and interest."

I wandered away, disappointed but not really surprised. How could I complain? I had far surpassed G2 and proven to Sundance that I was a fully capable auctioneer. So what if I didn't sell a Picasso this cruise? Who did I think I was, anyway?

I sat at the table and silently sipped my lukewarm latte. After a while I noticed Greg Gregg stealthily approaching me. Well, with as much stealth as possible from a man the size of a Kodiak bear.

"Tell me something," Greg asked. "Do you think a Picasso is a good investment?"

"I don't really look at it that way," I answered, gesturing for him to sit with me. "Most of the big name art we sell will likely raise in value, yes, but that should never be the reason to buy it. I hear stories all the time from collectors who bought a so-and-so twenty years ago and are shocked to hear what it's worth today. But that was never why they bought it. They just liked it."

"I'm curious," Greg said as he stroked his beard in thought. "If you had, for example, $50,000 to buy a new oil painting by Peter Max, or a 30-year old Picasso etching, which is one of a hundred, which would you buy?"

"That's easy," I replied. "I would buy the Picasso. I don't happen to like Peter Max's style so much, but I love Picasso. The only reason to buy art is because you like it. Be an art lover, not a gambler."

Greg chuckled to himself as he openly and appreciatively regarded the pornographic Picasso. Suddenly he asked, "How about an upgrade?"

"What do you mean?"

"If you drop everything that my wife bought this cruise, barring her favorite Peter Max 9/11, I'll buy this Picasso. You know, *Nasty Woman Eaten Out by Gay Boy.*"

My jaw wanted to drop, but I managed to keep cool by correcting, "*And a Cat.*"

"*And a Cat,*" Greg agreed.

"I think that is a brilliant idea," I agreed. "I think I can arrange that."

"I want to play a trick on her. I'll hang it in the living room. I can't wait to see her reaction."

"That will be something to see, all right," I deadpanned.

"I love it anyway, and Shirley will think this is absolutely hilarious. I just know it."

"You're so lucky," I said, sharing his grin. "Every man wishes his wife appreciates a fat whore's crotch shot."

Greg paused to review one final time the squatting, anatomically-correct woman receiving cunnilingus from the dandy with the huge penis.

"I think," he admitted.

We shook hands to seal the deal, and I couldn't help but tease, "So you *are* planning on spending the rest of the summer sleeping on the couch, then?"

"This is going in our living room," Greg answered, grinning hugely at his $60,000 prank. "Talk about a conversation piece!"

"Yeah, I think there'll be plenty of words, my friend."

Five minutes later Greg had sauntered away and I had cleared the sale through the ship's purser. I sat in the empty Rolls Royce Café and stared at nothing as it all sank in. I had surpassed all the goals set for me this cruise by the gallery, myself, and even Lucifer. Success. The realization of it trickled over me slowly, like a misty drizzle that creeps down the nape of your neck and drips down the small of your back. I had done it, and done it my way. While staying open to new ideas and heeding the advice of experts is important, sometimes you gotta stick to your guns.

I *am* the Frog Prince.

Three days later, I paused upon a steep brick road, trying to maintain my footing against the powerful gust of wet autumn wind. To my left ancient oaks thrashed, struggling to keep control of yellow and red leaves before winter muscled in too powerfully to resist. Rearing up to my right was a huge stone edifice, as indifferent to the onslaught of elements as it had been to that of the Huns.

Ship life was so hectic and crammed with so many strange sights and struggles that entire days were needed to stop looking over my shoulder. Immediately upon signing off *Ecstasy*, my focus had been on Romania. One transatlantic flight and seven time zones later, I was finally feeling that I had, indeed, made it back to the real world. If you could call Transylvania that, anyway.

The tale of Orpheus was foremost on my mind. In mythology, after his lover died, he traveled to the underworld to challenge Hades himself. The god of the afterlife allowed him to return to life, but Orpheus insisted that his lover Eurydice accompany him. Hades agreed, on condition that Orpheus lead and Eurydice follow. Should he ever glance back, Eurydice was doomed for eternity. Triumphantly Orpheus marched back, only succumbing to doubt on the very threshold of life. He peeked, then watched with horror as her spirit—who had indeed been faithful—was torn forever from him.

I felt brother to Orpheus, with even my own triumph over Lucifer. Now, on the brink of returning to life, was she really there? Or would my own doubts sabotage all I had already undergone? I spun about, but my Bianca did not vanish. The wind tussled her black hair and brought red to her round cheeks. Taking my clammy hand in her own, she said, "Do you remember that time in Jacksonville, when we kissed in the rain?"

"How could I forget?" I answered with a smile. "It was the most romantic moment of my life."

Having found our favorite spot in the world, I swept her back and kissed her deeply. We held the moment, hanging suspended in time, oblivious to the world. Alas, the world was not oblivious to us. A car honking its horn angrily jolted us to our feet.

"Get out of the middle of the road!" a driver cursed in Romanian, shaking his fist at us from inside a tiny, battered car. Sharing a laugh, we stepped to the side and continued our walk, hand in hand.

ABOUT THE AUTHOR

Born in Iowa, Mr. Bruns has since become a citizen of the world, traveling to nearly 50 nations. As an amateur art historian, he has delivered lectures to thousands aboard cruise ships. As an amateur adventurer, he has zip-lined over jungles in Costa Rica, parlayed with snake charmers in Morocco, entered the Pyramids of Giza, consulted the Oracle of Delphi, anted up in the Casino of Monte Carlo, and visited Dracula's house on Halloween night. Indeed, he has frequently summered in Transylvania, in the hometown of Vlad the Impaler.

Brian and his wife currently live in Las Vegas, where he divides his time between writing humor and horror, hiking, a few marathons, cigars, and bottles of Barbados rum.

Appendix A

The Department of Homeland Security on Brian David Bruns

Curious, indeed, are many things to me, things like women, reality TV, and basic arithmetic. Yet even a worn cynic will take pause at being detained by the Department of Homeland Security as representing a threat to the United States of America.

Looking in the mirror, I see a Midwestern college graduate (B.A. in Art History at the University of Northern Iowa), Boy Scout (from multiple generations of Scout Masters and Eagle Scouts), and proud member of the Civil War Preservation Trust (protecting the hallowed ground where our veterans fell). So what the Hell did the Department of Homeland Security see? Via the Freedom of Information Act, I resolved to find out.

I filled out the appropriate forms and sent them off. Figuring the bureaucratic nonsense would delay my request indefinitely, I soon forgot about the whole thing. I was surprised when in a timely fashion I received a rather bulky package from the U.S. Customs and Border Protection office in Washington, DC. Rather, and perhaps a bit cryptically, my parents received the package in Iowa, though I never mentioned my childhood address. Funny that they still got my birthday wrong. The following page is what the cover letter stated.

This is the final response to your Freedom of Information Act (FOIA)/Privacy Act (PA) request to the U.S. Customs and Border Protection (CBP), dated January 12, 2009, seeking information relating to you in the Automated Targeting System (ATS).

A search of the Passenger Name Record (PNR) from the ATS database is being provided to you under the Privacy Act 5 U.S.C. § 552a disclosure law and has produced five pages responsive to your request.

Furthermore, a search of CBP database has produced 23 pages responsive to your request. CBP has determined that certain portions of the enclosed documents are exempt from disclosure.

That's right: 28 pages of tracked behavior and an unknown amount of data still considered classified. What had I done that is considered classified? I slogged line by line through the mass of data, shocked to discover just how thoroughly Big Brother has been screening me. Eventually I realized there was not a single note regarding any of my trips to Morocco, Tunisia, Egypt, or Russia.

Of course they knew every time I entered and exited the U.S., and from where and when. Perhaps I shouldn't have been surprised that tracking my layover time in foreign airports was a natural extension of such information. They also knew *who* paid for my airline tickets, *what* bank account was used, *where* the purchaser was, both business and personal addresses, and *when* purchased in regards to flight date. The who, what, where, and when were covered. Their software concluded the *why*: Muslim extremist terrorist.

Appendix B

The 10 Most Expensive works of art sold in auction

1. ***Nude, Green Leaves and Bust***

Pablo Picasso—$106,482,500

This 1932 painting of Picasso's mistress Marie-Therese Walter measures 152 × 121 cm (about 5 × 4 feet). The painting has only once been exhibited in the U.S., in L.A. to commemorate Picasso's 80th birthday in 1961. Christie's auction house pre-sale estimate was $70M-$90M, but within a mere nine minutes of bidding it was sold to an anonymous buyer for $95M. The buyer's premium took the sale price up to $106.5M. Sold May 4, 2010.

2. ***L'Homme Qui Marche I***

Alberto Giacometti—$104,327,006

This 1961 metal figure of a walking man by Swiss sculptor Giacometti was expected to sell for up to 18 million pounds at the Sotheby's sale in London, but an anonymous telephone bidder paid out more than three times that amount. The life-size bronze figure, cast by the sculptor himself, was sold by a German bank. Sold February 4, 2010.

3. *Garçon à la Pipe*

Pablo Picasso—$104,100,000

Created during the Rose Period. The oil on canvas, measuring 100 × 81.3 cm (about 39 × 32 inches), displays a Parisian boy holding a pipe in his left hand. The record price auction at the time in Sotheby's was a bit of a surprise to the core art buyers, because it was painted in a style not usually associated with the artistic pioneer. Sold May 4, 2004.

4. *Dora Maar au Chat*

Pablo Picasso—$95,200,000

Dora Maar's portrait (and a cat!) was another enormous surprise, when nearly doubling its inaccurate pre-sale estimate and making a new record. Painted in 1941, Picasso's controversial portrait (one of his last) is sometimes described as an unflattering depiction of his mistress, who was an artist/photographer. Their relationship lasted ten years during the 1930s and 40s. Sold at Sotheby's May 3, 2006.

5. *Portrait of Dr. Gachet*

Vincent van Gogh—$82,500,000

This painting by the Dutch master became world-famous when Japanese businessman Ryoei Saito paid $82.5 million for it at auction in Christie's, New York. Saito was so attached to the painting he wanted it to be cremated with him when he died. Saito died in 1996, but the painting was saved. Vincent van Gogh actually painted two versions of Dr. Gachet's portrait.

6. *Moulin de la Galette*

Pierre-Auguste Renoir—$82,000,000

Bal au Moulin de la Galette, Montmartre was painted by French artist Pierre-Auguste Renoir in 1876. On May 17, 1990, it was sold for $78,000,000 at Sotheby's in New York City to Ryoei Saito, who bought it together with the Portrait of Dr. Gachet (see above).

7. *Massacre of the Innocents*

Peter Paul Rubens—$76,700,000

This painting by classic master Peter Paul Rubens, painted in 1611, is the only painting in this list which was not created in the 19th or 20th century. It was sold to Kenneth Thomson, 2nd Baron Thomson of Fleet for $76,700,000 at a 2002 Sotheby's auction.

8. *Portraite de l'Artiste sans Barbe*

Vincent van Gogh—$71,500,000

Portrait de l'Artiste sans Barbe (Self-portrait without beard) is one of many self-portraits by Dutch painter Vincent van Gogh. He painted this one in Saint-Rémy-de-Provence, France in September 1889. The painting is oil on canvas and is 40 cm x 31 cm (16" x 13").

This is an uncommon painting since his other self-portraits show him with a beard. The self-portrait became one of the most expensive paintings of all time when it was sold for $71.5 million in 1998 in New York.

9. *Rideau, Cruchon et Compotier*

Paul Cezanne—$60,500,000

This painting by color master Paul Cézanne, painted in ca. 1893-1894, sold at Sotheby's New York on May 10, 1999 to "The Whitneys". Whitney, born into one of America's wealthiest families, was a venture capitalist, publisher, Broadway show and Hollywood film producer, and philanthropist.

10. *Femme aux Bras Croisés*

Pablo Picasso—$55,000,000

This work, painted in 1901, was a part of Picasso's famous Blue Period, a dark, sad time in the artist's life. The beautiful and various tones of blue are typical of this period. The painting depicts a woman with her arms crossed staring at the endless nothing. *Femme aux Bras Croisés* was sold for $55,000,000 November 8, 2000, at Christie's Rockefeller in New York City.

Coming in 2012

Ship Happens

Book 3 of Brian David Bruns's award-winning Cruise Confidential series finally unveils all things Bianca, from the chance meeting to first multinational tryst, of exploring her home in Transylvania and falling in love under the suspicious eye of her father—a retired sergeant trained for decades under the Iron Curtain to kill Americans—and the years-long battle with cruise ships that both bring them together and pull them apart. Brian's ambitions as art auctioneer are scuttled on a murderous Carnival ship, reducing him to further training and another dreadful showdown with Lucifer. Brian earns placement on an exclusive six-star luxury liner, and is finally able to bring Bianca with him. But after three years of fighting to be together, is it too late?

Novellas of the Bizarre

A new series of weird fiction from Brian David Bruns, rich in setting and seasoned with odd characters that will take you in directions you never imagined!

The Ghost of Naked Molly

In old New Orleans the ghost of a gorgeous octoroon mistress complicates the political schemes of a local grandee by parading around his house in the nude.

"The macabre and supernatural add to the atmospherics in this beguiling collection."—Kirkus Reviews

The Finger People

During the attack on Confederate Fort Henry, a timid rebel cook discovers something grislier than the horrors of war.

"A fine study of Civil War squalor and carnage... a luridly ghoulish climax."—Kirkus Reviews

Luna Umbra

An odd guest comes daily to a shrimp buffet to gulp down vast quantities of shrimp, while his forlorn waitress appears to gain weight on his behalf.

"Bruns achieves a delightful balance of whimsy and grotesque with a glimmer of moonstruck romance."—Kirkus Reviews

The Penultimate Mr. Nilly

The crew of a ship trapped in the ice slowly go insane from hunger and paranoia, until salvation comes in the form of a toy wolf.

"Bruns drenches the tale in period detail that creates well-imagined, realistic settings for his lively characters."—Kirkus Reviews

Made in the USA
Charleston, SC
17 March 2012